Responsibility to Protect

Responsibility to Protect

The Global Effort to End Mass Atrocities

ALEX J. BELLAMY

polity

First published in 2009 by Polity Press

Polity Press
65 Bridge Street
Cambridge CB2 1UR, UK.

Polity Press
350 Main Street
Malden, MA 02148, USA

ISBN-13: 978-0-7456-4347-2
ISBN-13: 978-0-7456-4348-9(pb)

A catalogue record for this book is available from the British Library.

Typeset in 11.25 / 13 pt Dante
by Servis Filmsetting Ltd, Stockport, Cheshire
Printed and bound in Great Britain by
MPG Books Ltd, Bodmin, Cornwall

The publisher has used its best endeavours to ensure that the URLs for external websites referred to in this book are correct and active at the time of going to press. However, the publisher has no responsibility for the websites and can make no guarantee that a site will remain live or that the content is or will remain appropriate.

Every effort has been made to trace all copyright holders, but if any have been inadvertently overlooked the publishers will be pleased to include any necessary credits in any subsequent reprint or edition.

For further information on Polity, visit our website: www.polity.co.uk

For Sara
diligo usquequaque

Contents

Acknowledgements

This book had its genesis in Toronto, was drafted mostly in Brisbane, completed in Geneva and revised for the final time back in Brisbane. Along the way we launched the Asia–Pacific Centre for the Responsibility to Protect in Bangkok. I'm grateful to the University of Queensland for providing the time and wherewithal to complete this book.

Although I had worked in 2005–6 on the relationship between the Responsibility to Protect (R2P) and humanitarian intervention, especially in relation to the crisis in Darfur, it was a superb conference organised by the Peace and Conflict Society at the University of Toronto in early 2007 which showed me that R2P's potential extended well beyond the question of armed intervention and that the protection of civilians from genocide and mass atrocities involved everything from early warning to state capacity building. I am very grateful to Mike Lawrence and Max Kelly for inviting me to that conference and forcing me to think about – and learn about – the Responsibility to Prevent. The Toronto conference also gave me an invaluable opportunity to learn more about R2P from Gareth Evans and to discuss some of the most vexing problems with him. Gareth has since helped me to clarify my thoughts on the R2P and encouraged me to deepen my engagement with both the study and the practice of protection. His vision, commitment and wisdom are inspiring. As Lee Feinstein once put it, there would be no R2P without Gareth Evans. Despite his unbelievably intense workload, Gareth took the time to answer questions, set me straight and provide encouragement. When a few of us here began thinking about making a practical contribution to the furtherance of R2P, Gareth was an eager and active supporter and adviser, galvanising us into creating the Asia–Pacific Centre for the R2P. I am deeply grateful.

I was the fortunate recipient of advice, information and comments from many people who have been actively involved in creating, selling and operationalising the R2P. Their knowledge and insightfulness was humbling. Thomas Weiss in particular has been a rock throughout the writing of this book. He provided me with drafts of the ICISS report and with insightful and detailed answers to myriad questions; he also read, and offered incisive comments on, the first draft of this book. His influence can be seen on every page of it. Joanna Wenschler provided invaluable help and useful documents on the Security Council's deliberations about the protection of civilians. John Dauth, Australia's High Commissioner to New Zealand and former Permanent Representative to the UN, was extraordinarily generous in answering questions and follow-ups and in providing advice which helped to shape my interpretation of events and encouragement to take up and develop my interest in the R2P. Likewise, Allan Rock, Canada's former Permanent Representative to the UN, took the time to give detailed answers to my questions. Nicole Deller provided much assistance on the effort to engage civil society with the R2P and, deliberately or not, guided me towards the position I have ended up taking on the responsibility to prevent – a position quite at odds with the views I used to have before talking to her. Edward Luck travelled all the way to Bangkok to help us launch our Asia–Pacific Centre for the Responsibility to Protect; set out a clear and compelling vision for advancing the R2P; and was generous in answering questions and offering wise advice. Lloyd Axworthy, with whom the ICISS began, also came to Bangkok and took the time to impart advice on how to progress with the R2P agenda. Finally, Don Hubert shared his deep insight on R2P and offered wise advice during our panel at the International Studies Association Conference in San Francisco (2008) and later, over lunch. Between them, these people have not only profoundly shaped the way I think about R2P, they have also provided proof that there exists a constituency of determined, gifted and energetic people who have worked hard to get the R2P where it is today.

I have also benefited from the insights and advice of many academic colleagues. First is Paul Williams. Over the past decade I have had the honour of working with Paul on a number of projects relating to security, peacekeeping and R2P. I've said this before but it is worth saying it again – Paul is a brilliant scholar and a treasured friend. His handiwork and his ideas litter the pages of this book. Nicholas Wheeler has been a constant guide and an able advisor on every aspect of this project. It was his writings that first made me interested in all things related to the United Nations and framed the way I see the world. Working as a research assistant on his book *Saving Strangers* was a seminal experience and I have learned an awful lot from Nick – or at least I hope I have. Ramesh Thakur provided comments and advice on an earlier paper relating to this and other projects linked to R2P. He has offered guidance and support along the way and has played an absolutely pivotal part in the formation of the Asia–Pacific Centre, of which he is a patron. Luke Glanville, Richard Devetak and Hidemi Suganami shared with me their insights on the history of sovereignty and its relationship to human rights, an experience which has helped to shape my own thoughts. I am also grateful to all those who have shared their ideas with me and have lent their support to the establishment of the Asia–Pacific Centre for the Responsibility to Protect and its new journal, *Global Responsibility to Protect*. Apart from those already mentioned, these include (but are not limited to) Alistair Gee, Julia Roy, Brendan Ross, Andrew Hewett, Michael Smith, John Dowd, Amitav Acharya, Pranee Thiparat, Rizal Sukma, Noel Morada, Mely Cabellero-Antony, Shin-wha Lee, Vitit Muntarbhorn, Kyudok Hong, Paul Evans, Colin Keating, Muhadi Sugiono, Pang Zhongying, Yin He, Michael Barnett, Roberta Cohen, Kwasei Anning, Victoria Holt, Don Hubert, Michael Ignatieff, William Maley, Jennifer Welsh, Hugo Slim, Pierre Schorri, Adekeye Adebajo and Eli Stamnes.

As ever, Polity Press has been a pleasure to work with. Thanks to Louise Knight, and especially to Emma Hutchinson, who guided this book from conception to completion. I would also like to thank the anonymous reviewers for their insightful comments and suggestions. Thanks also to Manuela Tecusan, who did a brilliant job of translating the original draft into a much better text.

Next, I owe a debt of gratitude to my family. My brothers and sisters-in-law are the best siblings that an (often) desk-bound and over-opinionated brother-in-law could ask for. Alan and Marie are the best parents that a son-in-law could ask for – ever ready to lend a hand and to offer quiet, steadfast support, without concern for themselves. Polly – beautiful soul – has been through so much in such a short life. Her steely determination is a source of wonder; her love of life, a joy to behold; her perpetual yearning for food, a lesson in focusing.

Parts of the overall argument were field-tested at Macquarie University, Sydney, the Australian National University, Canberra and elsewhere. The whole book has been field-tested on my graduate students, some of whom have provided feedback and advice and are playing an important role in developing and advancing R2P. I'm especially grateful to Bryn Hughes, Matthew Bright, Sarah Teitt, Stephen Mcloughlin, Charlie Hunt, Jess Gifkins and Kimberley Nackers in this regard.

Finally and most importantly, I owe a massive debt of gratitude to my dear wife, friend and colleague, Sara. Sara is a brilliant scholar and guide and she has walked with me through every part of this book. She has read and discussed the whole book more than once, offering detailed comments on the first draft of the whole manuscript and forcing me to rethink many of my earlier ideas. In what little spare time she has, Sara has also played a huge role in advancing the R2P. She came up with the idea of establishing a journal, *Global Responsibility to Protect*, and then single-handedly went about piecing together an editorial board comprising most of the key figures and prominent scholars who engaged in R2P. And, as if that wasn't enough, she persuaded many of them to contribute articles for the first issues. She is my best friend, my inspiration and my light. She is a constant reminder that there is so much in the world that is good and ought to be protected. This book is dedicated to Sara.

AJB
Brisbane, May 2008

Abbreviations

ADF	Allied Democratic Forces
ASF	African Standby Force (AU)
AU	African Union
CIA	Central Intelligence Agency (US)
CIS	Commonwealth of Independent States
DPA	Department of Political Affairs (UN)
DPKO	Department of Peacekeeping Operations (UN)
DRC	Democratic Republic of Congo
ECOWAS	Economic Community of West African States
ECOSOC	United Nations Economic and Social Council
EISAS	Information and Strategic Analysis Secretariat for the Executive Committee for Peace and Security (proposed)
EU	European Union
EUFOR RD	European Union Reserve Deployment (DRC)
FAO	Food and Agricultural Organization
FDLR	Democratic Forces for Liberation of the Congo
FEWS	Famine Early Warning System
G8	Group of 8
G77	Group of 77
HEWS	Humanitarian Early Warning System
HLM	High-Level Mission of the United Nations Human Rights Council
HLP	United Nations High-Level Panel
HRC	United Nations Human Rights Council
ICC	International Criminal Court
ICG	International Crisis Group
ICISS	International Commission on Intervention and State Sovereignty
ICJ	International Court of Justice
ICRC	International Committee of the Red Cross
ICTR	International Criminal Tribunal for Rwanda

ICTY	International Criminal Tribunal for former Yugoslavia
IDP	Internally Displaced Person
IGAD	Intergovernmental Authority on Development
IICK	Independent International Commission on Kosovo
ILC	International Law Commission
IMF	International Monetary Fund
IMTF	Integrated Mission Task Force
IOM	International Organization for Migration
ISHR	International Service for Human Rights
JIU	Joint Inspection Unit (UN)
KFOR	Kosovo Force (NATO Mission in Kosovo)
KLA	Kosovo Liberation Army
MDGs	Millennium Development Goals
MONUC	United Nations Mission in Congo
NAM	Non-Aligned Movement
NATO	North Atlantic Treaty Organization
NGOs	Non-Governmental Organizations
OAU	Organization of African Unity
OCHA	Office for the Coordination of Humanitarian Affairs (UN)
OIC	Organization of Islamic Conferences
ORCI	Office for Research and Collection of Information (UN)
OSCE	Organization for Security and Cooperation in Europe
P5	Permanent Five Members of the UN Security Council
PBF	Peacebuilding Fund (UN)
PBC	United Nations Peacebuilding Commission
PBSO	Peacebuilding Support Office (UN)
RUF	Revolutionary United Front
R2P	Responsibility to Protect
R2P–CS	Responsibility to Protect – Engaging Civil Society
SADC	South African Development Community
SPITS	Stockholm Process on the Implementation of Targeted Sanctions
UN	United Nations
UNAMID	United Nations / African Union Mission in Darfur
UNAMIR	United Nations Assistance Mission in Rwanda
UNDP	United Nations Development Program
UNEPS	United Nations Emergency Peace Service (proposed)
UNHCR	Office of the United Nations High Commissioner for Refugees
UNIOSIL	United Nations Integrated Office in Sierra Leone

UNITA	Nacional para a Independência Total de Angola
UNICEF	United Nations Children's Fund
UNMIK	United Nations Mission in Kosovo
UNMIL	United Nations Mission in Liberia
UNMIS	United Nations Mission in Sudan
UNOCI	United Nations Mission in Côte D'Ivoire
UNPREDEP	United Nations Preventive Deployment in Macedonia
UNPROFOR	United Nations Protection Force
UNSC	United Nations Security Council
UNTAET	United Nations Transitional Administration in East Timor
UNTAC	United Nations Transitional Administration in Cambodia
UNTAG	United Nations Transitional Administration in Namibia
UPC	Union of Congolese Patriots
VIP	Very Important Person
WACSOF	West African Civil Society Forum
WFM–IGP	World Federalist Movement–Institute for Global Policy
WFP	World Food Program
WMD	Weapons of Mass Destruction

Introduction

Genocide and mass atrocities remain an all too frequently recurring phenomenon. In 1994, 800,000 Rwandans were butchered by *Interehamwe* militia and their supporters in just 100 days – a faster rate of killing than the Holocaust experienced. Elsewhere in sub-Saharan Africa, the 1990s delivered a bloody cocktail of state collapse and warlordism which killed more than five million people in the Democratic Republic of Congo (DRC), Sudan, Burundi and West Africa. In Asia, Indonesia's rule over East Timor came to an end in 1999, amidst an orgy of violence that left thousands dead. Nor was Europe spared. The wars of Yugoslav dissolution killed a quarter of a million people and gave the world a new phrase: 'ethnic cleansing'. In 1995, 7,500 men and boys were taken by Bosnian Serb forces from the town of Srebrenica, a UN-protected 'safe area', and killed. An act of genocide in the centre of Europe, fifty years after the end of the Holocaust. Thanks to concerted efforts by the UN, regional organisations, non-governmental organisations and internationalist-minded states, there are fewer wars and genocides today than there were ten years ago, but those who think that these tragedies are a thing of the past need only look to Darfur to see the durability of humankind's capacity for acts of shocking inhumanity.[1] There the government of Sudan and Arab militia groups collectively known as *Janjaweed* reacted to a rebellion over grazing rights and local autonomy by unleashing a reign of terror which killed 250,000 and forced more than two million to flee. The fighting has since then extended into neighbouring Chad and into the Central African Republic, spreading death and displacement.

All too frequently the world's response to genocide and mass atrocities is slow, timid and disjointed. Just as often it seems that political leaders are confronted with a choice between standing aside and sending in the Marines to wage war on the perpetrators of serious wrongs.[2] Sometimes, as in the case of Rwanda, the world's most powerful states simply lack the political will to step in and put an end to the bloodshed. Placing their own interests ahead of those of the victims, they stand aside in the face of conscience-shocking violence. In other cases, for instance Kosovo in 1999, collective action is blocked by political deadlock between states who are keen to intervene and those who oppose intervention on political, legal or other grounds.[3] More frequent in recent times than either of these two responses is one of a third type, whereby world leaders declare an interest in ending mass killing but find it difficult to muster anything better than tepid political responses and weakly mandated and equipped peace operations. In these cases, made evident in the world's slow response to the bloodshed in the DRC and Sudan, a combination of lack of will and political division produces slow, incoherent and under-resourced responses, which leave civilians facing enduring vulnerability.

The starting point for this book is the conviction that more needs to be done to protect civilians from genocide and mass atrocities. The very fact that the incidence of war and genocide has declined and that much of this decline can be ascribed to international activism suggests that this cause is far from being a hopeless one. Instead, it suggests that new knowledge about measures to prevent and stem the tide of genocide and mass atrocities can be developed, disseminated and translated into timely and effective political action. The single most important recent development in this regard was the creation, adoption and emerging operationalisation of a new international principle: the Responsibility to Protect (R2P).

The adoption of the R2P was one of the few real achievements of the 2005 World Summit hosted by the UN. World leaders unanimously declared that all states have a responsibility to protect their citizens from genocide, war crimes, ethnic cleansing and crimes against humanity and that they stood 'prepared' to take collective action in cases where national authorities 'are manifestly failing to protect their populations' from these four crimes. In April 2006, the UN Security Council unanimously reaffirmed the R2P and indicated its readiness to adopt appropriate measures where necessary (Resolution 1674, 28 April 2006) – albeit after almost six months of hard bargaining. The intellectual and political origins of the R2P lay in the concept of 'sovereignty as responsibility', developed by the UN Special Representative on Internally Displaced Persons, Francis Deng, and by Roberta Cohen, a Senior Fellow at the Brookings Institution. Amidst the controversy surrounding NATO's 1999 intervention in Kosovo, the concept was picked up by Kofi Annan, who challenged world governments to develop a way of reconciling the principles of sovereignty and fundamental human rights in a way which could protect individuals from arbitrary killing. That challenge was taken up by the Canadian government, which created the International Commission on Intervention and State

Sovereignty (ICISS). Chaired by Gareth Evans and Mohammed Sahnoun, the Commission set out the case for the R2P and identified its three main components: the responsibilities to prevent, to react and to rebuild. The adoption of the R2P at the 2005 World Summit was engineered by key states such as Canada and powerful norm entrepreneurs such as Kofi Annan, who incorporated the R2P into his blueprint for UN reform, guaranteeing it a place on the world agenda at the 2005 summit.

The purpose of the present book is twofold. First of all it examines the R2P's intellectual origins, the ICISS' proceedings and report and the effort to persuade world leaders to adopt the concept; this is done in order to understand what R2P means, how that meaning has changed and what are the political obstacles confronting it. The second part of the book focuses on the effort to operationalise the R2P; it asks what it takes to prevent, react and rebuild more effectively and it assesses progress towards achieving these goals. The argument that gradually unfolds may be considered controversial in some quarters. Although the R2P was initially conceived – and is, still often, presented – as a way of guiding policy-makers in their deliberations about whether or not to respond to genocide and mass atrocities with non-consensual military intervention, this is not where the principle has made its biggest difference; nor is it likely to do so in the future. Ultimately, even when armed with the criteria for using force set out by the ICISS in the report which gave birth to R2P (see Chapter 2), decisions about intervention will continue to be made in an ad hoc fashion by political leaders balancing national interests, legal considerations, world opinion, perceived costs and humanitarian impulses – much as they were prior to the advent of R2P. When a crisis gets to the point where only military intervention will do, it is in the hands of a combination of *Realpolitik* and the strength of individual leaders' moral commitments, and there is little that criteria can do to shape the leaders' calculations of interests, values, costs and benefits. When it comes to dealing with decisions about the use of force in individual cases, criteria cannot deliver consensus between the great powers, nor can they, by themselves, generate the political will necessary for leaders to commit resources to the protection of civilians in foreign countries.[4]

Where the R2P can make a real difference is in reducing the frequency with which world leaders are confronted with the apparent choice between doing nothing and sending in the Marines. Indeed, a careful reading of the ICISS report shows that, although much of the attention and focus was given to non-consensual military intervention, the commission itself believed that the *prevention* of genocide and mass atrocities was the single most important element of R2P (see Chapters 2 and 4). By starting with the needs of the victims and by outlining myriad ways in which those needs might be met, the R2P points towards a system of protection involving diplomacy, judicial measures, economic measures, peace operations deployed with local consent – albeit sometimes coerced – international assistance to help build responsible sovereigns with appropriate capacity and much more besides. If the institutional and political capacity necessary to maximise the effectiveness of these measures is developed, then the frequency with which governments are forced to choose between standing aside and going to war for humanitarian purposes will be reduced. This is not to say that such cases will never arise, or that the criteria for the use of force, which formed a large part of the ICISS' proposals on the R2P, do not provide guidance to decision-makers in these difficult cases. What I am saying is that, by reducing the frequency of all-or-nothing decisions, more civilians will be better protected from genocide and mass atrocities. That is the promise of R2P.

This position is seemingly at odds with the concerns which animated those most closely associated with the ICISS and with the concerns which have animated most of the commission's commentators.[5] We should acknowledge, however, that the commission itself certainly nodded in this direction when it identified prevention, not military intervention, as the single most important aspect of R2P. We should also recognise that the R2P endorsed by world leaders in 2005 and by the UN Security Council in 2006 did not include criteria for the use of force (see Chapters 3 and 5), but did point towards a heavy agenda of institutional reform and behavioural change geared towards preventing and mitigating genocide and mass atrocities. The understanding of R2P presented in the second part of this book, where I focus on the principle's operationalisation, is more in keeping with international consensus about what R2P actually entails than with R2P as originally conceived by the ICISS.[6]

Before that, however, I need to clarify briefly the terminology we use to describe the R2P.

Concept, Principle, Norm?

R2P is invariably referred to as a concept, a principle or a norm (usually an 'emerging norm'). Each of these terms confers a different status upon the R2P, so it is important to clarify the meanings behind these words, the reason why different actors use them and the way they will be used in this book.

R2P as concept

Most governments – supporters and critics of the R2P alike – refer to the R2P as a 'concept'. Examples of this abound in Chapters 3 and 5 especially.[7] Edward Luck, the UN Secretary-General's Special Adviser on matters relating to R2P, also describes the R2P as a 'concept', arguing that there is no consensus on whether the R2P has become a norm.[8] Originating from the Latin participle *conceptus* meaning 'conceived', the term 'concept' typically refers to an 'abstract idea'. When governments describe R2P as a concept, therefore, they mean that it is an 'idea' – a thought or suggestion about a possible norm or course of action. In other words it is a proposal, a suggestion, something requiring further development, elaboration or agreement before it can be turned into shared expectations of appropriate behaviour or into a plan of action for institutional reform. If, as the Chinese government argued in 2007 (but not, importantly, in 2006 or 2008), R2P is a concept, then it is inappropriate for the Security Council or other UN bodies to make use of it in their formal declarations or resolutions, because it is merely an idea warranting further discussion and elaboration and not an agreed principle or norm in need of operationalisation.[9]

The principal merit of describing the R2P as a concept is that this best reflects the language used by most governments themselves. Moreover, it is important to remember that, whilst the 2005 World Summit Outcome Document was unanimously endorsed by world leaders. It reflected not a determination by the assembly itself but a blueprint for the future direction of the UN. The decisions and proposals laid out in the Outcome Document were not self-authorising or self-executing but required further decisions by the General Assembly or other relevant Councils. Nor did the Security Council Resolution 1674 change this basic fact, since it was limited to endorsing the relevant paragraphs of the Outcome Document.

There are, however, problems with describing the R2P as a 'concept' in the post-World Summit era. First, the World Summit Outcome Document did not refer to R2P as a concept or idea requiring further deliberation. Its wording clearly indicated that R2P exists as something more than an idea – something to which all states pledge to adhere, both in their relations with their own citizens and in their behaviour as members of international society (see Chapter 3). Second, the Outcome Document did not *require* further decisions by the General Assembly in relation to the basic R2P commitment. Third, as chapters 4–6 of this book attest, the R2P has been incorporated into the practice of the UN, regional organisations and individual states.

R2P as principle

Sometimes R2P is referred to as a 'principle'. A 'principle' is commonly understood as a fundamental truth or proposition which serves as the basis for belief leading to action. Labelling the R2P a 'principle' rather than a 'concept' implies that it has acquired a status of shared understanding and that there is sufficient consensus to allow it to function as a foundation for action. Both the ICISS and the UN's High-Level Panel referred to the R2P as 'an emerging principle of customary international law'.[10] References to the R2P as a principle are not always associated with international law, however, and it is worth mentioning that the legal implications of the R2P remain controversial.[11]

Those who believe that the 2005 World Summit set out a clear understanding of the R2P and that world leaders actually committed to it rather than merely deliberating further are likely to argue that the R2P is a principle. Important in this regard, however, are those things which *are* typically referred to as 'principles' by world governments. Since 2001, international discussions about the the R2P have been punctuated by the insistence that it does not challenge or violate the well-established international 'principles' of sovereignty – non-interference and territorial integrity. Indeed, Paragraph 139 of the World Summit Outcome Document pointedly identified the 'principles' of the UN Charter and international law as a check on the advancement of the R2P.

Clearly the distinction between R2P as a concept and R2P as a principle is important. Conceptually, it determines whether the R2P is subordinate to traditional principles of sovereignty and non-intervention or whether – as a principle in its own right – it has the effect of altering the meaning of sovereignty itself. Practically, it has the effect of determining whether R2P remains primarily in the realm of rhetoric and deliberation for the next few years (the corollary of thinking of R2P as concept) or becomes the guide to institutional reform and behavioural change envisaged by UN Secretary-General Ban Ki-moon.[12]

R2P as norm

Academic commentators in particular prefer to describe R2P in relation to its status as a norm. At their most basic, norms are best understood as 'collective understandings of the proper behaviour of actors'.[13] Typically, the academic debate has centred not on the question of whether the R2P is a concept or principle, but on whether it is a norm and – if so – whether it is an emergent or an embedded norm.[14] But it is not only academics who have referred to R2P as a norm. The UN High-Level Panel, for instance, endorsed the 'emerging norm that there is a responsibility to protect' and confirmed the developing consensus that this norm was 'exercisable by the Security Council'.[15] In the same year (2004), Gareth Evans criticised the 'poorly and inconsistently' argued humanitarian justification for the war in Iraq, arguing that it 'almost choked at birth what many were hoping was an emerging new norm justifying intervention on the basis of the principle of "responsibility to protect"'.[16]

Describing the R2P in the language of norms both helps and complicates efforts to understand it. It complicates matters because, as commonly understood, 'norms' do not sit comfortably along a spectrum containing 'concepts' and 'principles' . Norms comprise elements of both concept and principle, involve actual behaviour and relate to a different standard of analysis. Given this, we should see the question of whether or not R2P is a norm, and what sort of norm it might be, as *parallel* to, but separate from, the question of whether it is a concept or principle. To be sure, both ways of understanding the issue ask similar questions, but the language of norms brings with it a host of concepts, distinctions and methods which are not easily tacked onto the language of concepts and principles. It is precisely the specificities associated with norms, however, that make this approach useful. For the language of norms allows us to make use of theories about different types of norm, norm entrepreneurs, and the development and evolution of norms.[17]

For the purposes of this study, however, I will use the language of 'concepts' and 'principles' rather than that of 'norms' because this reflects the terms in which governments themselves refer to the R2P. For the reasons set out above, I will treat the R2P as a 'concept' in the period between its articulation by the ICISS and adoption at the 2005 World Summit and as a 'principle' thereafter, noting that aspects of the R2P were altered, amended or simply ejected during this transition. Describing the R2P as a principle after 2005 reflects the fact that governments have indeed agreed on its content and have pledged to act in accordance with it.

1

Sovereignty and Human Rights

Sovereignty Versus Human Rights

Questions about preventing, reacting to and rebuilding after man-made catastrophes tend to be framed around an enduring struggle between sovereignty and human rights. By this account, sovereignty refers to the rights that states enjoy to territorial integrity, political independence and non-intervention, whilst human rights refer to the idea that individuals ought to enjoy certain fundamental freedoms by virtue of their humanity. Where sovereign states are either unwilling or unable to protect the fundamental freedoms of their citizens, sovereignty and human rights come into conflict.

This tension is evident in the UN Charter itself.[1] When it came to designing the post-war order, the horrors of the Second World War produced a contradictory response from world leaders. Three concerns pulled them in different directions. First, there was a strong impetus for the outlawing of war as an instrument of policy. Thus Article 2(4) of the UN Charter forbade the threat or use of force in international politics, with only two exceptions: each state's inherent right to self-defence (Article 51) and collective measures authorised by the UN Security Council (Chapter VII of the UN Charter). The second concern was the emergence of the idea that peoples had a right to govern themselves. This gave impetus to the process of decolonisation, which proceeded apace in the post-war era. How, though, would these new states be protected from the interference of great powers in their domestic affairs? The UN Charter's answer to this question came in the form of a commitment to 'mutual respect for sovereignty', the blanket ban on force mentioned earlier, and Article 2(7) prohibiting the UN from interfering 'in matters essentially within the domestic jurisdiction of states'.

The third concern was in large part a reaction to the Holocaust and the Second World War's many other horrors. Evidence of the depths to which humanity could sink persuaded the UN Charter's authors that aspirations for human rights had to be placed at the heart of the new order. But how might different conceptions of human rights be reconciled without under-mining the UN's other ambitions? The tension this problem created is evident in the preamble to the UN Charter, in which the members promise to 'reaffirm faith in fundamental human rights, in the dignity and worth of the human person', while also promising to 'practice tolerance and live together in peace with one another as good neighbours'. This set in train a critically important political dilemma: how should states behave in cases where maintaining faith in human rights meant refusing to be a good neigh-bour to genocidal and tyrannical states? Influenced by this tension, for the past sixty years debates about the relationship between sovereignty and human rights and the legitimacy of humanitarian intervention have boiled down to a single core question: should sovereignty and the basic order it brings to world politics be privileged over the rights of individuals, or should it be overridden in certain cases, so as to permit intervention for the purpose of protecting those fundamental rights?

There are good reasons for thinking that this tension goes to the very heart of international order, not least because those who argue against col-lective action aimed at reaffirming faith in fundamental human rights invoke sovereignty to support their case. Thus in 1977, when Vietnam invaded Cambodia and ousted the murderous Pol Pot regime, responsible for the death of some two million Cambodians, this state was widely con-demned for violating Cambodian sovereignty. China's representative at the UN described Vietnam's act as a 'great mockery of and insult to the United Nations and its member states' and sponsored a resolution condemning Vietnam's 'aggression'. The United States agreed. Its ambassador argued that the world could not allow Vietnam's violation of Cambodian sover-eignty to 'pass in silence', as this 'will only encourage Governments in other parts of the world to conclude that there are no norms, no standards, no restraints'.[2] France argued that 'the notion that, because a regime is detestable, foreign intervention is justified and forcible overthrow is legiti-mate is extremely dangerous. That could ultimately jeopardize the very maintenance of law and order.' Norway (among others) agreed, admitting that it had 'strong objections to the serious violation of human rights com-mitted by the Pol Pot government. However, the domestic policies of that government cannot – we repeat cannot – justify the action of Viet Nam.'[3]

More recently, in 2004, Pakistan argued against collective action in order to halt the mass killing and expulsion of civilians in Darfur sponsored by the Sudanese government on the grounds that 'the Sudan has all the rights and privileges incumbent under the United Nations Charter, including to sov-ereignty, political independence, unity and territorial integrity'.[4] Nowadays,

Western commentators sometimes put these sorts of arguments down to political posturing by recalcitrant states who invariably have their own human rights problems. But these arguments are still sometimes used by liberal states themselves. For example, in a March 2005 Security Council debate on whether to refer alleged crimes in Darfur to the International Criminal Court (ICC), the US representative argued that the court 'strikes at the essence of the nature of sovereignty' by purportedly sitting in judgement over the conduct of a state's internal affairs.[5]

At first glance, therefore, by insisting that sovereignty and fundamental human rights need not be antagonistic, the R2P stands at odds with what seems to be the main debate on how to respond best to humanitarian emergencies and on the legitimacy of such responses: namely the question whether sovereignty or human rights should be privileged. On closer inspection, however, there are four anomalies that this way of thinking about the problem cannot accommodate – which suggests the need to think differently about the relationship between sovereignty and human rights.

Sovereignty no barrier to intervention

Simon Chesterman has demonstrated that sovereignty has not in fact inhibited unilateral or collective intervention to protect fundamental human rights in other countries. Chesterman's argument was a response to lawyers who have engaged in the 'sovereignty versus human rights' dilemma by arguing that, in order to short-circuit the struggle and enable human rights to prevail, there ought to be a legal exception to the non-intervention rule in cases of gross human rights abuse. In response to this position, Chesterman argued that 'implicit in many of the arguments for a right of humanitarian intervention is the suggestion that the present normative order is preventing interventions that should take place. This is simply not true. Interventions do not take place because states do not want them to take place.'[6] From this point of view, it was not concerns about sovereignty that prevented timely intervention in Darfur or Rwanda, but rather the basic political fact that no state wanted to risk its own troops to save strangers.

What, though, of Vietnam's invasion of Cambodia? Was it not the case that Vietnam paid a heavy political and economic price because it was seen as violating Cambodia's sovereignty? If this is so, could it not be argued that violating sovereignty imposes inhibitive costs on the one who intervenes, acting as a potential deterrent to others? This position certainly has merit but needs to be viewed alongside two other considerations. First, Vietnam was not principally motivated by humanitarian concerns, nor did it justify its invasion as a humanitarian intervention. Second, and perhaps more importantly, we need to take the arguments levelled against Vietnam with a pinch of salt. Whilst not denying the fact that many states, particularly some members of the Non-Aligned Movement, opposed Vietnam on principled grounds, political considerations unrelated to sovereignty or human rights played an important part in shaping the way international society reacted to the Vietnamese intervention.[7] In the same year as Vietnam's invasion of Cambodia, Tanzania – a highly regarded state with a well-respected President, Julius Nyerere – invaded Uganda and deposed Idi Amin with barely a ripple of international condemnation. The vast difference between the way the world reacted to Vietnam and the way it reacted to Tanzania suggests that sovereignty was indeed doing less work than *Realpolitik* in shaping international reactions.

Sovereignty as a human right

The second set of issues surrounds the principle of sovereignty itself. This is a matter I will return to later in this chapter, so there is no need to labour the point here. At issue is the apparent disconnection between the idea that sovereignty stands in opposition to human rights and the fact that sovereignty is often claimed *in the name of human rights*. Typically, sovereignty claimed in the name of human rights is labelled 'popular sovereignty'. This manner of thinking about sovereignty began in earnest with the American and French Revolutions, in which the revolutionaries justified the violent overthrow of monarchs on the grounds that sovereignty derives from the people. In other words, sovereignty is based upon the people's right to choose their own form of government which is, in turn, grounded in the fundamental human right to liberty.[8]

Popular sovereignty lay at the heart of the decolonisation movement and emerged after the Second World War as the *only* means of legitimising government. That is, in order to win international recognition, states in the post-war era were obliged to demonstrate that they governed with the will of the people. Those which were patently unable to do so lost legitimacy and recognition. Thus in less than a decade colonialism was transformed from the world's most widespread form of governance into a moral pariah, on the grounds that it was wrong to deny people their right to govern themselves. Measures taken again apartheid South Africa were justified on precisely these grounds: as a racially based minority government, the South African government could not claim to represent the will of the people. Of course, the ascendancy of popular sovereignty raises as many questions as it answers. In particular, who are 'the people' supposed to be entitled to self-government and how is their 'will' to be ascertained? Democrats, communists, monarchists, Islamists and nationalists all have different answers to these questions, which is why we have different forms of government and disputes about the relationship between state rights and human rights. What is significant, however, is the post-1945 consensus that it is up to the people to determine their own form of government. Whichever logic is applied, ultimately this principle of consent is grounded in some conception of human rights.[9] Thus, the idea that sovereignty and human rights are locked in battle with one another makes little sense if one acknowledges the place of human rights in sustaining and legitimising sovereignty claims.

The limits of absolutism

The third issue looks at the problem from the opposite direction. Seeing sovereignty as a barrier to collective measures to protect fundamental human rights implies that sovereigns are entitled to act however they please within their own jurisdictions. This is commonly labelled 'absolutism' and was put forward most robustly by nineteenth-century German philosophers and scholars such as Hegel, Fichte, Ihering, Treitschke and Heller. Ihering maintained that sovereigns were limited only by their own will, whilst Treitschke argued that it was legitimate for a state to do anything at all to satisfy its interests and that these interests took priority over contractual obligations.[10] For the German absolutists, sovereignty implied not just the absence of a superior authority but also competence to the full reach of its material power. As a nineteenth-century French jurist, Fauchille, put it, 'to say a person is sovereign means not merely to say that he does not recognise any authority above his own, but that he may issue orders at his own discretion, that he may do freely and without limitation all that he considers fit to do'.[11] Historically, however, this vision of sovereignty has tended not to win support from the society of states. To illustrate this point, I will use two brief examples from the era of supposed sovereign absolutism.

To justify his decision to invade Belgium in 1914, violating its neutrality, which was guaranteed by international treaty, the German Chancellor von Bethmann-Hollweg argued that 'necessity knows no law'; that as a sovereign state Germany was entitled to take whatever measures it deemed necessary to protect itself.[12] This claim was widely rejected by international society and given as grounds for war by Britain. Coleman Phillipson, a London barrister, insisted that absolutist arguments can never 'convince men who possess reason and self respect that the rights and obligations established by solemn treaties can be destroyed at the pleasure of one contracting party'.[13] Likewise, British Prime Minister Lloyd George argued that Germany's repudiation of Belgian neutrality 'goes under the root of all public law. It is the straight road to barbarism.'[14] The point here is that Germany's attempt to claim a sovereign right to act as it pleased in relation to Belgian neutrality was rejected by Britain on the grounds that a sovereign was not entitled to repudiate international law.

But are sovereigns entitled to act as they please in their domestic affairs? Between 1880 and 1907, King Leopold of Belgium used terror to run his personal empire in the Congo as a profit-making entity. Most estimates agree that during this period Congo's population was halved from twenty million to ten million as a result of killings, forced labour, mass displacement and disease.[15] Under the 1884 Treaty of Berlin, Leopold was recognised as Congo's personal sovereign, which makes this a particularly apt case to test the scope of sovereignty. Leopold claimed to be an absolutist sovereign, arguing that 'the Congo has been and could have been nothing but a personal effort. There is no more legitimate or respectable right than that of an author over his own work, the product of his own labour . . . My rights over the Congo are to be shared with none; they are the fruit of my own struggles and expenditures.'[16] However, the Congo Free State was widely criticised and, after a sustained campaign of pressure by the British government which was supported by Germany and reluctantly by France, Leopold was forced to transfer sovereignty over the Congo Free State to Belgium.[17] Although painfully slow, ultimately the great powers pressured Belgium into removing Leopold's sovereignty.

What these two examples demonstrate is that, even in the period when the absolutist conception of sovereignty was advocated most strongly, these ideas did not win much support. Indeed, in both cases the advocates of absolutism eventually confronted coalitions of states determined to defend the idea that sovereigns have responsibilities both to each other and to their own people.

Sovereignty and non-intervention

The fourth concern relates to the relationship between sovereignty and non-intervention. The belief that sovereignty and human rights are fundamentally opposed to each other is based on the view that the principal duty owed to sovereigns is non-intervention. Human rights challenge sovereignty when they are used as a vehicle for outsiders to interfere in the sovereign's domestic affairs. But are sovereignty and non-intervention necessarily two sides of the same coin? The belief that they are is widespread. According to Hedley Bull, intervention is generally considered wrong because 'sovereign states or independent political communities are thought to have a right to have their spheres of jurisdiction respected, and dictatorial interference abridges that right'.[18] Barry Buzan recently defined non-intervention as the 'corollary' of sovereignty.[19] But this belief is misplaced, as has been made clear by Hidemi Suganami.

Before the UN Charter, sovereigns enjoyed a right to wage war.[20] Indeed, before the twentieth century sovereigns even had a legal right to expand their territory through armed conquest. Given that sovereignty goes back some four hundred years, it is fair to say that, for the bulk of its history, sovereignty was not accompanied by a right to non-intervention. Quite the opposite. Sovereignty involved a right to interfere in the territory of others and, for a long time, to transform that interference into an *entitlement* to rule – because victors were entitled to annex the territories of the vanquished. The point here is not to deny the power, utility or moral force of the non-intervention rule, but to demonstrate that it is *not* a corollary of sovereignty. Rather, it is a rule fashioned by sovereigns and designed to govern their relations with one another. Logically, therefore, one can have sovereignty without a rule of non-intervention. If this is the case, there is no *intrinsic* competition between sovereignty and the collective protection of human rights.

Together, these four concerns suggest that it is wrong to think that collective, sometimes coercive, measures to protect fundamental human rights 'strike at the very essence of sovereignty', as the American representative in the Security Council argued in 2005. Instead, the preceding discussion suggests that we need to move beyond thinking in terms of a struggle between sovereignty and human rights. In so doing, we should begin by acknowledging two fundamental points.

First, what academics and political leaders often present as a foundational struggle over the very essence of international order is, in actuality, a political conundrum about how to realise the ambitions set out by the preamble to the UN Charter. How do concerned states reaffirm faith in fundamental human rights *and* promote peace by behaving like good neighbours in cases where the two seem to require different courses of action? Second, sovereignty itself is not a settled norm. There are different ideas about what sovereignty is, where it comes from and what it requires and permits. Rather than the heart of the matter being a struggle between sovereignty and human rights, perhaps the issue revolves around different conceptions of sovereignty itself. This is how UN Secretary-General Kofi Annan presented the problem in a landmark article he wrote for the *Economist* in 1999.[21]

The first conception of sovereignty, what Annan labelled 'traditional sovereignty', holds that nations have a right to determine their own form of government and maintains that this right can only be protected through a robust rule of non-intervention which prohibits the strong from meddling in the affairs of the weak and from undermining their right to self-government. The second conception holds that sovereignty entails responsibilities and that a government's failure to fulfil those responsibilities might legitimise, indeed require, external interference in that sovereign's affairs. The preceding discussions demonstrate that such ideas are not entirely new, nor are they antithetical to sovereignty. Relations between rulers and the ruled have long been the concern of other states, and the title 'sovereign' has rarely – if ever – given states a free hand to act as they pleased. In the second part of this chapter I will outline these two concepts of sovereignty and discuss Annan's effort to bridge the divide between them – an effort which laid the groundwork for the development of the R2P.

Traditional Sovereignty

Traditional sovereignty draws its moral force from the argument that nations enjoy a fundamental right to self-determination. Proponents of this view argue that nations enjoy a 'common life' and should be free to determine their own form of culture and system of governance. This right is grounded in each individual's basic human rights and the non-intervention rule is an essential prerequisite for the realisation of these rights.[22] From this perspective there is a 'fit' between the nation and the state, and it should be assumed that states enable nations to develop and protect their own cultures and forms of government. Sovereignty protects this right to self-determination because it entails a presumption against external interference in their domestic affairs. This is sometimes labelled 'pluralism', principally because it has as its aim the preservation of cultural difference in world politics. At its heart, it holds that people might choose to live and be governed in many different ways and outsiders have no right to impose their particular way of life on others.

The argument that nations have a right to self-determination that can only be protected if sovereigns are granted a robust right of non-intervention has been used to defend traditional sovereignty since 1945.

Indeed, these concerns were aired by small states during the drafting of the UN Charter itself. Australia, Bolivia, Brazil and Norway all argued that the Charter's ban on the use of force should be worded in such a way as to eliminate potential loopholes.[23] Chief among the concerns of Latin American states was the stipulation that the new organisation should contain rules protecting their sovereign right to determine their own form of government.

Since then, the message from the postcolonial world has been loud and clear. In 1960, the General Assembly – the principal global voice for post-colonial states – issued its Declaration on the Granting of Independence to Colonial Countries and Peoples. Adopted by a majority of eighty-nine votes to none, with nine abstentions, the declaration proclaimed that 'all peoples have the right to self-determination; by virtue of that right they freely determine their political status and freely pursue their economic, social and cultural development'. The UN's subsequent resolutions on self-determination all use this wording, and in 1975 the International Court of Justice (ICJ) recognised the statement as the 'basis for the process of decolonisation'.[24] The insistence that all peoples have a right to self-determination, including a right to 'freely determine their political status' was also incorporated into the General Assembly's International Covenants on Human Rights in 1966.

For postcolonial leaders there is a direct relationship between a people's right freely to determine its political status and the non-intervention rule. After all, there can be no right of self-determination if powerful states feel entitled to interfere in the affairs of the weak. As such, the General Assembly's 1970 Declaration on Principles of International Law Concerning Friendly Relations stated categorically that:

> No state or group of states has the right to intervene, directly or indi-rectly, for any reason whatever, in the internal or external affairs of any other state. Consequently, armed intervention and all other forms of interference or attempted threats against the personality of the state or against its political, economic and cultural elements, are in violation of international law.

When viewed alongside its declarations on decolonisation, the Assembly's reasons for defending non-intervention so robustly are clear: non-intervention is necessary to protect the weak from the strong and to prevent the re-emergence of colonialism. On this account of sovereignty, there is a direct link between an individual's human right to determine his or her own way of life and form of government and the right of non-intervention.

Many academics support this argument and maintain that, because national communities are so different and because difference is a good worth preserving, international order can only be achieved by rigid adherence to the rule of non-intervention. In order to function properly, international society is based on legal rules which enable the world's diverse communities to enjoy their own ways of life without infringing on the rights of others to do likewise. In a world characterised by radical cultural, religious, economic, social and political disagreements, a relaxed attitude to intervention would create disorder, as states would wage war to protect and export their own cultural and political preferences.[25] From this perspective, it is a short road from relaxing non-intervention to legitimising colonialism. Moreover, states have shown a distinct predilection towards 'abusing' humanitarian justifications to legitimise wars that were anything but humanitarian. Most notoriously, Hitler insisted that the 1938 invasion of Czechoslovakia was inspired by a desire to protect Czechoslovak citizens of German nationality whose 'life and liberty' were threatened by their government.[26]

For these reasons, states developed a framework of positive law comprising a comprehensive ban on the use of force (Article 2(4)), except in self-defence or where authorised for the collective good by the UN Security Council. According to Simon Chesterman, a humanitarian exception to the ban on force would not enable more humanitarian interventions, but it would make it easier for states to justify self-interested invasions through spurious humanitarian arguments.[27]

Because this conception of sovereignty is predicated on human rights, it does not go as far as the 'absolutist' view in implying that sovereigns are entitled to act as they please. On the one hand, its association with a conservative view of international law means that advocates of traditional sovereignty welcome the view that states are obliged to conduct their international relations with due respect to the legal rules – the principle of non-intervention being chief among them. On the other hand, because it draws a straight line from individual human rights to sovereign rights, this approach to sovereignty does not rule out all forms of intervention per se.[28] Contemporary advocates of traditional sovereignty do not argue that sovereigns are entitled to commit genocide. Nor do they deny that the UN Security Council is entitled to authorise collective measures against member states which abuse their citizens. Instead they insist that the Security Council is alone in enjoying this prerogative, and they set a high threshold for when it may act. Acting otherwise would undermine the rule of law and the fundamental human right to self-determination. Collective action authorised by the Security Council might be occasionally acceptable, however, because the Council's seal of approval provides albeit imperfect assurance that the measures taken are aimed at achieving collectively agreed goals.

International commitment to traditional sovereignty remains widespread and steadfast. It is a position rhetorically endorsed by a majority of states in the General Assembly (especially a majority of members in the G77 and NAM), by many international lawyers and by notable groups of politicians and activists in the West. It manifests itself in two principal ways in debates relating to the R2P. First, traditional sovereignty requires a presumption against intervention by placing a high threshold on when outsiders are entitled to intervene to ameliorate human suffering against the wishes of the host government. It is hard to deny the merits of unilateral intervention in cases like that of Rwanda, where 800,000 people were killed in a hundred days. But where the rate of killing is lower and slower, advocates of traditional sovereignty tend to be either sceptical or hostile towards uninvited coercive interference, pointing to the potential for abuse by the great powers. Second, this position insists that any intervention should be properly authorised by the UN Security Council and that, if the Council is to become proactive in judging the domestic affairs of states, reforms to make that body more representative are imperative.

Advocates of the R2P do not dismiss these arguments lightly. Gareth Evans, for example, recognised that sovereignty hard won through decolonisation is not lightly given away.[29] In similar vein, Ramesh Thakur has repeatedly argued that the R2P is not an 'intervener's charter', but an attempt to restrain unilateral intervention while guiding genuine collective measures.[30] The link between individual human rights, self-determination and the rule of non-intervention is certainly valid, though the problem nowadays is not that there are *too many* humanitarian interventions but too few – as Rwanda and Darfur attest. Nonetheless, students of contemporary history would recognise merit in the claim that relaxing the non-intervention rule could weaken already weak states and open the door to neo-colonialism. Moreover, because this is a position held by the majority of states, the R2P cannot evolve and spread if it ignores these concerns. There are, however, avenues for advancing the cause of human protection within this framework. After all, traditional sovereignty is founded on human rights. Today's advocates of traditional sovereignty do not typically argue that sovereigns may act as they choose, or that mass killing is acceptable. Nor do they rule out intervention in every case. Instead, they worry about how collective action and the potential for the R2P to grant licences to neo-imperialists; they express scepticism about the utility of force; and they are concerned that the R2P is the thin end of the wedge when it comes to the imposition of basically Western values on the rest. Of course, sometimes the position is simply advocated by despotic governments who seek cover for abusing the human rights of their citizens in the most chronic fashion. The challenge is to distinguish the legitimate arguments from the self-justifications of tyrants.

Sovereignty as Responsibility

The second conception of sovereignty identified by Annan is 'sovereignty as responsibility'. According to Annan,

> state sovereignty, in its most basic sense, is being redefined . . . States are now widely understood to be instruments at the service of their peoples, and not vice-versa. At the same time individual sovereignty – by which I mean the fundamental freedom of each individual, enshrined in the Charter of the UN and subsequent international treaties – has been enhanced by a renewed and spreading consciousness of individual rights. When we read the Charter today, we are more than ever conscious that its aim is to protect individual human beings, not to protect those who abuse them.[31]

This account shares the traditional view that the sovereignty of states is ultimately derived from individual human rights. Sovereignty thus entails both rights and responsibilities. Only those states that cherish, nurture and protect the fundamental rights of their citizens and thereby fulfil their sovereign responsibilities are entitled to the full panoply of sovereign rights. Sovereignty therefore is not 'suspended' or 'overridden' when external bodies act against (or to assist) a government that fails in its responsibilities by abusing its citizens on a massive scale. Instead, sovereignty is protected and promoted in such cases because such international activism seeks to create the conditions necessary for individual sovereigns to determine their own fate.

Sovereignty as responsibility rests on two foundations. First, it rests on the proposition that individuals have *inalienable* human rights that may never be rescinded. These rights are universal, not culture-specific. They are also prior to politics. As such, an individual's basic rights are never secondary to the rights of national groups, as the traditional concept of sovereignty implies. According to Lynn Hunt, these rights have three innate qualities: they are *natural* (inherent in human beings), *equal* (the same for everyone), and *universal*.[32] Second, governments have the primary responsibility for protecting their citizens' rights, but where they abuse those rights international society acquires rights *and duties* to take measures to protect the rights in question.[33]

This is often touted as a new or radical conception of sovereignty. But it is neither new, having been enunciated for the first time in 1776, nor radical. The doctrine of sovereignty as responsibility was written down by Thomas Jefferson and proclaimed in America's Declaration of Independence on 4 July 1776. Thus:

> We hold these truths to be self-evident, that all men are created equal, that they are endowed by their Creator with certain inalienable Rights, that among these are Life, Liberty and Happiness.

> [T]o secure these rights, Governments are instituted among Men, deriving their just powers from the consent of the governed – That whenever any Form of Government becomes destructive of these ends, it is the Right of the People to alter or abolish it, and to institute new Government. . .

> [W]hen a long train of abuses and usurpations, pursuing invariably the same Object, evinces a design to reduce them under absolute Despotism, it is their right, it is their duty, to throw off such Government, and to provide new Guards for their future security . . .

In short, governments which fail to protect the fundamental rights of their citizens or wantonly abuse those rights fail in their sovereign responsibilities. This gives the people, as individual sovereigns, the right and duty to overthrow the government and to replace it with one more conducive to the satisfaction of their rights. These ideas were repeated thirteen years later by the French National Assembly, which in 1789 proclaimed the 'Rights of man and of citizen', insisting that 'the principle of all sovereignty rests essentially in the nation. No body and no individual may exercise authority which does not emanate expressly from the nation.'

Of course, these ideas were not widely supported in their own time. American independence was won through the force of arms, not through the power of persuasion. The French Revolution gave way to the 'Terror', Napoleonic despotism and imperial expansion. Paradoxically, the Napoleonic wars discredited popular sovereignty while spreading it to new parts of Europe and inspiring later Italian, Hungarian and German nationalists. Although its meaning and fortunes ebbed and flowed, sovereignty as responsibility survived into the twentieth century. Among its champions were three members of the Roosevelt dynasty.

In May 1918, former US President Theodore Roosevelt insisted that the massacre of Armenians by the Turks invalidated Turkey's claim to rule over

Armenia. He argued that 'the perpetuation of Turkish rule is the perpetuation of infamy', continuing: '[w]e are guilty of a peculiarly odious form of hypocrisy when we profess friendship for Armenia and the downtrodden races of Turkey, but don't go to war with Turkey. To allow the Turks to massacre the [Armenians] and then solicit permission to help the survivors . . . is both foolish and odious.' He ended by referring to America's reasons for joining the First World War: 'when we now refuse to war with Turkey we show that our announcement that we meant "to make the world safe for democracy" was insincere claptrap'.[34] After the war, Woodrow Wilson defended the idea that sovereignty be based on the principle of self-determination, though this did not extend to self-determination for Armenians because Congress rejected a proposed American trusteeship.

In the 1941 Atlantic Charter, Theodore's nephew, Franklin Roosevelt, succeeded in persuading British Prime Minister Winston Churchill to subscribe to the principles of self-determination and individual human rights. The charter proclaimed 'the right of all peoples to choose the form of government under which they will live' and that the Allied powers would establish a peace in which 'all the men in all the lands may live out their lives in freedom from fear and want'.[35] After the Second World War, a third Roosevelt, Eleanor, played a key role in cajoling the world into adopting a Universal Declaration of Human Rights, chairing the UN Human Rights Commission and shepherding the draft declaration through eighty-three commission meetings and some 170 amendments.[36] The Declaration proclaimed that 'recognition of the inherent dignity and of the equal and inalienable rights of all members of the human family is the foundation of freedom, justice and peace in the world'. Among its thirty articles, Article 1 declared that '[a]ll human beings are born free and equal in dignity', whilst Article 3 insisted that '[e]veryone has the right to life, liberty and security of person'. Missing, however, was the second component of sovereignty as responsibility: the idea that a government's failure to satisfy these rights granted others a responsibility to ensure their realisation.

Sovereignty as responsibility was given new impetus after the Cold War. The immediate catalyst was Boutros Boutros-Ghali's appointment of Francis Deng, a well-respected former Sudanese diplomat, as his Special Representative on Internally Displaced People (IDPs) in 1993. In appointing Deng and in highlighting the problem of IDPs, Boutros-Ghali was responding both to urgent humanitarian need and to a vexing political dilemma. As wars became less of a matter between states and more of a struggle between forces within states, the number of internally displaced people exploded. When Deng was appointed, there were some twenty-five million

IDPs globally.[37] If these civilians crossed an international border, the majority would be entitled to claim refugee status, on condition that their host was a signatory to the 1951 Refugee Convention or a state accepting help from the UNHCR.[38] As IDPs, however, they were afforded no special protection and remained critically vulnerable to the whims or failings of their home state.

Deng recognised both sides of the problem. On the humanitarian side, he noted that IDPs 'remain within the borders of a country at war with itself, and even when they move to safer areas, they are viewed as strangers, discriminated against, and often harassed . . . those persons who are uprooted from their home have been shown to be especially vulnerable to physical attack, sexual assault, abduction, disease and deprivation of basic life needs. They suffer higher rates of mortality than the general population, sometimes as high as fifty times greater.'[39] He also recognised the politically problematic status of IDPs. To return to Deng:

> In many countries experiencing internal conflicts, the internally displaced are not only disposed [of] by their own governments but are outside the reach of the international community because of the negative approach to sovereignty as a barrier against international involvement. While international humanitarian and human rights instruments offer legally binding bases for international protection and assistance to needy populations within their national borders, needy populations are for the most part at the mercy of their national authorities for their security and general welfare. International access to them can be tragically constrained and even blocked by states in the name of sovereignty, by the collapse of states, or by rampant insecurity.[40]

In order to argue their way around the use of sovereignty to deny international assistance for IDPs, Deng and Cohen proposed sovereignty as responsibility. The starting point for this new, positive account of the relationship between sovereignty and fundamental human rights was a recognition that the primary responsibility for protecting and assisting IDPs lay with the host government – an idea which came to sit at the heart of the R2P.[41] No legitimate state, they argued, could quarrel with the claim that it was responsible for the well-being of its citizens; and indeed, as we noted earlier, no governments have in fact quarrelled with this proposition. Where a state was unable to fulfil its responsibilities, it should invite and welcome international assistance to 'complement national efforts'.[42] Deng and Cohen argued that international involvement actually aided the realisation of effective national sovereignty by increasing a state's capacity to fulfil its sovereign responsibilities. The best way for a vulnerable state or one failing to protect its sovereignty, they argued, was by inviting international assistance.

The corollary of sovereignty as responsibility is accountability. Through this concept, the host state is made accountable both to its citizens and to international society, and the latter acquires a responsibility to assist the host state or, in extreme cases, to act without the state's consent in order to protect the fundamental rights of IDPs. At its heart, therefore, sovereignty as responsibility was based on Deng's positive account of sovereignty. As Deng and his collaborators on another project – on conflict management in Africa – put it:

> Sovereignty carries with it certain responsibilities for which governments must be held accountable. And they are accountable not only to their national constituencies but ultimately to the international community. In other words, by effectively discharging its responsibilities for good governance, a state can legitimately claim protection for its national sovereignty.[43]

Whether assistance is requested or is non-consensual, the logic of sovereignty as responsibility gives troubled states an interest in cooperating with international agencies as the best way of realising their sovereignty. Troubled states faced a choice: to work with international organisations and other interested outsiders so as to realise their sovereign responsibilities; or to obstruct international efforts and forfeit their sovereignty.[44] As a 1992 human rights conference on IDPs concluded, 'if governments failed to meet their obligations, they risked undermining their legitimacy'.[45]

But at what point can a state be judged to have forfeited its sovereignty, and what body has the right to decide it? Deng and his collaborators were sketchy on these questions, but usefully suggested that sovereignty as responsibility implied the existence of a 'higher authority capable of holding supposed sovereigns accountable' and that this higher authority should place the common good ahead of the national interests of its member states. Clearly, the UN Security Council is closest to fitting the bill, but it falls short of Deng's ideal by a considerable degree. It is important to keep this point in mind: the more the Security Council is asked to do and adjudicate on, the more important the Council's own legitimacy becomes – the extent to which Council members place the common good ahead of their own interests, the extent to which it is representative and the extent to which it is accountable and transparent. Given this, there is little wonder that Boutros-Ghali's successor, Kofi Annan, insisted that the success of the R2P and wider UN reform was intimately linked to the reform of the Security Council.

In the late 1990s, two permanent members of the Security Council, the US and UK, began putting forth their own ideas about sovereignty as responsibility. For American policy-makers associated with both the Clinton and the Bush administrations, responsible sovereignty was tied not just to human rights, but also to security imperatives such as WMD non-proliferation and anti-terrorism cooperation. In 1998, Philip Zelikow, who was later to become executive director of the 9/11 Commission and author of the 2002 National Security Strategy, co-authored a report on global responses to 'catastrophic terrorism' which set out the case for a wider doctrine of responsible sovereignty. The report concluded that 'international norms should adapt so that such states are obliged to reassure those who are worried and to take reasonable measures to prove they are not secretly developing weapons of mass destruction. Failure to supply such proof, or prosecute the criminals living in their borders, should entitle worried nations to take all necessary measures for their self-defence'.[46]

A key advocate of the American conception of sovereignty as responsibility was Richard Haass, President of the Council on Foreign Relations and former Director of Policy Planning in Colin Powell's State Department. Haass argued that sovereignty should be conditional on human rights as well as on a commitment to WMD non-proliferation and counter-terrorism. Thus in 2002 he insisted that 'sovereignty does not grant governments a blank check to do whatever they like within their own borders'.[47] Two years later, Stewart Patrick, one of Haass' colleagues at the State Department, elaborated on this idea, insisting that:

> Historically, the main obstacle to armed intervention – humanitarian or otherwise – has been the doctrine of sovereignty, which prohibits violating the territorial integrity of another state. One of the striking developments of the past decade has been an erosion of this non-intervention norm and the rise of a nascent doctrine of 'contingent sovereignty'. This school of thought holds that sovereign rights and immunities are not absolute. They depend on the observance of fundamental state obligations.[48]

This doctrine of sovereignty later became an official part of America's defence strategy, with the 2005 National Defense Strategy declaring that 'it is unacceptable for regimes to use the principle of sovereignty as a shield behind which they can claim to be free to engage in activities that pose enormous threats to their citizens, neighbors, or the rest of the international community'.[49] This doctrine partly informed Clinton's decision to intervene in Kosovo in 1999 and was subsequently associated with the 2001 intervention in Afghanistan and the 2003 invasion of Iraq. However, this link between sovereignty as responsibility and George W. Bush's unpopular foreign policy helped to create significant obstacles for those seeking to forge a global consensus on the R2P (see Chapter 3).

NATO's 1999 intervention in Kosovo provided the catalyst for Tony Blair to put forth his own ideas about sovereignty as responsibility. Shortly after NATO began its bombing campaign, Blair travelled to the US to help Clinton in shoring up domestic support for the war. It was there that he gave a landmark speech – the first draft of which was penned by the British academic Lawrence Freedman – setting out his 'doctrine of the international community' and his concept of sovereignty as responsibility. Blair anchored sovereignty as responsibility into the changing nature of international order. He maintained that sovereignty should be reconceptualised because globalisation was changing the world in ways that rendered traditional sovereignty anachronistic. Argued Blair:

> We live in a world where isolationism has ceased to have a reason to exist. By necessity we have to co-operate with each other across nations. Many of our domestic problems are caused on the other side of the world . . . We are all internationalists now, whether we like it or not. We cannot refuse to participate in global markets if we want to prosper. We cannot ignore new political ideas in other countries if we want to innovate. We cannot turn our backs on conflicts and the violation of human rights within other countries if we want still to be secure.

According to Blair, global interconnectedness created two sets of responsibilities. First, enlightened self-interest created international responsibilities for dealing with egregious human suffering because, as President Kennedy argued, in an interdependent world 'freedom is indivisible and when one man is enslaved who is free?' Second, sovereigns had responsibilities to the society of states because problems caused by massive human rights abuse could spread across borders. Thus Blair continued:

> The most pressing foreign policy problem we face is to identify the circumstances in which we should get actively involved in other people's conflicts. Non-interference has long been considered an important principle of international order. And it is not one we would want to jettison too readily ... But the principle of non-interference must be qualified in important respects. Acts of genocide can never be a purely internal matter.[50]

To balance respect for non-interference with concern for human rights, Blair proposed five tests to ascertain the legitimacy of intervention – setting in train a debate about the use of criteria to guide intervention which crystallised in the work of the ICISS (see Chapter 2). These tests were:

1 Are we sure of our case?
2 Have we exhausted all diplomatic options?
3 Are there sensible and prudent military options?
4 Are we prepared for the long-term?
5 Are there national interests involved?

The British Foreign Office's Policy Planning staff followed up by circulating a draft paper among the P5 in late 1999 on intervention criteria.[51] The paper went through several revisions on the basis of feedback from governments and the Foreign Office's own change in thinking, but it was never made publicly available and the endeavour was quietly dropped at around the same time as the controversy sparked by Annan's endorsement of the need to rethink the relationship between sovereignty and intervention (see below).[52]

The adoption of variants of the concept of sovereignty as responsibility by the US and UK attracted international criticism, especially when this doctrine was associated with the 2003 invasion of Iraq (see Chapter 3). Critics argued that the US and the UK were abusing and selectively applying a partial account of human rights to justify armed intervention in weak and mainly postcolonial states. They also insisted that the UN Security Council should properly validate measures carried out in the name of fundamental human rights. Tellingly, however, criticisms like these were aired well before sovereignty as responsibility was picked up by Washington and London.

When Francis Deng started talking about sovereignty as responsibility, he attracted withering criticism. During a 1993 discussion on IDPs in the UN's Human Rights Commission, China, whilst stressing human rights and fundamental freedoms as a 'lofty goal of mankind', delivered a broadside on sovereignty as responsibility. China argued against interference in the internal affairs of states on the grounds of 'self-interested' concepts of human rights and ideologies held by 'a few countries'. Its argument ran: 'the practices of distorting human rights standards, exerting political pressure through abuse of monitoring mechanisms, applying selectivity and double-standards have led to the violation of principles and purposes of the UN Charter, and the impairing of the sovereignty and dignity of many developing countries. Thus the beautiful term of human rights has been tarnished.' According to China, advocacy of sovereignty as responsibility amounted to nothing but an attempt to legitimise the interference of the strong in the affairs of the postcolonial world. The Chinese representative continued:

> The urgent issue is to remove as soon as possible the imposition of their own human rights concepts, values and ideology by a few countries who style themselves as 'human rights judges': and the interference in internal affairs of other countries by using human rights as a means of applying political pressure. The victims of such practice are developing countries who[se] people suffered from violation of human rights and fundamental freedoms for a long time before and are now making great efforts to safeguard their sovereignty and independence for their survival and development.[53]

Cuba joined the assault, linking Deng's work on IDPs to a doctrine of humanitarian intervention which constituted an attempt 'to forcibly impose certain ideological conceptions of human rights on a number of countries, chiefly, though not exclusively, in the Third World'.[54] Advocates of traditional sovereignty worried that, by propounding sovereignty as responsibility, the West was setting itself up as both judge and jury in relation to a doctrine which lent the veneer of legitimacy to coercive interference in the affairs of sovereigns. Moreover, it allowed the West to further its own interests by interfering in the affairs of others under the banner of human rights.

Bridging the Gap? Kofi Annan on Intervention

Matters came to a head in the late 1990s. In March 1998, Serbian forces began a wave of ethnic cleansing in Kosovo. Western states led by Tony Blair and Bill Clinton pushed for a decisive international response. It was clear from the outset, however, that there would be little likelihood of consensus in the Security Council, owing to Russian and Chinese opposition to intervention. It was in this atmosphere that Annan took on the role of 'norm entrepreneur' and decided to change the topic of his 1998 lecture to the Ditchley Foundation – an annual gathering of the British foreign policy elite – from 'the challenge of governance' to 'intervention'.[55] Insiders write that, even after asking Edward Mortimer – his recently appointed speech writer, who had formerly been a columnist for the *Financial Times* – to draft a speech on intervention, Annan remained unclear about his own position. On the one hand he recognised that the UN's failure to prevent or halt the bloodshed in Rwanda and Bosnia had badly hurt the organisation and undermined its credibility. On the other hand he believed in the sanctity of the UN Charter, including Article 2(4). He also knew that it would be difficult, if not impossible, to make the case for intervention so as to persuade a large enough majority of member states. But the role of the UN Secretary-General, as Annan recognised better than any holder of that office since Dag Hammarskjöld, is to act as a source of moral vision and to present ideas which might be unpopular and ahead of their time.[56] This is precisely what Annan did at Ditchley.

The Ditchley speech contained two key moves. First of all, the Secretary-General insisted that certain responsibilities were inherent to sovereignty and embedded in the UN Charter. He argued that:

> In reality, this 'old orthodoxy' [traditional sovereignty] was never absolute. The Charter, after all, was issued in the name of the 'the peoples', not the governments, of the United Nations. Its aim is not only to preserve international peace – vitally important though that is – but also 'to reaffirm faith in fundamental human rights, in the dignity and worth of the human person'. The Charter protects the sovereignty of peoples. It was never meant as a license for governments to trample on human rights and human dignity. Sovereignty implies responsibility, not just power.[57]

Annan then appealed to supporters of traditional sovereignty by pointing out the dangers associated with permitting individual states to decide on a case for intervention for themselves. In the Secretary-General's words: 'Can we really afford to let each state be the judge of its own right, or duty, to intervene in another state's internal conflict? If we do, will we not be forced to legitimise Hitler's championship of the Sudeten Germans, or Soviet intervention in Afghanistan?' In place of unilateralism, Annan argued that measures designed to interfere in the domestic concerns of states be genuinely collective. 'Surely', he continued, 'the only institution competent to assume that role is the Security Council of the United Nations. The Charter clearly assigns responsibility to the Council for maintaining international peace and security. I would argue, therefore, that only the Council has the authority to decide that the internal situation in any state is so grave as to justify forceful intervention . . . humanity is ill-served when the Council is unable to react quickly and decisively in a crisis.' The real challenge, Annan maintained, was to prevent crises from emerging in the first place. To do this, member states should work through UN bodies and agencies to tackle the underlying causes of humanitarian crises. This is what Deng was getting at in his call for a positive approach to sovereignty and fundamental human rights.

The 'Ditchley formula', as it became known, was put to the test by the crisis in Kosovo. The international community failed to stem the tide of Serbian ethnic cleansing through diplomacy, sanctions and threats and, when the Rambouillet negotiations broke down without reaching a settlement, the Serbs launched a new wave of killings and forced expulsions. NATO responded with a campaign of aerial bombardment. Crucially, the intervention was not authorised by the Security Council, on account of threatened vetos from Russia and China. However, two days into the campaign, the Council also emphatically rejected a Russian draft resolution condemning NATO and calling for an immediate cessation of hostilities. The draft was rejected by twelve votes to three, with only Namibia joining Russia and China in support of the resolution. Kosovo thus posed a hard test for the Secretary-General. Would Annan criticise what seemed to many to be a clear violation of the UN Charter, or would he accept that 'individual sovereignty' grounded in human rights created a higher legitimacy in this case?

The intervention sparked fierce debate within Annan's office. Some, such as Annan's American Special Adviser John Ruggie, his deputy Iqbal Riza and Edward Mortimer supported NATO and recommended the Secretary-General to do likewise. Whilst calling on both sides to end the violence, in Resolution 1199 the Security Council had identified Serbian ethnic cleansing as a threat to international peace and security and had issued a strong condemnation. They also argued that the Serbs and their supporters were doing precisely what Annan had criticised at Ditchley – using sovereignty as a veil to protect the committing of gross human rights abuses. Others, such as Kieran Prendergast – Head of the Department of Political Affairs – and Sashi Tharoor – future candidate for Secretary-General – criticised the violation of Article 2(4) and argued that Annan should do the same.[58] The two sides squabbled over the wording of UN memos and reports, over the culpability of the KLA and the extent of ethnic cleansing. On one occasion Riza had to reprimand Alvaro de Soto, a high-ranking official in the Department of Political Affairs, for describing the crisis as 'an ongoing dispute in whose resolution we have no involvement' – a view significantly at odds with the vision set out by Annan at Ditchley.[59] Trying to pick his way through the morass, the Secretary-General issued an even-handed statement the day after the bombing began. Noting that NATO should not have acted without seeking authorisation from the Security Council, he went on to argue:

> I deeply regret that in spite of all the efforts made by the international community, the Yugoslav authorities have persisted in their rejection of a

political settlement, which would have halted the bloodshed in Kosovo and secured an equitable peace for the population there. It is indeed tragic that diplomacy has failed, but there are times when the use of force may be legitimate in the pursuit of peace.'[60]

In NATO countries, Annan's statement was seen as tacit endorsement, a view only strengthened by the Security Council's rejection of the Russian draft resolution and subsequent adoption of Resolution 1203, authorising a post-war NATO-led peacekeeping mission (KFOR) in Kosovo.

Whilst Annan's position might have helped to smooth out difficulties, relations between the UN and NATO remained tense. Albright took offence at a statement by Annan deploring the loss of civilian lives caused by the bombing. When Yeltsin proposed that Annan be invited to broker a political settlement, Clinton rejected it on the grounds that he would not permit the UN to negotiate on NATO's behalf.[61] To make matters worse, the perception that Annan had tacitly supported the intervention did nothing for the Secretary-General's ambition to sell a new doctrine of intervention. The Non-Aligned Movement (NAM) itself responded by issuing a declaration condemning the 'so-called right of humanitarian intervention' which, it argued, 'has no legal basis'.[62] Two months after his initial statement, Annan tried to clarify his position by emphasising his frustration at the fact that NATO had failed to bring its case before the Security Council. In a speech at The Hague, Annan recognised the difficulty of obtaining Security Council approval for intervention in difficult cases but insisted that 'patient and careful' diplomacy could have achieved this aim. Most worrying for the Secretary-General 'has been the inability of states to reconcile national interests when skilful and visionary diplomacy would make unity possible'. He continued by reiterating the theme of Security Council legitimacy, which both he and Deng thought was so intimately connected to the management of sovereignty as responsibility: 'unless the Security Council is restored to its pre-eminent position as the sole source of legitimacy on the use of force, we are on a dangerous path to anarchy'.[63]

In the wake of Kosovo, the UN Secretary-General created a working group including people from both sides of the debate, to explore the question of the post-Kosovo security framework. Over time, the group became more sceptical about Annan's association with humanitarian intervention. Lakhdar Brahimi, a diplomat of high standing and chair of the UN's high-profile panel on peace operations, argued that, by associating itself with humanitarian intervention, the UN risked being abused by powerful states to the detriment of the organisation as a whole. On the other side, Edward Mortimer pointed out that it was the UN's failures in Rwanda and Bosnia that had done more than anything else to discredit the organisation.[64] Grasping for a way to bridge the divide meaningfully and to chart a course which might help Annan to avoid a repetition of the divisive debate on Kosovo, Mortimer agreed that it was necessary to find a new way of talking about intervention, a way which emphasised 'relieving human suffering' rather than military action and the legal rights of interveners.[65] The Secretary-General, in other words, needed to adopt the positive language of sovereignty and fundamental human rights advocated by Francis Deng six years earlier.

Over the coming months, Annan tackled the issue head-on, writing the 'two concepts of sovereignty' essay described earlier and using his opening address to the 1999 General Assembly to frame the terms of the forthcoming debate. Annan used the address to set out the problem and to challenge world leaders to find a solution:

> To those for whom the greatest threat to the future of international order is the use of force in the absence of a Security Council mandate, one might ask . . . in the context of Rwanda: If, in those dark days and hours leading up to the genocide, a coalition of States had been prepared to act in defence of the Tutsi population but did not receive prompt Council authorization, should such a coalition have stood aside and allowed the horror to unfold?
>
> To those for whom the Kosovo action heralded a new era when States and groups of States can take military action outside the established mechanisms for enforcing international law, one might ask: Is there not a danger of such interventions undermining the imperfect, yet resilient, security system created after the Second World War, and of setting dangerous precedents for future interventions without a clear criterion to decide who might invoke these precedents, and in what circumstances?[66]

Tacitly adopting Deng's approach to sovereignty, Annan argued that the state was the servant of the people and that the 'sovereignty of the individual' was enhanced by a growing respect for human rights. State sovereignty therefore implied a responsibility to protect individual sovereigns. The role of the UN was to assist states in the fulfilment of their responsibilities and achievement of their sovereignty. This much was clearly set out in the UN Charter, Annan reiterated. The question, however, was one of how to determine the 'common interest' in particular cases. In a case such as that of Kosovo, did sovereignty as responsibility require intervention, and, if so, who was entitled to take this decision?

Answering his own questions, Annan developed the three benchmarks set out at Ditchley. First, a principle of intervention should be 'fairly and consistently applied'. Second, it should embrace a 'more broadly defined, more widely conceived definition of national interest'.[67] In other words, as Deng had argued, decision-makers should take decisions on the basis of the common good, not on the basis of national interests. Third, the proper authority was the Security Council, but the Council should accept its responsibilities and make a commitment to respond to humanitarian emergencies. Repeating his warning to those who would stand in the way of genuine collective humanitarian action, Annan told the Assembly that, 'if the collective conscience of humanity . . . cannot find in the United Nations its greatest tribune, there is a grave danger it will look elsewhere for peace and for justice'.[68]

The Secretary-General did not have to wait long for the debate to begin, and the shift in emphasis did little to stem the tide of opposition. The third speaker following Annan, President Abdelaziz Bouteflika of Algeria, issued a strong rebuke to the Secretary-General, insisting that his country was

> extremely sensitive to any undermining of our sovereignty, not only because sovereignty is our final defence against the rules of an unjust world, but because we have no active part in the decision-making process in the Security Council nor in monitoring the implementation of decisions . . . We firmly believe that interference in internal affairs may take place only with the consent of the State in question.[69]

Later that day, Theo-Ben Gurirab, the Namibian Ambassador and President of the General Assembly, used a toast at a diplomatic cocktail party to criticise Annan's speech still further – a move described as 'an astonishing breach of etiquette'.[70]

The Secretary-General's efforts had, however, helped to re-focus the debate. The question was now not whether sovereigns had responsibilities but what those responsibilities were, how they were best realised and what role international society should play. That much had been set out clearly by Deng and Annan and had been accepted by a growing number of governments and NGOs – the latter's views on the matter being set out in a 2002 report by the International Council on Human Rights Policy.[71] Answering Annan's challenge, the baton was picked up by the Canadian government, which in 2000 announced the creation of the International Commission for Intervention and State Sovereignty (ICISS) – the subject of the following chapter.

Conclusion

The whole concept of the R2P rests on the idea that sovereignty and human rights are two sides of the same coin, and not opposing principles locked in interminable struggle, as is often portrayed. If this is the case, then the question of the rights and responsibilities of states in cases of genocide and mass atrocities is a question not of the relative weight of sovereignty and human rights but of which account of sovereignty holds sway. Historically, sovereignty has almost always entailed responsibilities in one form or another. What changes is not the connection between sovereignty and responsibility, but the scope of the relevant responsibilities, the identity of those to whom sovereigns are responsible (the Pope, the people and so on) and the practical effect of that relationship. It is these issues that animate the contemporary contest between 'traditional sovereignty' and 'sovereignty as responsibility'. Both accounts admit that sovereigns have responsibilities – to their people and to international society. They disagree on the precise nature of the responsibility to the people (traditional sovereignty focusing on self-determination; sovereignty as responsibility on fundamental human rights) and on the role of international society (traditional sovereignty views it as a horizontal relationship between equals with no external oversight of sovereign behaviour; sovereignty as responsibility holds that international society should collectively oversee the domestic behaviour of sovereigns in some circumstances) – though both to some extent concede that the UN Security Council has the authority to police sovereign affairs. As this chapter has demonstrated, traditional sovereignty and sovereignty as responsibility have more in common than appears at first. This common ground provided the opportunity to build a consensus around the R2P.

This chapter has also surveyed some of the precursors to the R2P. It is important to recognise that the concept had its origins in two distinct settings, which creates something of a tension between those who believe that the R2P is primarily about prevention and protection and those who think that its focus ought to be on questions concerning military intervention.[72] The first root was the concept of 'sovereignty as responsibility', an idea with a long history, which was given new life and focus by Francis Deng and Roberta Cohen in the 1990s. Their approach focused on highlighting the responsibilities that sovereigns have towards their own population and on developing ways of encouraging and enabling states to live up to their responsibilities. The second root of the concept was the debate about humanitarian intervention sparked by NATO's 1999 intervention in Kosovo. It was this setting that provided the immediate catalyst for the creation of the ICISS, ideas about sovereignty yielding to external inter-vention during major humanitarian crises, and the notion that decisions about when to use force should be framed by criteria.

Having briefly surveyed the debate about sovereignty and human rights and charted the R2P's predecessors, the following chapter focuses on the ICISS itself.

2

The International Commission on Intervention and State Sovereignty

In early 2000, Canadian officials Don Hubert, Heidi Hulan and Jill Sinclair began advocating an 'International Commission on Humanitarian Intervention'. Canada's Foreign Minister Lloyd Axworthy recognised that, to be effective, any such commission would need 'serious political sponsorship'. Axworthy persuaded Annan to endorse the commission and to accept its report, but the Secretary-General maintained that it should sit outside the UN for obvious political reasons. At Annan's encouragement, Axworthy agreed that Canada would sponsor the new commission.[1]

In his 2000 Millennium Summit report, the Secretary-General set the scene for the proposed commission by revisiting the question of intervention and challenging the UN membership to resolve the perceived tension between sovereignty and human rights. Annan identified three specific concerns which had been raised in response to his 1999 address. Some worried that humanitarian intervention 'could become a cover for gratuitous interference' in the affairs of sovereigns. Others were concerned that it might encourage secessionists to use violence to provoke intervention-triggering human rights abuse. A third group expressed scepticism about the selectivity with which any principle of humanitarian intervention would be applied. Annan acknowledged that 'the principles of sovereignty and non-interference offer vital protection to small and weak states'. But, he continued, 'if humanitarian intervention is, indeed, an unacceptable assault on sovereignty how should we respond to Rwanda, to Srebrenica – to gross and systematic violations of human rights that offend every precept of our common humanity?' According to the Secretary-General, 'surely no legal principle – not even sovereignty – can ever shield crimes against humanity . . . Armed intervention must always remain the option of last resort, but in the face of mass murder, it is an option that cannot be relinquished.' World leaders confronted what Annan described as a 'real dilemma': 'Few would disagree that both the defence of humanity and the defence of sovereignty are principles that must be supported. Alas, that does not tell us which principle should prevail when they are in conflict.'[2]

The Canadian Prime Minister, Jean Chrétien, responded to Annan's call by announcing the establishment of an International Commission on Intervention and State Sovereignty (ICISS).[3] The name change from Axworthy's proposed 'commission on humanitarian intervention' was driven by concerns about the politically controversial language of 'humanitarian intervention', concerns subsequently borne out in the commission's global consultations (see below). Axworthy had set out the reasoning behind Canada's position some months earlier, endorsing Deng's positive approach to sovereignty and arguing that 'international promotion of human security does not weaken sovereignty, but strengthens it by reinforcing democratic, tolerant, open institutions and behaviour'. Axworthy maintained that Canada would take up Annan's gauntlet and identified three issues which required urgent attention: the norm of civilian protection; the political will to act when necessary; and the development of military and civilian capacity.[4]

But how should difficult decisions about military intervention be made when the world is confronted by severe humanitarian crises? Axworthy maintained that the bar should be set high and limited to 'egregious acts of violence . . . deliberately committed against the innocent'. Who had the right to make such decisions? He recognised that the Security Council had 'primary responsibility' for international peace and security but that all too often the council had failed to fulfil its responsibility. If the council failed, states still had an obligation to act but unauthorised intervention must be limited to exceptional cases and linked as closely as possible to the Security Council.

Announcing the ICISS' terms of reference in September 2000, Axworthy argued that it would build a broader understanding of the issues surrounding intervention and sovereignty to 'foster global political consensus'. The ICISS was to outline appropriate and politically feasible international responses to massive human rights violations and to set out ways of preventing such violations.[5] He also pointed towards a model of how the ICISS might do this. In the late 1980s, the Brundtland Commission had reconciled the apparently irreconcilable concerns of environmental protection and economic development by devising the phrase 'sustainable development' – which covers the idea that environmentalism and development are interdependent. Axworthy hoped that the ICISS would repeat the Brundtland Commission's achievement by finding a way to reconcile intervention and sovereignty.[6]

If commissions are to reflect a genuine consensus, they should be representative in their composition. At the invitation of the Canadian government, the ICISS was chaired by former Australian Foreign Minister Gareth Evans and by Mohammed Sahnoun, a former Algerian diplomat who served the UN as special adviser on the Horn of Africa and special representative in Somalia and the Great Lakes of Africa. The position was first offered to another Algerian, Chair of the UN Special Panel on Peace Operations Lakhdar Brahimi, who declined it owing to his concerns about interventionism and the expansion of the UN's role in the domestic affairs of states. Of the ten other commissioners, five were from the 'West' – Gisele Côte-Harper and Michael Ignatieff (Canada), Lee Hamilton (US), Klaus Neumann (Germany) and Cornelio Sommaruga (Switzerland) – and there were single representatives from Africa (Cyril Ramaphosa (South Africa)), East Asia (Fidel Ramos (the Philippines)), South Asia (Ramesh Thakur (India – though Thakur is also an Australian citizen)) and Latin America (Eduardo Stein Barillas (Guatemala)). There was also one Russian on the commission, Vladimir Lukin – deputy speaker of the Duma. Of course, none of the commissioners was meant to 'represent' their country or region of origin in any direct sense. Apart from quibbles about the underrepresentation of significant parts of the planet (such as South America, Africa, East Asia and the Middle East), the most obvious problem with the commission's composition was its gender bias. Of the twelve commissioners, only one was a woman. It is not surprising, therefore, that the ICISS was criticised as 'gender blind'.[7]

The commission was overseen by an advisory board appointed by Axworthy's successor as foreign minister, John Manley, and chaired by Axworthy himself. The role of the advisory board was to help the commissioners to 'ground their report in current political realities' and to assist in the building of a global consensus. To that end, the board had one full meeting with the commissioners in London on 22 June 2001. In addition, ICISS had a research directorate led by Thomas Weiss at the City University of New York, an eminent figure in the study of UN and global humanitarianism, and by Don Hubert, one of Weiss' former postdoctoral fellows, given leave from the Canadian Ministry of Foreign Affairs. The directorate was charged with conducting research to assist the commission's work. Some of this material was published as Volume 2 of the final report. Another part of the directorate was fronted by Stanlake Samkange, former speechwriter to Boutros-Ghali, who acted as rapporteur. In addition to funding and administrative support from the Canadian government, a range of foundations, including the Carnegie Corporation, the Hewlett Foundation, the MacArthur Foundation and the Rockefeller Foundation funded various aspects of the commission's work, as did the British and

Swiss governments. The ICISS was given one year to complete its work and to issue its findings.[8]

Global Consultations

The whole commission met five times and met once with the advisory board.[9] Naturally, some commissioners played a more active role than others. The final report was essentially written by three commissioners – Gareth Evans, Michael Ignatieff and Ramesh Thakur – but reflected a unanimous consensus among the commissioners. Sometimes commissioners changed their position as a result of debates within the commission and the global consultations. Sometimes, though, positions did not change and consensus was achieved only through compromise. For instance, some commissioners preferred wider thresholds to trigger intervention, while others preferred narrower thresholds. Likewise, the commissioners disagreed on the scope for intervention outside the Security Council, some arguing for greater flexibility and others insisting upon council primacy.[10] The finished report proposed compromise positions on both questions. This had the advantage of embedding the commission's mandate to develop politically feasible recommendations within its working practices, but in at least two instances it resulted in the commission being more conservative than even the Security Council (see below).

The commission also organised a series of eleven regional roundtables and national consultations attended by commissioners and participants from the academy, governments and the non-governmental sector. Parallel to these meetings was a series of other workshops and roundtables aimed at addressing the relationship between intervention and sovereignty. Most prominent among these parallel processes were the Pugwash workshops on 'Intervention, sovereignty and international security', the 'Working group on humanitarian intervention' of the 'Rio Group' and a meeting at Wilton Park in the UK.[11] In July 2001, the Pugwash Study Group held a joint meeting with key figures associated with the ICISS (Stanlake Samkange and Heidi Hulan), whilst the work on humanitarian intervention by the 'Rio Group' helped to set the terms of discussion for the ICISS roundtable in Santiago. Finally, the commission hastily organised a special late September 2001 session in Brussels to discuss what revisions, if any, should be made to the report to recognise the impact of the 9/11 terrorist attacks in New York and Washington. Thomas Weiss made a conscious decision not to attend the meeting, arguing that it was a 'distraction' from the commission's purpose. In the end the commission agreed not to alter its report substantively, the co-chairs maintaining that there was a 'funda-mental difference' between human protection claims in other states (the stuff of R2P) and the principles which should guide the way states react to terrorist attacks against their own citizens.[12]

Precursors to ICISS

The first meeting of the Pugwash Study Group (Venice, 10–11 December 1999) was held immediately after Annan's 1999 address to the General Assembly. Comprising current and former senior officials as well as leading academics, the group maintained that criteria to guide decision-making about humanitarian intervention could help to circumvent what was portrayed as the gradual emergence of two competing norms: the unac-ceptability of genocide, massive war crimes and crimes against humanity; and a norm emphasising the peaceful settlement of disputes. Delegates argued that criteria could help to justify intervention in the worst cases of human suffering; would provide a mechanism for others to test those justifications; and would contribute to identifying the areas where 'inter-national law and custom should be evolving'.[13] This, delegates believed, would increase the likelihood of future interventions enjoying the widest possible international support.[14]

The group identified four clusters of criteria, arranged on a continuum from the clearest-cut to the most controversial. At the clear-cut end were massive and systematic human rights abuse and genocide. Next came the suppression of the clearly expressed will of the people, either through the violent overthrow of democratically elected governments (as in Haiti) or through the denial of an internationally sanctioned right to self-determination (as in East Timor). The third category covered 'clear cases of failed states' such as Somalia. Finally and most controversially, there was the use of 'inhumane' violence in civil wars. Expressing concerns about the utility of criteria, however, delegates noted that the latter's applicability to actual cases would be hotly contested, that there were grey areas within each of the categories and that some cases might fall into more than one category. Sceptics responded by arguing that interventionism amounted to a selective imposition of western values and by noting that it was unlikely that western states would ever be subject to intervention, despite their breaches of human rights. Chinese delegates, for instance, argued that China was not opposed to collective action but rejected selective and unlawful intervention.[15]

The second Pugwash workshop (Como, 28–30 September 2000) focused on regional responses to intervention, especially those of Russia, China,

South Asia and Africa. In many ways, the workshop represented a step back-wards, as delegates agreed that it was precipitate to address questions about the criteria and modalities of intervention. Criteria were quickly dismissed on the (correct, it later transpired) grounds that it was unlikely that the P5 would accept measures which constrained their freedom of action.[16] Likewise, three of the four commissioned papers painted a broadly nega-tive picture. Writing about Russian attitudes, Vladimir Baranovsky stressed concerns about the 'messianic' strains of the West's commitment to the forcible imposition of human rights and the extent to which humanitar-ian intervention legitimised self-interested interference in the affairs of others.[17] Chu Shulong, writing about China's attitudes, reiterated that, whilst China was not hostile to collective action in every case, its experience of colonisation made it deeply sceptical about Western interventionism.[18] Likewise, Radha Kumar's account of South Asian attitudes pointed to the centrality of decolonisation in framing the region's commitment to tradi-tional sovereignty.[19] African attitudes, by contrast, were more open to new understandings, argued Adekeye Adebajo and Chris Landsberg. African states had shown themselves willing to cooperate with global institutions, to contemplate redrawing boundaries and accepting secessionism, and to use regional bodies as peacekeepers and enforcers. However, Africans remained sceptical about the Western approach to intervention and were convinced that the P5's commitment to Africa was wafer thin.[20]

At first glance, these discussions painted a gloomy picture for the ICISS. But on closer inspection they revealed that even determined opponents were not opposed to intervention in every case. The heart of the problem seemed to lie in determining the circumstances in which intervention might be required and in clarifying the locus of authority to make such deci-sions.[21] Importantly for ICISS, delegates also agreed that humanitarian intervention should be viewed as one stage in a continuum of international support for efforts to prevent and limit human suffering. Situated alongside a global commitment to prevention, peacebuilding and statebuilding, armed intervention would be a rare and exceptional measure, aimed at sup-porting this broader agenda. Echoing Francis Deng's views on sovereignty as responsibility, the delegates maintained that intervention would be about supporting sovereignty in contexts where it was endangered by state failure.[22]

The idea of using criteria to make judgements about the legitimacy of humanitarian intervention was given a further boost by the working group on humanitarian intervention created by the 'Rio Group', and also by the Independent International Commission of Kosovo (IICK). In October 2000, the Permanent Representatives to the UN of the 'Rio Group' members held two meetings on humanitarian intervention. The meetings exposed divisions between defenders of traditional sovereignty (such as Cuba and Uruguay) and others (such as Chile and Argentina), who were prepared to consider moving the issue forward. The parties compromised by releasing a concepts-paper calling for more work to ascertain thresholds for humanitarian intervention.[23] Working towards its finding that the intervention in Kosovo was 'illegal but legitimate', the IICK lent support to the idea of using criteria as thresholds for determining whether or not to use force to alleviate humanitarian emergencies. The Kosovo Commission recognised that, whilst the UN Charter's restrictions on the use of force contributed to international peace and security by prohibiting aggressive war, there may be circumstances – as in Kosovo – where intervention is needed as a last resort but is not likely to be authorised by the Security Council because of a threatened veto. Criteria, the commission reasoned, might guide the Security Council's deliberations (reducing the likelihood of a veto) and create pathways for states to intervene legitimately in the most extreme emergencies without council authorisation.[24]

ICISS begins: The Ottawa roundtable

The first ICISS roundtable was held a few months later, on 15 January 2001. Each subsequent one had a different composition. Some, such as the Santiago roundtable (conducted at the invitation of the Chilean government) and the first Paris roundtable, comprised mainly government officials and parliamentarians. Others had almost exclusively academic audiences (e.g. the one in Beijing). The majority contained a mixture of officials, NGOs and academics. Much of the early discussion centred around the three concerns identified by the Pugwash and 'Rio' Groups: criteria for intervention, institutions / authority and modalities. At this stage in the process there was no R2P, no clear indication that the ICISS intended to embed intervention within a broader regime of prevention and rebuilding (indeed the ICISS co-chairs were almost entirely focused on intervention at this point), and no clear sense of what sort of authority structure was needed.

Opening deliberations in Ottawa, the ICISS co-chairs advised that they would follow the Brundtland example and seek 'to re-frame a concept in order to build consensus on a divisive issue'. 'Changing the discourse of intervention', they argued, 'may constitute a great step forward'. The co-chairs remained unclear as to how they would do this but touted as possibilities a reframing of the concept of national interest or looking at the problem from the victim's point of view. This latter view was precisely what the commission ended up doing.[25]

The first hurdle, however, was terminological: it involved the relationship between 'humanitarian' and 'intervention'. NGO representatives argued that it was disingenuous to pair the term 'humanitarian' – which typically refers to politically neutral activities aimed at saving human lives where there is greatest need – with 'intervention' – which implies the coercive use of military force, a view vigorously supported by Sommaruga.[26] These concerns were repeated at subsequent roundtables in Maputo, Cairo and Paris and played a part in influencing the commissioners to drop the label 'humanitarian intervention' altogether.[27] The NGOs argued that it was wrong to associate the term humanitarian with acts of war, whilst others maintained that the association between humanitarianism and intervention made it harder for human rights activists to lobby governments about human rights abuse.[28] Rightly or wrongly, it became clear in subsequent negotiations that the phrase 'humanitarian intervention' was deeply unpopular and tainted by association with the coercive interference of the powerful in the affairs of the weak. As Ramesh Thakur later put it: 'the weight of historical baggage is too strong for a new consensus to be formed around the concept of humanitarian intervention. If major powers wish to help victims instead of helping themselves, they would do well to abandon talk of "humanitarian intervention".'[29] In place of 'humanitarian intervention', participants argued that armed intervention should be placed within a continuum of measures to address humanitarian crises – an idea first raised by Francis Deng and endorsed in the Pugwash meetings.

The idea of situating intervention within a continuum of engagement chimed well with the co-chairs' interest in recasting the problem from the victims' point of view. The Ottawa roundtable helped in singling out this approach by casting doubt on the co-chairs' other proposed route: changing national interest. Whilst it was widely agreed that political will, not sovereignty, was the main barrier to intervention, participants noted that directly refashioning the national interests of great powers was a tall order. Proposed avenues included turning to 'middle powers' or 'internationalist'-minded states, or emphasising the role of NGOs. However, neither path offered much potential for advancing the debate and building consensus.

The remainder of the Ottawa meeting focused on criteria and modalities. The participants agreed that criteria to guide decision-making about the use of force would be helpful, but doubts were expressed about their ability to generate political will and consensus in specific cases – a point which was widely shared and became increasingly evident. Some suggested a 'conflict certification' procedure whereby an independent body would adjudicate on whether a particular case met the criteria for intervention. Variants of this proposal were suggested at other roundtables, but the consensus view was that such a body would be unlikely to overcome barriers to intervention and that states were unlikely to endorse some sort of 'automatic' mechanism. In relation to modalities, participants suggested the need to coordinate between different civilian and military agencies in developing long-term strategies to prevent massive human suffering. This was linked directly to the only solid conclusion produced by the roundtable: that the net should be cast wider than intervention, to include long-term strategies for prevention.[30]

R2P and the Geneva roundtable

Between the Ottawa and the Geneva roundtables, Gareth Evans came up with the idea of reframing the debate in terms of a 'responsibility to protect'.[31] The phrase was aired as a way of reconciling sovereignty and human rights and of resolving four problems, set out in a discussion paper put before the 31 January 2001 Geneva roundtable. First, the almost exclusive focus on military intervention was misplaced. If the aim was to strengthen international protection for basic human rights, it was necessary to consider a much wider continuum of activities. Second, resistance to humanitarian intervention was grounded in legitimate historical sensitivities about colonialism and self-determination. Third, the search for new legal rules to govern intervention was not a promising avenue of enquiry. Not only was the possibility of consensus slim, but new legal rules would not guarantee the protection of endangered peoples. Finally, more attention should be given to the responsibilities of different actors.[32] The participants at Geneva endorsed 'the possible approach' of the R2P as a way of responding to these issues, but several argued that the commission continued to place undue emphasis on the military dimension.

Like in Ottawa, the subsequent discussion in Geneva addressed criteria (briefly) and modalities. Participants acknowledged the value of criteria and reviewed yet another list, similar to that espoused by Tony Blair (see Chapter 1). Much of the remainder of the discussion turned to the wider aspects of the potential R2P. In addition to prevention, participants at Geneva insisted that any consideration of intervention should include long-term plans for rebuilding after conflict. But expanding the R2P in this way raised the spectre of potential neo-colonialism. To avoid this problem, participants returned to the idea of seeing the problem from the victim's point of view and of focusing on rebuilding around local empowerment.

After Geneva, the regional roundtable discussions crystallised around the four themes of R2P terminology: criteria, institutions/authority and modalities. In the forthcoming discussion I will provide a brief overview of the debate relating to these four concerns before I go on to focus on one of the most important roundtables, the one in Beijing.

Changing the language

The R2P was warmly received almost everywhere it was discussed, although participants in the St Petersburg roundtable (16 July 2001) declined to discuss it despite promptings from the commissioners.[33] The concept was first aired in Geneva, and by the subsequent London round-table (3 February 2001) it had been fleshed out as a more 'holistic' approach, which went beyond the so-called 'right of intervention' by encompassing prevention and 'the responsibility to mend war-torn societies'.[34] The shift in language was particularly well received at the Maputo roundtable (10 March 2001), where participants welcomed the commitment to prevention and rebuilding and supported the shift away from the military dimension.[35] Similar sentiments were evident in the second Paris roundtable (23 May 2001) of NGOs and other interested parties. The Paris participants welcomed the R2P's focus on prevention and on the victims' point of view.[36]

Other endorsements offered portents of future political struggles. Participants in the Washington DC roundtable (10 March 2001) welcomed the R2P, calling attention to the idea, first put forth by Deng and Cohen (see Chapter 1), that local authorities had the *primary* responsibility to protect. From the very outset, however, this was a double-edged sword. On the one hand, as the Washington participants noted, local authorities might have more legitimacy and be able to act more effectively than international agencies. Also, stressing the primacy of host state responsibility reaffirmed respect for sovereignty and made good on Deng's positive approach to sovereignty and human rights. This was the logic used by participants in the Paris roundtable who argued that sovereignty was an essential prerequisite for economic development and for the realisation of human rights.[37] On the other hand, local primacy might limit international responsibility. At Washington this was portrayed as a good thing, and there are certainly positive elements to it. One participant argued that without local primacy 'there is a risk that people would automatically start looking outside their own borders for others to protect them'.[38] On the downside, however, local primacy could enable outsiders to limit their commitment both to the R2P itself, as John Bolton – America's Permanent Representative to the UN – did during the 2005 World Summit negotiations, and to the protection of civilians in specific cases, as much of the West did in relation to Darfur between 2004–8 (see Chapters 3 and 5).

Elsewhere, though, doubts were expressed about the value of changing terminology. Participants in London argued that the ICISS should reaffirm support for the rule of non-intervention (a suggestion taken up by the commission), humanitarian intervention being seen as an 'extraordinary exception' to the norm. Hubert Védrine, the French foreign minister, echoed this view at the Paris roundtable (23 May 2001). The London participants argued that, while potentially significant, the change of terminology did not tackle the fundamental problems associated with international law – a position endorsed at the Paris roundtable.[39] Those problems were further clarified at a joint ICISS–Pugwash meeting held in Nova Scotia (20–1 July 2001).[40]

On balance, the introduction of new R2P terminology was broadly welcomed because it shifted the focus from military intervention to a wider continuum of responsibilities; it implied a focus on the victim's perspective; and it assumed the primacy of local authorities. However, sceptics questioned whether changing the terms of the debate would have practical impact and worried that it might avoid the core issues.

Criteria

Broad support for criteria to guide decision-making about intervention was expressed in the Pugwash meetings, the earliest ICISS deliberations, and the speeches of figures including Kofi Annan, Tony Blair, Lloyd Axworthy and Hubert Védrine. After Geneva, however, a division began to emerge between those who were sceptical and sometimes outright hostile to criteria and those who were strongly supportive of them. The strongest support came from the developing world, which accredited Thakur's view that, far from being an enabling 'charter for interveners', the commission's criteria might actually restrain intervention.[41] An alternative interpretation proposed at the Washington roundtable supported criteria on the grounds that they might legitimise unilateral intervention in cases where the Security Council was deadlocked.[42] This question of whether criteria would be primarily constraining or enabling became a key part of the debate about the R2P (see Chapter 3).

Strong support for criteria was voiced at the Cairo and New Delhi round-tables. Participants in Cairo argued that clear and universally agreed crite-ria were necessary to improve the Security Council's accountability. They maintained that the application of criteria to specific cases be done in an 'objective' way, by a representative body, and they expressed doubts about a commissioner's suggestion that a body of eminent people should be set up to scrutinise the application of criteria. Instead, the participants endorsed a reformed and more representative Security Council as the most appropriate body.[43] If anything, support for criteria was amplified at New Delhi (10 June 2001). The participants were adamant that criteria were nec-essary if the world was to commit to the R2P. They proposed a compre-hensive list, including a requirement that interveners should address the root causes of conflict and should conduct themselves impartially. The New Delhi roundtable also reiterated Cairo's insistence for criteria to be applied by a legitimate and representative body, concluding that a reformed and expanded Security Council was the best candidate for this role.

Opposition to criteria was strongest in the West. There was some support at the London roundtable, on the grounds that criteria might reduce the risk of states using humanitarian justifications as a pretext for the self-interested use of force. In general, though, participants were scep-tical. Some doubted the ability of criteria to shape political decision-making, noting that they would only form one out of many considerations weighing on political leaders. One participant rejected the very idea of having a debate about criteria, on the grounds that this would be 'poiso-nous' and 'divisive'. Others suggested that a better way forward was to rely on the emergence of customary practice, which would change interna-tional law over time.[44] These views were amplified in the commission's meeting with French government officials and parliamentarians. French officials correctly argued that criteria would have little practical impact, because individual states would interpret them differently. They also main-tained that criteria might worsen humanitarian crises by encouraging groups to escalate hostilities in order to draw intervention.[45]

Institutions and authority

Opinion was also divided on the question of which institutions had the authority to sanction the use of force or other coercive measures for R2P purposes. There was broad agreement that the UN Security Council should play the primary role in authorising enforcement measures, but beyond that few roundtables wanted to address the problem in black-and-white terms. Only three roundtables (Cairo, New Delhi and Beijing) agreed that the Security Council was the *sole* source of authority. Writing two weeks after the Cairo roundtable, one of the participants, Mohamed Sid-Ahmed, maintained that state sovereignty was being 'demolished' because the UN was failing to balance American hegemony. Responding to Evans' suggestion that changing the terminology of the R2P might help to overcome reservations, Sid-Ahmed insisted that 'the problem is not one of terminology; it is one of substance. The very legitimate reservations on the issue of intervention can only be overcome if the United Nations replaces the United States as the super-actor.'[46]

Elsewhere attitudes were more complex. In Maputo, St Petersburg and Santiago, participants were reluctant to reject a priori the legitimacy of interventions not authorised by the Security Council, primarily because this might entail rejecting interventions by regional organisations. Thinking in particular of the ECOWAS intervention in Liberia, which was only endorsed after the fact by the Security Council, participants in Maputo maintained that intervention by regional organisations could be legitimate even when not authorised by the Security Council. The role of the UN, they argued, would be to support regional efforts, though the Maputo meeting did not address the question of how interventions by regional organisations should be authorised, apart from expressing a preference for host state consent.[47] Regional measures also prompted the delegates at St Petersburg to refrain from denouncing all non-UN sanctioned interventions, primarily because Russia has itself intervened in several conflicts in the former Soviet space (e.g. in Abkhazia) through the Commonwealth of Independent States (CIS). As in Maputo, however, participants emphasised the importance of host-state consent.[48] The reasoning was slightly different in Santiago (4 May 2001), where the participants – mostly government officials – refused to rule out the potential legitimacy of an intervention not authorised by the Security Council, noting only that the legitimisation of unauthorised operations would be 'very difficult'.

The view that the Security Council should not be seen as the sole source of authority was not articulated strongly in any of the three roundtables – London, Washington DC, Paris – where it might have been most expected. In London, the question of authority was not widely discussed. In Paris, Hubert Védrine argued that, whilst unauthorised interventions such as NATO's in Kosovo might sometimes be necessary, the real challenge was not to uncover ways of legitimising action outside the Security Council but to develop proposals for making the council work better. He proposed a P5 'code-of-conduct' which would enable the council to respond more decisively to humanitarian emergencies. The code would contain clear thresholds for what counted as a humanitarian crisis requiring a Security Council response and an agreement by the P5 not to cast their veto in cases where there was a council majority in favour of intervention and where no vital national security interests were at risk.[49]

Of these three roundtables, the clearest arguments against Security Council primacy were expressed in Washington DC. One participant argued that the Security Council was not the sole source of authority for intervention, and another pointed to a US State Department document arguing that council authorisation was 'preferable' but not always necessary. As indicated earlier, participants in Washington DC conceptualised criteria primarily as a way of holding the Security Council to account and of legitimating humanitarian intervention conducted without council authorisation.[50]

All things considered, there was surprisingly broad agreement on the question of authority. Almost all the roundtables agreed that the Security Council had primacy in authorising intervention, but there was also wide recognition that intervention might be legitimate in other circumstances, especially those involving regional organisations and where the host state gave its consent. There was little support for the 'preferable not necessary' formula aired in Washington DC and, whilst the Cairo, New Delhi and Beijing roundtables were adamant in their insistence that the only legitimate interventions were those authorised by the Security Council, this view was not endorsed in Europe (including St Petersburg), Santiago and Maputo. For the commissioners, Védrine's proposed 'code of conduct' offered a way of making the Security Council work better and provided arguably the best way of navigating through the complex debate. It also provided a neat link between the R2P and the criteria: the Security Council should be encumbered with a responsibility to protect and empowered to make effective and timely decisions in the discharge of its responsibilities. The commissioners adopted this line of reasoning in their approach to the question of authority.

Modalities

The fourth element of the debate involved the modalities of R2P. There was broad agreement that, in addition to intervention, prevention and rebuilding should also be embedded in the R2P, though strikingly little detail was offered at the roundtables about what this would mean in practice and how it might be operationalised. There was also broad agreement on the need to learn the lessons of past failures (most notably in Rwanda and Bosnia) – although, once again, specific recommendations did not go beyond those already put forward elsewhere, most notably in the Brahimi report.

There was broad agreement that the R2P should be operationalised in such a way as to empower local communities. The Maputo roundtable, for instance, called for 'adequate and thorough discussions with involved parties' prior to intervention.[51] Likewise, participants in the roundtable with French officials argued that the best measure of legitimacy was the local population's perception of an intervention. The roundtables also suggested different ways of operationalising prevention. Participants at Maputo suggested the creation of an early warning-and-response mechanism to alert the world to potential crises and to coordinate responses.[52] French officials and parliamentarians proposed the creation of an international conflict prevention agency, which would include an early warning mechanism of the sort envisaged at Maputo. They also argued that the International Criminal Court had an important preventive role and that regions ought to build the capacity to respond quickly to crises, as Europe had done with the Rapid Reaction Force. Finally, whilst there was broad agreement on the importance of making a long-term commitment to peacebuilding, there was much less discussion of what this commitment would look like and great sensitivity to the potential of new UN trusteeships becoming a form of neo-imperialism.

Beijing

The penultimate roundtable was a meeting with the China Institute of International Studies (Beijing, 14 June 2001). If common ground could be found in Beijing, then it might be possible to build a global consensus on the R2P. If not, ICISS advocates would have a very hard time making a good case and persuading the world. The omens were not good. Chinese participants ignored the R2P almost entirely, focusing instead on humanitarian intervention – which they denounced. The meeting opened with a paper which argued that humanitarian intervention was 'a total fallacy' because it had no basis in law, being derived from a fallacious view of human rights as 'transcending' sovereignty, and that its Western advocates had not seriously pursued a policy of protecting human rights. All was not lost, however. The Chinese went on to argue that, whilst humanitarian intervention was fallacious, humanitarianism was not. In fact, humanitarianism was a 'lofty virtue' which could be pursued through the Security Council. Thus the Chinese participants argued that it was legitimate for the Security Council to authorise peacekeeping missions where there are threats to international peace and security, but that such missions should remain neutral.[53] This left open the possibility that China might contemplate acquiescing to the R2P if the latter operated under the authority of the Security Council.

Summary

Early in the process, Gareth Evans identified the R2P as a way of emulating the Brundtland Commission's feat of reconciling seemingly irreconcilable principles by changing the terms of the debate. The roundtables revealed a broad consensus on the view that sovereignty implied certain responsibilities.[54] As a way of framing the issues, the R2P focused on the victim's perspective rather than on that of the perpetrator or intervener, and this too was broadly welcomed. The roundtables also helped to impart the idea that the R2P would have to be about more than just intervention. The R2P could only make sense if it also encompassed prevention and rebuilding. This, in turn, reduced the centrality of non-consensual military force by situating it alongside a range of other measures which might be used to discharge the responsibility.

The regional roundtables also helped to clarify matters in relation to the question of authority. Somewhat surprisingly – given the tenor of the debate described in the previous chapter – they showed that the global consensus lay somewhere between the following poles: 'intervention must always be authorised by the Security Council' and 'UN approval is preferable but not necessary'. Crucially, they also revealed a broad consensus around the proposition that it was best to avoid outcomes which would discredit the council.[55] This opened up an important middle position, suggested by Védrine but tacitly endorsed by others: the principal task was not to identify alternatives to the Security Council but to identify ways of making the council work better. The roundtables suggested at least three ways of doing this: the creation of criteria to guide decision-making; the establishment of a P5 'code-of-conduct'; and a reform of the council itself, to make it more representative. For sceptics, this approach dodged rather than tackled the question of whether it is legitimate for groups of states to use force for humanitarian purposes without a Security Council mandate, as NATO had done in Kosovo. Others shared Kofi Annan's optimism that, with careful and patient diplomacy, NATO could have persuaded Russia and China of its case for intervention in Kosovo and therefore secured a Security Council mandate.

The Responsibility to Protect

The report was completed in mid-August 2001, shortly before the 9/11 attacks on New York and Washington. As I noted earlier, the commission responded to 9/11 by holding a special meeting in Brussels and delaying the report's release until December. Thankfully, commissioners left the report largely intact, inserting some new paragraphs but leaving the focus and rationale intact. 9/11, ICISS argued, simply confirmed its view that human security was indivisible – that complex conflicts in faraway lands could have direct consequences for the security of powerful states and of their citizens.[56] As it turned out, the report's relatively narrow focus proved to be one of its greatest strengths, especially when it came to lobbying governments to adopt the R2P as a new international principle (see Chapter 3).[57] There is little doubt that the commission's findings would have been much less durable had commissioners been sidetracked by 9/11.

Releasing the report on 18 December 2001, Paul Heinbecker – Canada's Ambassador to the UN – declared his confidence that 'the thoughtfulness of this report, with its clear political and practical focus, provides a solid basis for advancing this issue within the UN system'.[58] As promised, Annan endorsed the report a few weeks later, describing it as 'the most comprehensive and carefully thought-out response we have seen to date'. Addressing the co-chairs, Annan commented:

> I admire your diplomatic skill in redirecting the debate, and – believe me – I wish I had thought of this myself. It would have saved me quite a few explanations of just what I was proposing in my speech.
>
> I say this because your title really describes what I was talking about: the fact that sovereignty implies responsibilities as well as powers; and that among those responsibilities, none is more important than protecting your citizens from violence and war.[59]

Modelling its approach on the Brundtland Commission's success, the 'responsibility to protect' sought to change the terms of the debate to encourage and enable intervention in genuine humanitarian emergencies, while constraining the use of humanitarian arguments to justify other types of force. Adopting the position first elaborated by Francis Deng and

Roberta Cohen, the R2P insisted that states have the primary responsibility to protect their citizens from genocide, mass killing and ethnic cleansing and that, whenever they proved either unwilling or unable to fulfil their duties, the responsibility to protect was transferred to international society. The R2P comprised three interrelated sets of responsibilities: to prevent, to react and to rebuild.

Responsibility to prevent

ICISS described the 'responsibility to prevent' as the 'single most important dimension of the responsibility to protect'.[60] In saying this, the ICISS pointed to two sets of issues raised in the global consultations and elsewhere. First and most importantly, if the overarching goal of the R2P is to save lives, it stands to reason that the focus should be on prevention, not on reaction. Second, a focus on prevention was essential for moving the debate forward by making military intervention a small part of a much wider continuum – of engagement with the protection of civilians and attempts to reduce the frequency of cases in which the world is confronted with a choice between armed intervention and standing aside.

In a stinging critique of the commission's stance on prevention, Thomas Weiss argued that 'it is preposterous to argue that to prevent is *the* single most important priority'. He continued:

> [M]ost of the mumbling and stammering about prevention is a superficially attractive but highly unrealistic way to try and pretend that we can finesse the hard issues of what essentially amounts to humanitarian intervention. The ICISS's discourse about prevention is a helpful clarification, but it nonetheless obscures the essence of the most urgent part of the spectrum of responsibility to protect those caught in the crosshairs of war.[61]

This goes to the heart of the question of the place which prevention and rebuilding take in the R2P schema. Weiss was quite right to point to the unsatisfactory way in which the commission dealt with prevention, and it is hard to disagree with his view that prevention and rebuilding were 'tagged on' to R2P in order to make military intervention more palatable.[62] The report is conceptually confused about the nature, scope and place of prevention and adds little new to the way we think about the practice of prevention. Much the same can be said of the commission's findings on rebuilding. There is a vast gulf between the commission's sophisticated and nuanced treatment of intervention and its brief, confused and unoriginal take on prevention and rebuilding. This presents analysts and advocates with two options. On the one hand, they could argue – as Weiss does – that the R2P is *primarily* concerned with military intervention and that prevention and rebuilding are at best distractions and, at worst, threats to the R2P's conceptual clarity. This runs the risk of alienating governments which remain concerned about the potential abuse of humanitarian arguments – a prospect made real in the minds of many by the use of human rights to justify the 2003 invasion of Iraq. This first option also undermines the novelty of the R2P, upon which the shaky consensus that emerged in 2005 is based (see Chapter 3). The alternative, which will be presented in the second half of this book, is to accept the ethos of a continuum of R2P measures and to argue for the further development and clarification of the responsibilities to prevent and rebuild. I would go as far as to argue, for example, that the commission should rewrite its chapters on prevention and rebuilding.

The need to do better in relation to prevention was a constantly recurring theme of the ICISS' global consultations.[63] Reflecting long-standing views about the different types of prevention, the commission divided its recommendations into the areas of 'early warning', tackling root causes, and 'direct prevention'. ICISS opened its discussion by noting that failings associated with early warning are often overstated and that the nub of the problem tends to lie not in predicting the outbreak of violent conflict but in generating the political will to act on these predictions.[64] As it is now known only too well, the carnage of Bosnia, the genocide in Rwanda and the reign of terror in Darfur were all predicted before the event. However, the commission found that a more accurate analysis of warning signs might identify earlier opportunities for constructive third-party engagement. The commission recommended that UN headquarters should develop the capability to collate this information, including sensitive intelligence, from member states.[65]

Given the sheer diversity of the potential root causes of violent conflict, it is unsurprising that the commission's recommendations in this area were somewhat more opaque. In keeping with the overall tenor of its findings, the ICISS called for the Security Council to play a leading role and identified four key dimensions in the prevention of root causes: a political one (relating to good governance, human rights, confidence building); an economic one (relating to poverty, inequality and economic opportunity); a legal one (relating to the rule of law and to accountability); and a military one (relating to disarmament, reintegration and sectoral reform).[66] These four dimensions also shaped the commission's recommendations in relation to direct prevention. The political dimension was made to refer to the Secretary-General's preventive diplomacy; the economic dimension, to the use of positive and negative inducements by the Security Council; the legal dimension, to a range of measures, from mediation to legal sanctions; and the military dimension – considered the most limited one in scope – to preventive deployments.[67] To actualise this agenda, the report called for the creation of a pool of unrestricted development funding that might be used for root cause and direct prevention and for the centralisation of efforts by UN headquarters.[68]

The commission identified two potential problems with prevention. First, states 'at risk' were likely to resist external efforts on the grounds that 'internationalisation' is the start of a slippery slope towards intervention.[69] Second, states worried that third-party intervention might inadvertently legitimise rebels by awarding them the status of negotiating partner – a concern identified by Annan in his 'Millennium report' and in the global consultations. As a remedy for these problems, ICISS recommended that international actors should display sensitivity and craft preventive efforts carefully, in a 'non-intrusive' fashion.[70]

Despite stressing the critical importance of conflict prevention, the commission stopped short of making concrete proposals other than the call to centralise the world's conflict prevention efforts and to develop capacity in relation to early warning. It also stopped short of offering guidelines for prevention equivalent to those set out for guiding decisions about the use of force. What is more, the commission avoided explicit discussion of the single most pressing dilemmas in relation to the 'responsibility to prevent': the questions of how to translate early warning signs into a commitment to act and a consensus on how to act.

Responsibility to react

On the question of when to intervene, ICISS commissioners struggled to find a compromise and adopted the commonly held view that intervention should be limited to 'extreme' cases, which sets a high threshold. Intervention, it concluded, was warranted in cases where there was large-scale loss of life or ethnic cleansing, 'actual or apprehended', either deliberately caused by the state or facilitated by neglect or incapacity.[71] In addition to these 'just cause' thresholds, the commission set out a series of 'precautionary principles' to guide decision-making (see Box 2.1).

The question of authority proved to be just as thorny, and ultimately the commission was unable to reach a clear consensus on the legitimacy of interventions not authorised by the Security Council. In its place, the ICISS proposed a three-layered distribution of responsibility. Primary responsibility lay with the host state, which is in line with the general ethos of sovereignty as responsibility. Secondary responsibility lay with the domestic authorities working in partnership with outside agencies. If the primary and secondary levels failed to ameliorate a humanitarian emergency, responsibility was transferred to international society.[72] At this level, the ICISS accepted the view that primary legal authority for action was vested in the Security Council. If the Security Council rejects a proposal for intervention in a humanitarian emergency that crossed the 'just cause' thresholds, the commission concluded that potential interveners should approach the General Assembly for declaratory support and, if that failed, they should work through regional organisations, or even coalitions of the willing.[73]

To improve the chances of consensus in the council, the ICISS adopted Védrine's proposed code of conduct. It recommended that the council should adopt criteria relating to the use of force in humanitarian emergencies. ICISS suggested that states should always seek Security Council authorisation before using force; that the council should commit itself to dealing promptly with humanitarian emergencies involving large-scale loss of life, recognising – as Annan himself had argued in his 1999 address to the General Assembly – that its credibility and legitimacy would be impaired by a failure to act; that the P5 should bind states not to cast a veto so as to obstruct humanitarian action where a majority was in favour of it – unless their own vital national interests were involved; and that Security Council members should admit that, if they fail to fulfil their responsibility to protect, other states and organisations may take it upon themselves to act.[74] The commission insisted that the question of military intervention should be placed firmly on the Security Council's agenda if either of the 'just cause' thresholds was satisfied (see Box 2.1).[75]

In order to reconcile sovereignty and intervention, the commission required a formula to avoid future situations like that of Kosovo, where division paralysed the Security Council and a group of states decided to take matters into their own hands. In addition, the aspiration to avoid future disasters like the one in Rwanda, where the world stood aside as genocide unfolded, meant that the commission also had to say something about the thorny issue of political will. I will briefly focus on the remedies proposed by the ICISS for both sets of problems.

There are two accounts of the cause of deadlock in the Kosovo case.[76] According to one account, deadlock was caused by 'unreasonable' threats of Security Council vetos by Russia and China. The alternative holds that Russia and China had genuine concerns as to whether the situation was so dire as to warrant intervention. To prevent future Kosovos, therefore, ICISS

Box 2.1   The Responsibility to protect: Principles for military intervention

(1) The Just Cause Threshold

Military intervention for human protection purposes is an exceptional and extraordinary measure. To be warranted, there must be serious and irreparable harm occurring to human beings, or imminently likely to occur, of the following kind:

    A   large scale loss of life, actual or apprehended, with genocidal intent or not, which is the product either of deliberate state action, or state neglect or inability to act, or a failed state situation; or

    B   large scale 'ethnic cleansing', actual or apprehended, whether carried out by killing, forced expulsion, acts of terror or rape.

(2) The Precautionary Principles

    A   Right intention: The primary purpose of the intervention, whatever other motives intervening states may have, must be to halt or avert human suffering. Right intention is better assured with multilateral operations, clearly supported by regional opinion and the victims concerned.

    B   Last resort: Military intervention can only be justified when every non-military option for the prevention or peaceful resolution of the crisis has been explored, with reasonable grounds for believing lesser measures would not have succeeded.

    C   Proportional means: The scale, duration and intensity of the planned military intervention should be the minimum necessary to secure the defined human protection objective.

    D   Reasonable prospects: There must be a reasonable chance of success in halting or averting the suffering which has justified the intervention, with the consequences of action not likely to be worse than the consequences of inaction.

(3) Right Authority

    A   There is no better or more appropriate body than the United Nations Security Council to authorize military intervention for human protection purposes. The task is not to find alternatives to the Security Council as a source of authority, but to make the Security Council work better than it has.

B   Security Council authorization should in all cases be sought prior to any military intervention action being carried out. Those calling for an intervention should formally request such authorization, or have the Council raise the matter on its own initiative, or have the Secretary-General raise it under Article 99 of the UN Charter.

C   The Security Council should deal promptly with any request for authority to intervene where there are allegations of large scale loss of human life or ethnic cleansing. It should in this context seek adequate verification of facts or conditions on the ground that might support a military intervention.

D   The Permanent Five members of the Security Council should agree not to apply their veto power, in matters where their vital state interests are not involved, to obstruct the passage of resolutions authorizing military intervention for human protection purposes for which there is otherwise majority support.

E   If the Security Council rejects a proposal or fails to deal with it in a reasonable time, alternative options are:

     I.   consideration of the matter by the General Assembly in Emergency Special Session under the 'Uniting for Peace' procedure; and

    II.   action within area of jurisdiction by regional or sub-regional organizations under Chapter VIII of the Charter, subject to their seeking subsequent authorization from the Security Council.

F   The Security Council should take into account in all its deliberations that, if it fails to discharge its responsibility to protect in conscience-shocking situations crying out for action, concerned states may not rule out other means to meet the gravity and urgency of that situation – and that the stature and credibility of the United Nations may suffer thereby.

(4) Operational Principles

A   Clear objectives; clear and unambiguous mandate at all times; and resources to match.

B   Common military approach among involved partners; unity of command; clear and unequivocal communications and chain of command.

C   Acceptance of limitations, incrementalism and gradualism in the application of force, the objective being protection of a population, not defeat of a state.

D   Rules of engagement which fit the operational concept; are precise; reflect the principle of proportionality; and involve total adherence to international humanitarian law.

E   Acceptance that force protection cannot become the principal objective.

F   Maximum possible coordination with humanitarian organizations

SOURCE: ICISS, 'The responsibility to protect', pp. xii–xiii.

needed to pay heed to both of these accounts, by making it more difficult for the P5 to use their veto capriciously, particularly in the face of humanitarian emergencies, *and* by making it harder for states to abuse humanitarian justifications – which thereby addressed Russian and Chinese concerns over Kosovo. The principal device for achieving this goal consisted in the commission's criteria to guide decision-making on the use of force. The criteria are set out in full in Box 2.1.

The ICISS maintained that, if states committed to these principles, it would be harder for some to oppose genuine humanitarian intervention, as China and Russia did, and harder for others to abuse humanitarian justifications, because it would be very difficult for interveners to satisfy all the criteria unless they were acting for genuinely humanitarian reasons. This would help to address mainly Western concerns about the capricious use of the veto, as well as Russian and Chinese concerns about Western interventionism in less than conscience-shocking cases of human distress.

Preventing future Rwandas – that is, cases where the 'just cause' thresholds are clearly breached but where governments lack the political will to act – boils down to overcoming a single obstacle: that of persuading states, particularly powerful states, to accept risk in order to save people in distant lands, when there are but few strategic interests at stake. The commission's approach to this problem was to try to persuade states to acknowledge both their responsibility to protect and the 'just cause' thresholds. This would help to create expectations in an indigenous population about when its government ought to act to save imperilled people. Thus, in cases of mass killing and ethnic cleansing, governments would be put under pressure from the public to fulfil their international undertakings. Moreover, the commission reiterated that the UNs legitimacy would be gravely damaged if, having given an undertaking to respect the R2P, the council failed to act in the face of large-scale loss of life or ethnic cleansing.[77]

Responsibility to rebuild

The idea that potential interveners should make a long-term commitment to rebuilding was aired in the commission's earliest consultations. The ICISS concluded that potential interveners should have a strategic plan about how they intend to 'rebuild' post-conflict societies. That is, 'there should be a genuine commitment to helping to build a durable peace, and promoting good governance and sustainable development'.[78] In taking on a responsibility to rebuild, interveners were required to consider three areas: security, justice and reconciliation, and development.[79]

In relation to security, the ICISS argued that interveners acquired a moral duty to protect those in their care and should also work towards disarming and demobilising former combatants and establishing effective and legitimate national armed forces. To engender justice and reconciliation, peacebuilders should establish a local judicial system, foster local opportunities for reconciliation and guarantee the legal rights of returnees – people forced to flee their homes. Finally, interveners should use all possible means to foster economic growth.[80] In doing so, they should turn responsibility over to local leadership as rapidly as possible. The practicalities of how one goes about transforming war-torn societies have long been hotly contested (see Chapter 6). The ICISS only maintained that interveners acquired responsibilities for the post-war society, but it stopped short of offering practical guidance or elaborating on the relationship between rebuilding and the other aspects of the R2P.

Too Much, Too Little, Too Vague?

The ICISS report was widely scrutinised and highly commended. For instance, Anthony Lewis, former columnist for the *New York Times*, commented that the report 'captured the international state of mind'.[81] The report's critics, however, tended to fall into one of three camps: those who believed that the report gave too much ground to interveners, those who argued that it did not go far enough, and those who maintained that the report left important questions unanswered.

Too much

The first camp maintained that the report advocated the imposition of Western values and the diminution of sovereignty. David Chandler, a left-leaning British academic, is one of the most consistent proponents of this view.[82] He presented three main arguments against the R2P, which have resonated widely.

First, the R2P ultimately translates into a right of intervention. According to Chandler, although the report rejected 'right of intervention' language, it 'smuggled' rights back in by giving individuals a right to protection. This individual right to protection, he argued, translates into a duty for states to take concrete measures to operationalise those rights. For Chandler, this amounts to a mere rephrasing of the 'right to intervene'.[83] Second, he maintains that 'sovereignty as responsibility' is, in fact, a diminution of sovereignty – a 'fundamental downgrading', in Chandler's words. Because sovereignty as responsibility implies accountability to both citizens and the society of states, sovereigns are stripped of exclusive jurisdiction. According to Chandler, 'a power which is "accountable" to another external body clearly lacks sovereign authority'.[84] Third, Chandler argues that far from demilitarising humanitarianism by embedding intervention within a wider set of responsibilities, 'the Commission makes external intervention more legitimate and extends the rights of a "continuum" of mechanisms of less and more coercive international interference'.[85] From this perspective, therefore, the R2P merely changes the terminology of intervention to make it more palatable.

These arguments have found many ready sympathisers, but they do not stand up to scrutiny. First, whilst Chandler was correct to argue that the R2P is not devoid of 'rights', he was quite wrong to imply that ICISS ever maintained it would be. The regional roundtables revealed a broad consensus on human rights and on the notion that states have responsibilities relative to those rights. Nowhere was it argued that intervention for humanitarian purposes was wrong in every instance. The R2P fundamentally alters the locus of rights – from a 'right' of the interveners to the globally acknowledged rights of victims.

Chandler's second argument amounts to a straightforward defence of a traditional account of sovereignty with absolutist leanings (see Chapter 1) which bears little resemblance to contemporary world politics. This account overlooks the fact that almost every state has consented to a degree of international accountability by joining the UN and by signing up to a Charter which grants the Security Council the authority to prescribe enforcement measures whenever and wherever it identifies a threat to international peace and security. Moreover, most states are today voluntary members of a whole host of institutional arrangements which cede sovereign authority to higher bodies: the World Trade Organisation, World Health Organisation, International Criminal Court – all have this effect in one way or another. The bottom line is that sovereigns have almost always been accountable to their peers.[86] If we take Chandler's standard, few states (if any) are sovereign. Chandler's third argument is based on a very selective reading of the report. The report clearly sets out that the triggers for military intervention are the 'just cause' thresholds, and it is not clear how embedding intervention within a continuum of measures including prevention and rebuilding alters that fact. The report also clearly indicates that ownership of rebuilding processes should be handed over to the local population as quickly as possible.

Too little

The second camp maintains that the report was not ambitious enough. It holds that the commission was overly conservative – a product of its need to find a consensus among all the commissioners. Advocates of this view hold that in at least two areas the commission was more conservative than it needed to be.

First, the commission's 'just cause' thresholds set the bar too high ('large-scale loss of life . . . actual or apprehended' and 'large-scale ethnic cleansing').[87] The thresholds were apparently the result of a compromise between groups of commissioners who wanted wider and narrower thresholds respectively.[88] Importantly, they set the bar higher than the actual practice of the Security Council does, by excluding measures to protect democratic governments from violent overthrow and measures to protect civilians in cases which amounted to less than large-scale or genocidal killing. The ICISS thresholds excluded the overthrow of democratically elected governments, despite the fact that in 1994 the Security Council had identified the violent overthrow of Bertrand Aristide's government in Haiti as a 'threat to international peace and security' and had authorised enforcement measures to restore the elected government. Three years later, ECOWAS intervened in Sierra Leone to restore an elected government, a move subsequently endorsed by the Security Council.[89] In addition, the requirement of large-scale killing or ethnic cleansing precludes Security Council action in circumstances where the threat to civilians is somewhat lower. Once again, it would appear that Security Council practice is in advance of the

R2P. Security Council Resolution 1265 (17 September, 1999) stated the council's readiness to take appropriate steps to protect civilians who were being deliberately targeted, without insisting that this targeting had to be genocidal or 'large-scale'. In 2005, the Security Council authorised its peace operation in Côte D'Ivoire (UNOCI) to use force in order to protect civilians, even though the level of killing had not reached 'just cause' thresholds. In relation to thresholds, therefore, we can agree with Thomas Weiss that the ICISS took a conservative position and was 'neither forerunner nor pacesetter'.[90]

Additionally, the report had almost nothing to say about gender, despite significant moves by the Security Council to identify the role of women in peace and security. Resolution 1325 (October, 2000) had recognised the importance of female participation in all peace and security initiatives; the requirement for UN personnel to receive gender training; the need to protect women and girls and their human rights during and after armed conflict; and the need to mainstream gender throughout the UN system. Despite this clear statement, the ICISS report mentioned women only three times, and never in relation to including them in the process of protection or in terms of recognising their 'unique needs and contributions' in conflict and post-conflict contexts.[91] The report mentions 'rape' eight times, and two of the three references to women relate to this. Critics point out that the 'just cause' thresholds provide that rape is a cause for intervention only 'if it occurs as a means of ethnic cleansing'. The report therefore failed to develop the agenda set out in Resolution 1325, having nothing to say about the unique experiences (other than rape) of women and girls in wartime, about their contribution to peace and protection, or about the importance of gender training for interveners and gender mainstreaming across the whole UN system.

Too vague

A third group welcomed the report but maintained that it left important questions unaddressed and succumbed to the need for consensus by presenting vague wording which failed to advance the debate. The central weakness, often overlooked, was the report's failure to articulate a conceptually coherent, innovative and realisable account of the responsibilities to prevent and rebuild. This failure did nothing to dispel the perception that these components were tacked onto the R2P in order to make military intervention more palatable and helped to fuel the opposition to the R2P charted in the following chapter. This problem is discussed in greater detail in the second half of the book.

A second criticism levelled by this group focused on the relationship between the 'just cause' thresholds and the authority to intervene in cases where the Security Council is deadlocked.[92] The commission avoided specifying what it meant by 'large-scale' killing and ethnic cleansing or clarifying the meaning of 'actual or apprehended'.[93] In the absence of a clear understanding of what the thresholds are or when they are triggered, their ability to create moral authority for intervention is reduced.

Finally, both Francis Deng and Kofi Annan admitted that sovereignty as responsibility implied that sovereigns should be made accountable to a higher authority and that this required the creation of a legitimate and representative global body. It was commonly accepted that the Security Council was best placed to fulfil that role, but that the council had to become more efficient, representative and accountable in order to do it. If we accept these propositions, Security Council reform becomes a necessary component of the R2P, not an optional extra.[94] While recognising the problem ('uneven performance', 'unrepresentative membership'),[95] ICISS sidestepped the question of Security Council reform almost entirely. Limiting its reform proposals to the P5 'code-of-conduct', the commission concluded that 'there is no doubt that reform of the Security Council, in particular to broaden and make more genuinely representative its composition, would help in building its credibility and authority', but noted that such a reform would not necessarily improve the council's performance and that the question of reform itself was beyond its purview.[96]

The report was also criticised for being too vague in its operational recommendations. Adam Roberts, for instance, suggested that the ICISS failed to flesh out how it would actualise the prevention component.[97] The same might also be said in relation to rebuilding. In addition, the report's call for clarity of mandate contradicted its obvious preference for international consensus; the commission's call for 'unity of command' overlooked the reluctance of the great powers to place their forces under the command of others; and, although the commission noted the difficulty and importance of civil–military coordination, it offered no guidance on how to improve it.[98] Finally, Roderic Alley noted that the commission avoided discussion of the rebuilding role of the World Bank and IMF.[99]

It was inevitable that a relatively short report would leave many questions unanswered. Furthermore, ambiguity on questions such as authority and Security Council reform – itself a product of differences between the commissioners – made it harder for sceptical states to dismiss the R2P altogether. Given the damage inflicted on the R2P agenda by the 2003 invasion of Iraq, the concept's survival and integrity was an issue in itself.

The commission called upon the General Assembly to adopt a declaration affirming the principle of sovereignty as responsibility, asserting its responsibility to prevent, to react and to rebuild, and articulating the decision-making criteria. It maintained that the Security Council should adopt a resolution committing itself to the commission's 'principles for military action' and that the P5 should adopt the code of conduct relating to the (non-)use of the veto on resolutions authorising the use of force for human protection purposes. Finally, the commission called upon the Secretary-General to develop measures to realise the ICISS agenda.[100] This Kofi Annan did with gusto, playing an important role in getting R2P onto the international agenda by incorporating it into his blueprint for UN reform.[101] Nonetheless, the R2P faced an uphill battle against determined opposition, which only got stiffer thanks to the 2003 invasion of Iraq.

Conclusion

Given the task of reconciling the principle of state sovereignty with the idea that international society cannot simply stand aside when a government perpetrates, or fails to ameliorate, acts of genocide and mass atrocities within its borders, the ICISS developed the novel concept of the R2P. As conceived by the commission, the R2P started by insisting that all governments have a responsibility to protect their citizens from genocide and mass atrocities and that international society had responsibilities to prevent, react and rebuild – with an emphasis very much on the responsibility to react and on the question of when it was legitimate to intervene militarily to protect endangered populations. For example, although the commission described the 'responsibility to prevent' as the 'single most important dimension' of R2P – a view later restated by Thakur[102] – it dedicated only nine of its eighty-five pages to prevention. Indeed, the responsibilities to prevent and rebuild received only sixteen pages, compared with thirty-two pages on the question of intervention (chapters on 'reaction', 'authority' and 'operational aspects').

R2P succeeded in reframing the debate largely by stressing the primary responsibility that states had towards their own citizens; by situating non-consensual intervention within a wider continuum of measures – including prevention, rebuilding and non-forcible means of reaction; and by identifying a wide range of practices other than armed intervention which could contribute to the prevention and amelioration of genocide and mass atrocities. However, the prevention and rebuilding components did not receive the same degree of attention as intervention, and some of the core aspects of the commission's position on the latter (especially criteria, but also restrictions on the use of the veto) were deeply unpopular among governments of all stripes.

These facts made it difficult for advocates to build international support for the R2P after the commission released its report in 2001. The commission's own regional roundtables, post-report consultations with NGOs and governments organised by the Canadian government, and other dialogues all highlighted widespread hostility to 'humanitarian intervention' and a broad consensus against the idea of a so-called 'right of intervention', especially where that right was associated with unilateralism. Moreover, it was made clear that the association of the R2P with 'humanitarian intervention' would be a key barrier to consensus.[103] However, this deep-seated scepticism towards intervention did not necessarily translate into a rejection of the underlying purpose of the R2P – the prevention and amelioration of genocide and mass atrocities. Indeed, in the commission's own consultations, there was a clear consensus on the importance of shifting away from the non-consensual use of force to protect civilians, within a broader continuum of measures, including prevention. The commission's adoption of language focusing on the rights of endangered civilians rather than on the rights of potential interveners helped to illuminate a broad constituency of states and civil society actors prepared to acknowledge that sovereignty entailed responsibilities and the legitimacy of the international involvement in protecting people from genocide and mass atrocities. However, the commission's focus on non-consensual intervention and apparent openness to intervention not authorised by the Security Council meant that the R2P was unlikely to make the transition from being a 'twinkle in the eye' of an international commission to becoming a principle which could command the unanimous endorsement of world leaders without some important revisions. It is not surprising, therefore, that the R2P principle which emerged from the 2005 World Summit was different in some respects from the concept espoused by the ICISS, even if the name and the central idea remained the same. The next chapter focuses on the campaign to persuade international society to adopt the R2P.

3

The 2005 World Summit

World leaders formally adopted the R2P at the 2005 World Summit – the centrepiece of Kofi Annan's reform programme, which aimed at renewing a global organisation in crisis on account of its past inaction in the face of genocide, of divisions over Kosovo and Iraq, and of 'oil-for-food' and sexual abuse scandals. Paragraphs 138 and 139 of the summit's Outcome Document declared:

> 138. Each individual state has the responsibility to protect its populations from genocide, war crimes, ethnic cleansing and crimes against humanity. This responsibility entails the prevention of such crimes, including their incitement, through appropriate and necessary means. We accept that responsibility and will act in accordance with it. The international community should, as appropriate, encourage and help States to exercise this responsibility and support the United Nations in establishing an early warning capability.
>
> 139. The international community, through the United Nations, also has the responsibility to use appropriate diplomatic, humanitarian and other peaceful means, in accordance with Chapters VI and VIII of the Charter of the United Nations, to help protect populations from war crimes, ethnic cleansing and crimes against humanity. In this context, we are prepared to take collective action, in a timely and decisive manner, through the Security Council, in accordance with the Charter, including Chapter VII, on a case-by-case basis and in cooperation with relevant regional organisations as appropriate, should peaceful means be inadequate and national authorities are manifestly failing to protect their populations from genocide, war crimes, ethnic cleansing and crimes against humanity. We stress the need for the General Assembly to continue consideration of the responsibility to protect populations from genocide, war crimes, ethnic cleansing and crimes against humanity and its implications, bearing in mind the principles of the Charter and international law. We also intend to commit ourselves, as necessary and appropriate, to helping States build capacity to protect their populations from genocide, war crimes, ethnic cleansing and crimes against humanity and to assisting those which are under stress before crises and conflicts break out.[1]

This chapter charts the global effort to persuade states to adopt the R2P and evaluates the significance of this declaration. That the R2P survived until 2005 was an achievement in itself. That it was adopted by a consensus of the General Assembly was momentous, though the form of words finally agreed upon was less comprehensive than the summit's organisers and R2P advocates had hoped for. Indeed, some go as far as to suggest that what the World Summit proposed was 'R2P lite' – the basic principle divested of almost all its substance.[2] Although the summit document disappointed those who wanted to see greater progress on questions concerning non-consensual intervention and more robust action in defence of human rights, Paragraphs 138 and 139 and other elements of the document do provide a mandate for a wide range of institutional reforms and international activities aimed at preventing and protecting people from genocide and mass atrocities.[3] It is this mandate, by and large, that animates the analysis of the operationalisation of R2P in the following three chapters.

The Setting Sun of Humanitarianism?

In its first two years, all the indicators suggested that there was little likelihood of the R2P being adopted in a UN declaration or resolution. Not only were the P5 and many other governments sceptical about the ICISS report's implications; the use of humanitarian justifications by supporters of the 2003 US-led invasion of Iraq only heightened global sensitivity about perceived affronts to sovereignty.

Several P5 governments were sceptical from the outset. At the Security Council's annual retreat, in May 2002, the US rejected the idea of criteria to guide decision-making on the grounds that it would not bind itself in ways that might constrain its right to decide when and where to use force.[4] This led prominent observers to write in 2004 that 'the Bush administration does not and will not accept the substance of the report or support any formal declaration or resolution about it'.[5] The Chinese were also unconvinced about the R2P and insisted that all questions relating to the use of force should be deferred to the Security Council. Russia shared China's concern and argued that the UN was already equipped to deal with humanitarian crises, noting that, by countenancing unauthorised intervention, the R2P risked undermining the Charter.[6] Although the UK and France advocated R2P and (along with the US) flatly rejected the view that unauthorised intervention should be prohibited in all circumstances, they too expressed concerns. In particular, they worried that agreement on criteria would not necessarily deliver the political will and consensus required for effective responses to humanitarian crises.[7]

Opinion outside the Security Council was similarly divided. The Non-Aligned Movement (NAM) flatly rejected the R2P. India, a leading member of the NAM, argued that the council was already sufficiently empowered to act in humanitarian emergencies and observed that the failure to act in the past was caused by a lack of political will, not of authority. India's ambassador to the UN, Nirupam Sen, insisted that the R2P should 'be addressed with necessary caution and responsibility', since 'we do not believe that discussions on the question should be used as a cover for conferring any legitimacy on the so-called "right of humanitarian intervention" or making it the ideology of some kind of "military humanism"'. The rule of international law, Sen argued, 'should protect weak and vulnerable states from the arbitrary exercise of power by the strong'.[8] Speaking on behalf of the NAM, Malaysia argued that the R2P represented a potential reincarnation of humanitarian intervention, for which there was no basis in international law.[9] The Group of 77 (G77) was more equivocal. Failing to reach a consensus, it suggested that the report should be revised so as to emphasise the principles of territorial integrity and sovereignty.[10]

To make matters worse, constructive debate about the R2P was hampered by the US-led invasion of Iraq. It certainly did not help that a prominent ICISS commissioner – Michael Ignatieff – initially defended the invasion on human rights grounds, before he changed his mind.[11] Gareth Evans rightly claimed that the 'poorly and inconsistently' argued humanitarian justification for the war in Iraq 'almost choked at birth what many were hoping was an emerging new norm justifying intervention on the basis of the principle of "responsibility to protect."'[12] This view was widely shared: Ian Williams argued that the Iraq war brought 'humanitarian intervention into disrepute'; Richard Falk lamented that the war risked undermining consensus at the UN; Bruce Jentelson observed that it 'exacerbated suspicions about humanitarian justifications for the general use of force'; Karl Kaiser insisted that 'Washington has lowered [consensus on] the humanitarian intervention approach to an unprecedented level'; John Kampfner suggested that 'there has been no better time for dictators to act with impunity'; and The Fund for Peace project found that Europeans were reluctant to support humanitarian intervention for fear of tacitly legitimising the invasion of Iraq.[13] David Clark, a former special advisor to the British Foreign Office, bluntly maintained that 'Iraq has ruined our case for humanitarian wars. As long as US power remains in the hands of the Republican Right, it will be impossible to build a consensus on the Left behind the idea that it can be a power for good. Those who continue to insist that it can, risk discrediting the concept of humanitarian intervention.'[14]

Of course, many states opposed the R2P before the invasion of Iraq, which led some analysts to doubt Iraq's negative impact.[15] However, in addition to giving succour to the R2P's traditional opponents, Iraq encouraged some R2P supporters to limit the scope of what they would ask the world to sign up to, thus laying the foundations for important changes to the R2P concept that helped forge global consensus in 2005. For example, immediately after the Iraq war (14 July 2003), a forum of social democratic political leaders rejected sections of a draft communiqué proposed by Tony Blair and Jean Chrétien endorsing the R2P and supporting the idea that it ought to override sovereignty in grave humanitarian crises. Blair's draft text used language clearly reminiscent of R2P: 'where a population is suffering serious harm, as a result of internal war, insurgency, repression or state failure, and the state in question is unwilling or unable to halt or avert it, the principle of non-intervention yields to the international responsibility'. Germany, Argentina and Chile – all supporters of the R2P – opposed this wording, reportedly 'believing it could be used to justify the military campaign in Iraq'. In the end, the communiqué made no mention of human rights trumping sovereignty or criteria to govern intervention; it called instead upon the General Assembly to discuss the R2P, whilst reiterating that 'the Security Council remains the sole body to authorise global action'.[16]

After this meeting, the German government began emphasising a different understanding of what the R2P entailed in relation to non-consensual force, arguing that such measures should be sanctioned by the Security Council. Gerhard Schroeder told an audience in 2004 that 'Germany is committed . . . to its responsibility to protect people from wars, violence, genocide, terror, injustice, and oppression', before going on to insist that whilst 'prevention does not rule out timely military intervention . . . this must be based on criteria that are in keeping with our values and basic political convictions'. The chancellor concluded: 'no country can guarantee security, peace, and prosperity for itself and deal with the new challenges that face us by acting alone . . . German security policy is based on the primacy of international law and the strengthening of the United Nations.'[17] Another case of links being drawn between the R2P and the Iraq war was the Sudanese government's portrayal of American activism on Darfur as analogues with its strategy in Iraq: both were oil-oriented and anti-Islamic. Although disingenuous, this argument helped to reinforce African and Middle Eastern hostility to the idea of western interference in

Darfur.[18] Neither of these cases clearly indicates an increased reluctance to support R2P per se, but it is clear that, at the least, the invasion of Iraq intensified sensitivity about intervention without Security Council approval and weakened the moral standing of those states associated with the invasion.

Given all this, it is not surprising that early efforts to persuade the General Assembly to commit to R2P were unsuccessful. In these first two years, Canada stood 'almost alone' in trying to persuade states to commit to R2P.[19] In late 2002, the NAM blocked a Canadian draft of a technical General Assembly resolution which bound the Assembly to deliberate on the ICISS report. Opponents feared that technical deliberations would lead to substantive discussion of the report's findings. In response, Canada revised the draft resolution so that it merely asked the Secretary-General to facilitate dialogue on R2P, but this failed to win support as well.[20]

Shortly afterwards, participants in a Canada-sponsored roundtable suggested slowing the diplomatic effort to sell the R2P, in order to allow sufficient time for the norm to evolve and avoid a potential backlash from the General Assembly. A full-scale effort to persuade the assembly to subscribe to criteria in guiding military intervention could 'backfire terribly', it was argued. Patrick Wittmann, Deputy Director for Humanitarian Affairs in the Canadian Foreign Ministry, maintained that, although there was broad support for the R2P, there was a small, determined and influential group of 'rejectionists' capable of swaying the majority's opinion.[21] These rejectionist states were undoubtedly behind the failed 2002 bid in the General Assembly, and this experience encouraged Canada to adopt a longer-term approach.

By early 2003, therefore, R2P looked like a stillborn concept, tainted by an (albeit misplaced) association with the deeply unpopular Iraq War. Nevertheless, the Canadian government still harboured plans to return to the General Assembly with the draft of a substantive resolution. What kept alive the concept and the promise of adoption by the General Assembly and/or Security Council was the confluence of four factors. The first two – public advocacy by the Canadian government and ICISS Commissioners and the adoption of the R2P by the UN Secretary-General after a proposal by the High-Level Panel commissioned to explore the challenges confronting the organisation in the twenty-first century – were critical in terms of placing the concept on the international agenda. The other two factors – a growing American willingness to consider the R2P as part of a broader package of UN reform and the adoption of R2P-like principles by the African Union – created the potential for a global consensus.

Turning the Tide

Canada and the ICISS commissioners

The Canadian government was the R2P's principal advocate. As soon as plans for the 2005 World Summit were announced, the Canadian government began to advocate the R2P at every level. In particular, government officials and diplomats focused on persuading the UN High-Level Panel (HLP) to endorse the R2P and on encouraging the UN Secretary-General to do likewise in his response. This was because they saw these two as the most important milestones in terms of placing the R2P on the international agenda.[22]

Canada's advocacy of the R2P actually began almost as soon as the ICISS report was released. It attempted to mobilise civil society to act both as advocate and as agent of implementation, while at the same time leading an inter-governmental process to gauge support for the R2P, to identify political obstacles and to build a group of 'like-minded' 'friends' – states which may advocate and operationalise the concept. It was through these processes that the Canadians identified two avenues for selling the R2P. The first was through persuading states to adopt the R2P in various resolutions and declarations. This was called 'norm building'. The second was through focusing on practical initiatives towards increasing the physical protection of civilians. This was labelled the 'just do it and don't call it a doctrine approach' by Paul Heinbecker, Canada's ambassador to the UN.[23] In 2003–4, Canada pursued initiatives along both tracks through which it became convinced that, even if 'norm building' was important, 'operationalisation' was likely to deliver more consensus and actual protection.

Having ascertained that NGOs were interested in advancing the R2P agenda, Canada invited the World Federalist Movement–Institute for Global Policy (WFM–IGP) to organise a series of roundtables with NGOs to seek feedback on the report, advice about the best way of advancing the R2P agenda, and suggestions about the potential role of civil society. Canada also asked WFM–IPG to play a continuing role in involving NGOs in the process. This eventually became the 'Responsibility to Protect – Engaging Civil Society' (R2P–CS) project, led by WFM–IPG and Oxfam. R2P–CS played an important role by continuing global consultations (for example, hosting a seminar on R2P at the 2003 World Social Forum of 100,000 NGOs, held in Brazil), by marshalling the support of NGOs globally, fostering efforts to inform the public better, and by actively lobbying permanent delegations in New York.

The WFM–IPG roundtables yielded some important insights on how best to advance the R2P agenda, identifying a 'three track' approach to potential civil society engagement. The first track involved persuading decision-makers of the moral imperative for action in response to R2P-triggering crises; embedding a change of language from 'right of intervention' to 'responsibility to protect'; and emphasising the priority of prevention. Indeed, one of the key recommendations was that 'the best approach [for furthering R2P] is to focus on the prevention of conflict/protection of civilians aspects of the Report, and to allow discussion of the appropriate circumstances for military intervention to flow from there'.[24] The roundtables identified a number of ways in which civil society groups could advance this agenda – for instance by promoting global dialogue, by disseminating the report's findings and by making connections between the R2P and other relevant policy agendas.[25] One such dialogue, conducted in 2005, revealed that, although south-east Asians remained deeply sceptical about 'humanitarian intervention', they were open to the idea that sovereignty entailed responsibilities and that the protection of individuals, if handled appropriately, could be a matter of legitimate international concern.[26] Developing this approach, the R2P–CS also became an important advocate, promoting the R2P in policy circles.[27]

The second track focused on the creation of political will within governments. NGOs could gather and disseminate information about potential and actual crises, monitor the activities of the Security Council (a role ably fulfilled by *Security Council Report*), lobby for the inclusion of R2P-related issues on the council's agenda and advocate the incorporation of the R2P into the operational mandates of international operations.

The third track focused on operational questions and advocated strengthened capacity for international institutions. Chief among recommendations in this area was advocacy for the commitment of resources for conflict prevention and support for the development of international policing capacity and the mandates of UN representatives and advisers on protection issues such as IDPs and the prevention of genocide. Across all three tracks, there was broad agreement that R2P initiatives should be grafted onto pre-existing policies rather than sold as entirely novel.[28]

In addition to encouraging civil society engagement, the Canadian government also ran an inter-governmental process. It organised a series of workshops with other governments and hosted meetings with permanent missions in New York. This process helped to persuade Canada that, although the R2P was resolutely opposed by a small and determined group of states within the NAM, a majority could be won over. The key to doing this, Canadian officials believed, lay in emphasising that the R2P involved a continuum of measures, from prevention to rebuilding, and involved more, not fewer, rules relating to the use of force. This view sat comfortably with the emerging preference among NGOs for the 'operational' over the 'norm building' approach; it also fitted in with the view that specific initiatives should be grafted onto work already underway in the UN and elsewhere.[29]

In light of this feedback and of the 2002 General Assembly experience, the Canadian government and high-profile ICISS commissioners duly emphasised aspects of the ICISS report that would constrain the freedom of states to justify the use of force for humanitarian purposes. In particular, the Canadian government insisted that intervention should be authorised by the Security Council and stressed that the threshold for action should be set high – higher, in fact, than Security Council practice in the 1990s (see Chapter 2).[30] In his 2004 address to the General Assembly, Canadian Prime Minister Paul Martin argued that the R2P filled a gap in international law: 'it says that we [the members of the UN] should have a legal right to intervene in a country on the grounds of humanitarian emergency alone when the government of that country is unwilling or unable to protect their people from extreme harm'.[31] Of course, Martin was pointing to the fact that the Security Council had already exercised a legal right to intervene on humanitarian or other grounds during the 1990s. Martin continued by arguing that 'the Security Council should establish new thresholds for when the international community judges that civilian populations face extreme threats', finally insisting that 'the responsibility to protect is not a license for intervention; it is an international guarantor of international accountability'.[32] In short, Martin argued that, whilst a commitment to the R2P created international duties, the Security Council should only license intervention when the 'just cause' thresholds were satisfied. The problem of unauthorised intervention, raised so divisively by Kosovo and Iraq, was carefully bypassed. Thus tying non-consensual force under the banner of the R2P *exclusively* with Security Council authorisation – rather than *primarily*, as proposed by the ICISS – became a key part of the R2P and was an essential component of the 2005 consensus.

The place of this new understanding of the R2P (sometimes labelled 'R2P lite') in Canada's position was stated more clearly in its non-paper, submitted to the High-Level Panel (HLP) established by Kofi Annan to explore options for UN reform (see below). The non-paper reiterated the centrality of sovereignty, going as far as to maintain that sovereignty should trump humanitarianism if the latter can only be 'undertaken at the cost of undermining the stability of the state-based international order'.[33] The R2P, it argued, should be grounded in the UN Charter's demand for sovereignty to yield to international peace and security; and the UN members should resolve or declare that, 'while the primary responsibility to protect rests with individual states, there is a corollary responsibility on the part of the international community to act in extreme cases'.[34] The threshold for intervention, Canada argued, should be set high and the Security Council should carefully assess the modalities of action before authorising intervention.[35] In short, the Canadian government proposed a new understanding of the R2P by dissociating the original concept from unauthorised intervention of the type illustrated in Kosovo or Iraq, by insisting that coercive humanitarian action remained the prerogative of the Security Council and by limiting council activism to cases which crossed the 'just cause' threshold. Conspicuous by their absence from the non-paper were core elements of the ICISS report, most notably the P5 code of conduct and guidelines for cases where the council fails to take timely and decisive action in threshold-crossing cases.

Ramesh Thakur, one of the most prominent ICISS commissioners, adopted a similar tone. Drawing on a body of thought dating back to the 1970s, Thakur argued that the 'just cause' thresholds and precautionary principles should be viewed as constraints limiting governments' ability to 'abuse' humanitarian justifications.[36] According to Thakur, the criteria would 'make it more difficult for coalitions of the willing to appropriate the language of humanitarianism for geopolitical and unilateral interventions', while making the Security Council's deliberations more transparent.[37] Prophetically, Thakur argued that a post-Iraq consensus could be forged if these constraining elements were emphasised. Consensus on criteria, he insisted, would make it more rather than less difficult for states to claim a humanitarian mantle for armed intervention.[38]

In their bid to build consensus on the R2P in the wake of the deeply divisive Iraq War, key advocates attempted therefore to buy consensus by watering down the concept and offering the world a new understanding of the R2P.[39] First, the question of unauthorised intervention was sidestepped in favour of a concept of R2P which was wedded to Security Council authorisation. Second, having placed the legitimation of intervention squarely under the rubric of the Security Council, these advocates further limited the scope of council activism by insisting that it should be guided by the 'just cause' threshold and by the precautionary principles. Finally, in order to win over great powers which were reluctant (especially the US, Russia and China), the P5 'code-of-conduct' – widely considered central to making the council work more effectively – was dropped. At the very beginning of the World Summit negotiations, not even ardent supporters were advocating the wholesale adoption of the commission's recommendations. Instead, they wedded the R2P to the Security Council, while dropping the very measures which, as ICISS maintained, were necessary to make the council better able to discharge its responsibilities.

Annan and the UN

The adoption of the R2P by the Secretary-General's High-Level Panel (HLP), and its subsequent place in Kofi Annan's agenda for renewing the UN ('In larger freedom'), paved the way for the incorporation of the R2P into the 2005 World Summit declaration.[40] The HLP's endorsement opened up the possibility of a declaratory commitment to the R2P, but it also confirmed the principle's transformation away from the vision set out by the ICISS. Kofi Annan commissioned the HLP, which included Gareth Evans, in September 2003, instructing it to examine challenges to international peace and security and the contribution that the UN could make to addressing those challenges more effectively. In its December 2004 report, the panel endorsed the 'emerging norm that there is a responsibility to protect' and confirmed the developing consensus that this norm was 'exercisable by the Security Council'.[41] The task, it argued, was not to resolve the dilemma of how to proceed when the council is deadlocked, but to make the council itself work better.[42] Yevgeny Primakov, a panel member and former Russian prime minister, explained that, while a minority of states (especially NATO members) maintained that humanitarian intervention required a departure from the UN framework, the overwhelming majority believed that intervention should only occur if duly authorised by the Security Council.[43]

In order to make the Security Council work better, the panel endorsed the R2P's 'just cause' thresholds and precautionary principles with minor revisions. It broadened and clarified the 'just cause' thresholds by adding 'serious violations of humanitarian law' to a list containing genocide, large-scale killing and ethnic cleansing.[44] Just as significantly, it narrowed the preventive component of the 'just cause' criteria slightly, insisting that the criteria would be satisfied if the threat was actual or 'imminently apprehended' – as opposed to simply 'apprehended', as ICISS had proposed.[45] The panel also endorsed, and renamed, the four precautionary principles. It recommended the Security Council to adopt the guidelines in a declaratory resolution, but it overlooked the P5 'code of conduct'. In its place, the HLP proposed a somewhat weaker constraint on the use of the veto, in a passage on Security Council reform. Instead of a commitment not to veto collective action in response to threshold-crossing crises where the majority is in favour unless vital national interests are at stake, the HLP suggested a system of indicative voting, whereby council members could call for states to declare themselves publicly and to justify their positions prior to an actual vote.[46] Rather optimistically, the HLP hoped that members would be reluctant to declare publicly their opposition to collective action in conscience-shocking cases and that this would reduce the threat of veto.

Annan accepted almost all the HLP recommendations in his own blueprint for UN reform.[47] He endorsed the idea of criteria to guide the Security Council in its decision-making about the use of force, seeing criteria as a potential mechanism for avoiding the damaging divisions caused by Iraq. In order to distinguish the R2P from humanitarian intervention and the use of force still further, Annan changed the R2P's place in the broader reform agenda. The HLP had placed the R2P in a chapter on 'collective security' and under the banner of 'Use of Force', primarily in an attempt to sell the concept as a device for re-characterising humanitarian intervention. Annan separated the commitment to the R2P from the proposal for criteria, placing the former in a section on the rule of law and leaving the latter in a section on the use of force. He did this in order to reinforce the view that the R2P was not only about the use of force but, in the words of William Pace and Nicole Deller, about 'a normative and moral undertaking requiring a state to protect its own citizens'.[48] This underlined the broader moral principle and helped to distance the R2P from 'humanitarian intervention' – an attempt to head off potential criticism from the NAM and G77.

Like those before him, Annan implied that the Security Council was the sole source of authority for R2P interventions and that criteria should serve as a constraint on its decision-making. He noted the 'sensitivities involved in this issue', but insisted that 'we must embrace the responsibility to protect and, when necessary, we must act upon it'. The Secretary-General reiterated that primary responsibility lay with the host state, adding that only if a state proved unwilling or unable to protect its citizens would responsibility shift to international society. If all else failed, 'the Security Council may out of necessity decide to take action', but should 'follow the principles' outlined by the HLP.[49]

The adoption of the R2P by the HLP and Annan was undoubtedly critical to getting it on the agenda of the 2005 World Summit. Without this adoption, it is unlikely that the Canadian government and high profile ICISS commissioners would have succeeded in persuading governments to discuss the R2P, let alone include it the final text. However, the UN secretariat's advocacy of R2P-related ideas involved much more than these two high profile reports. Since the 2000 Brahimi report on peace operations, UN officials worked in various ways to operationalise principles associated with the R2P into the working practice of the Security Council and other UN bodies. Most obviously, it is has become common practice for UN peace operations to be given a mandate to protect civilians (see Chapter 5). This accumulation of experience had a significant cushioning effect on the way the world received Annan's recommendations. Not only had the UN established itself in the civilian protection business, but some of those states most sceptical about the R2P had made a physical contribution to protection through their involvement in UN peace operations. For instance in the UN missions in Haiti and the DRC, troops and police from Jordan, Brazil, China, Pakistan and India have used force against gangs and militia. Such front-line examples indicate a wide consensus around the notion that, when properly authorised and managed, the protection of civilians can sometimes trump the principle of non-interference.

This gradual shift in the way the UN conducts peace operations was not, however, uncontroversial. Speaking to the General Assembly on behalf of the NAM, Morocco insisted that the 'establishment by the United Nations of any peace operation under Chapter VII of the United Nations Charter, or extension of a mandate, should not only be based on the consent of the parties, but also on the non-use of force, except in self-defence'.[50] Likewise, the G77 was less than effusive in its response to the use of the R2P in Annan's 'In larger freedom'. Unable to reach a consensus, it insisted only that reform should promote equity and protect 'the rights and interests of all states'.[51]

Africa and the Ezulwini consensus

Although many governments outside the West were sceptical about the R2P, seeing it as a potential licence for intervention, a significant shift in attitudes was afoot in Africa. Indeed, one study found 'little or no unease among African stakeholders', noting that the reinterpretation of sovereignty (as responsibility) 'does not trigger the same alarm bells in Africa as it does in other regions of the world'.[52] This change in attitudes, characterised by the African Union (AU) as one from 'non-intervention to non-indifference', helped in creating a constituency of states in the developing world which were willing to endorse the R2P.[53] This significantly altered the balance in the global debate by challenging the idea that the R2P pitched the West against the rest.

In 2003, the Organisation for African Unity (OAU) was formally replaced by the AU. Among the factors precipitating the new organisation was a belief that the developed world had neglected African problems and that the continent must take its own measures to improve peace and security.[54] As the African heads of state themselves declared, 'the international community has not always accorded due attention to conflict management in Africa, as it has consistently done in other regions, and . . . the efforts exerted by Africans themselves in the area of peacekeeping . . . are not given adequate financial and logistical support'.[55] Under the Constitutive Act of the AU, African leaders awarded the new organisation a right of intervention but balanced this by reaffirming the principle of non-interference. Article 4(h) of the Act established 'the right of the Union to intervene in a Member State pursuant to a decision of the assembly in respect of grave circumstances, namely war crimes, genocide and crimes against humanity'. The article was amended in 2003 to cover other 'serious threats to legitimate order', and an additional paragraph (Article 4 (j)) formalising the members' right to request intervention was added. The seemingly contradictory Article 4(g), meanwhile, insisted that the member states should refrain from interfering in the domestic affairs of others. Together, these articles provide a legal framework for collective intervention. As Ben Kioko, senior legal advisor to the AU, explained: 'Article 4(h) was adopted with the sole purpose of enabling the African Union to resolve conflicts more effectively on the continent.'[56]

There are at least two problems, however, with the way in which the AU's intervention mechanism has developed in practice. First, the AU remains unclear about both the procedural and the substantive conditions under which this mechanism would be utilised. Second, as the Darfur case demonstrates, the AU's regional mechanisms may be used to block collective action through the UN. I will consider both of these problems in turn.

There remains confusion about the legal relationship between the AU and the Security Council. Under the Constitutive Act, the AU Peace and Security Council, which includes fifteen members, would recommend action to the AU Assembly. The assembly is authorised to defer its responsibility to the AU Peace and Security Council. The problem here is that the assembly meets only once a year and takes decisions on the basis of consensus or, failing that, of a two-thirds majority. The process of activating Article 4(h) against the will of the relevant member state would therefore be time-consuming and fraught with political obstacles. Moreover, given the continent's traditional reluctance to endorse interventionism and its fractious sub-regional alignments, the likelihood of securing a two-thirds majority in the face of a hostile host must be considered to be slim at best. It is no surprise that both of the AU's peace operations, in Burundi and Darfur, were conducted with host state consent.

The relationship between AU initiatives and the Security Council is equally problematic. The Constitutive Act strongly implies that the AU, not the UN Security Council, may assume primary responsibility in the face of humanitarian emergencies. Indeed, Africa's sub-regional organisations have a long track-record of intervention and peacekeeping. Often, as in the case of the ECOWAS intervention in Liberia, these initiatives were welcomed by the Security Council. Sometimes, however, they were quite unhelpful and attracted international criticism, as in the case of the Zimbabwe-led intervention in the DRC, which was carried out under the auspices of SADC.[57] Moreover, when it comes to matters outside their own region, African states have a track-record of opposing Security Council activism. In 1999, Namibia voted to condemn NATO's intervention in Kosovo, a position publicly shared both by South Africa and by Nigeria, and in early 2007 South Africa joined China and Russia in arguing that political oppression in Myanmar was a domestic issue in which the council should not be involved – an argument which had not been seriously aired in the council for a decade.[58]

This gets us to the second problem associated with African regionalism, namely that it could be used to thwart efforts to mobilise action through the Security Council. On the one hand, the old adage of 'African solutions to African problems' permits the P5 to defer its responsibilities to the AU in cases where the former lacks the political will to act – and to do it regardless of the actual capacity of the AU to protect civilians. On the other hand, it may lend credence to arguments against UN activism by fostering the idea that the Security Council should avoid imposing its will on Africans. Both of these possibilities were evident in the Security Council's deliberations on how best to respond to the Darfur crisis. In one of its first discussions on the matter, in July 2004, the US, UK, Germany, Chile and Spain (those states generally most supportive of action against the Sudanese government) argued that the Sudanese government had failed in its responsibility to protect, but they refrained from arguing that the R2P should be taken up by the council. Instead, they referred to the AU as bearing primary responsibility, should the government of Sudan continue to fail.[59] This position was endorsed by Francis Deng, who argued that, since the Sudanese government had declared its hostility to UN intervention, the best way forward was to encourage the AU to establish a presence in Darfur with Sudanese consent.[60] This was supported by some African states primarily concerned with averting international intervention. Algeria, a strident opponent of the R2P, used ongoing regional initiatives to justify rejecting American proposals for overflights to verify compliance with the ceasefire – proposals which it deemed 'unacceptable assaults on Sudan's sovereignty'.[61] Likewise, an 'African mini-summit' on Darfur led by Libya and Egypt – two other opponents of the R2P – rejected 'any foreign [i.e. UN or 'Western'] intervention by any country whatsoever in this pure African issue', insisting that regional solutions should take precedence over globally orchestrated action.[62]

What all this meant for Africa's position on the R2P became clear when the Union's Executive Council met to develop a common position on UN reform in March 2005. The so-called 'Ezulwini consensus' went some way towards resolving the procedural problems but left the substantive problem intact. The consensus endorsed the HLP's criteria for guiding the Security Council but, at the insistence of South Africa – one of the most persistent advocates of the R2P in Africa – observed that these guidelines 'should not undermine the responsibility of the international community to protect'.[63] On the relationship between the AU and the Security Council, the consensus endorsed the idea that, although the AU was the primary instrument of peace and security in Africa, its interventions should be approved by the Security Council – though, 'in certain circumstances, such approval could be given "after the fact"'. The consensus endorsed the R2P within the framework of the Security Council, though it went marginally further than the HLP in granting leeway to regional organisations. However, this position was balanced by two key assertions. First, the AU insisted that the R2P should not be used 'as a pretext to undermine the sovereignty, independence and territorial integrity of states'.[64] Second, the use of force should comply scrupulously with Article 51 of the UN Charter (self-defence) and Article 4(h) of the AU Constitutive Act.[65] This paragraph clearly aimed to limit Security Council activism and to assert the AU's primacy.

These concerns aside, the development of a regional peace and security mechanism in Africa and its incorporation of a regional 'right to intervene' certainly implied support for the ICISS concept.[66] The 'Ezulwini consensus' should not be understood as an endorsement of the R2P as outlined either by the ICISS or by the HLP, but as an insistence that, even if regional bodies *may* decide to intervene, such decisions must be subject to sovereignty considerations and regional deliberations must take precedence over global deliberations even when the relevant regional bodies decide not to act or are incapable of acting effectively. Despite South Africa's insistence that the continent needed to develop a proactive doctrine to protect its people, others (e.g. Libya, Algeria, Zimbabwe) were mainly concerned with limiting council activism. Nevertheless, the agreement helped to open the door to the possibility of a global consensus on R2P and helped identify African champions for the concept.

Gingrich/Mitchell and American policy

A subtle yet important shift in American attitudes was also critical to getting the R2P to the table. As we have noted earlier, the US remained somewhat aloof, expressing concern that a public commitment to the R2P might compel the US to deploy forces in ways which were inimical to its perceived national interests and that criteria would limit its flexibility in deciding when and where to use force to protect the common good.[67] These sentiments were encouraged by an anti-UN political atmosphere in Washington DC which was fuelled by Annan's criticism of the Iraq War and by the UN's 'oil-for-food' scandal. In 2004, Henry Hyde introduced into Congress legislation aimed at halving America's dues to the UN. This would have caused a financial crisis for the organisation overnight.

The Hyde Bill prompted serious debate in Washington DC on the value of the UN and provided the catalyst for a shift in the Administration's public position on both the UN and the R2P. Although critics argue that the White House could have struck down the bill at any time, some Administration officials did come out against it and, in doing so, offered a robust defence of the UN. Under-Secretary of State, Nicholas Burns, told the *New York Times*: 'we are the founder of the UN. We're the host country of the UN. We're the leading contributor to the UN. We don't want to put ourselves in the position where the United States is withholding 50 percent of the American contributions to the UN system.' The bill passed Congress nonetheless, which led some commentators to suggest that, if the White House was to kill it off in the Senate (as it subsequently did), it would need a good outcome at the World Summit. According to insiders, the Hyde Bill would be 'unstoppable' if the summit failed to deliver.[68]

Meanwhile, a high profile task force organised by the US Institute of Peace and chaired by George Mitchell and Newt Gingrich – the latter being a renowned UN-sceptic – was exploring the relationship between US interests and Annan's reform agenda. The task force's report was published on the same day when the White House finally declared its opposition to the Hyde Bill.[69] It argued that the UN's failure to respond to past genocides was a failure of those member states who had 'blocked or undermined' collective action.[70] To remove this stumbling block, it recommended that UN members affirm their responsibility to protect their own citizens from genocide, mass killing and massive human rights violations.[71] In cases where a government failed to protect its citizens, 'the collective responsibility of nations to take action cannot be denied'. Disputing the emerging consensus that the use of force for humanitarian purposes be authorised by the Security Council, it argued that the failure of the Security Council to act 'must not be used as an excuse by concerned members to avoid protective measures' – precisely the position taken on Darfur in the Security Council by the US, UK and France between 2003 and 2007.[72] Furthermore, it insisted that the US should compel states opposed to intervention to justify their position in public.

The task force argued that in practice, the US should adopt a four-stage approach to dealing with genocidal regimes:

1   The government implicated in genocide, mass killing or massive violations of human rights should be warned that it has a responsibility to protect.

2   If it fails to remedy the problem, the government should have its financial assets frozen and 'targeted sanctions' should be imposed.

3   If these measures fail, the Security Council should consider military intervention. But, 'in the event that the Security Council is derelict or untimely in its response, states – individually or collectively – would retain the ability to act'.[73]

4   Individuals guilty of mass murder should be identified and held accountable.

The Mitchell-Gingrich report thus laid the groundwork for a renewed US engagement with the R2P. It was publicly endorsed by Nicholas Burns and praised by the *New York Times* for offering 'constructive recommendations on mobilizing Washington's powerful influence to promote urgent and necessary reforms'.[74] In UN circles, the report was widely taken to indicate a new and more constructive American engagement. Moreover, by de-coupling the R2P from criteria and expressly permitting unauthorised intervention, the task force spoke directly to the Administration's two principal concerns about the concept. Of course, these aspects of the American position put it somewhat at odds with the emerging global consensus, but they certainly facilitated America's engagement with the R2P.

The 2005 World Summit

In September 2005, world leaders gathered in New York to celebrate the six-tieth anniversary of the UN and to debate Annan's proposed reform package. Commitment to the R2P was a significant part of that package. The effort to draft a reform document, based on Annan's 'In larger freedom', which could command a consensus in the General Assembly began in late 2004, when Jean Ping, Foreign Minister of Gabon and Assembly President, began consulting with the permanent delegations. Ping brought together ten ambassadors, including two from the western bloc (Australia and the Netherlands), to act as summit 'facilitators'. This strategy was later criticised by US Ambassador John Bolton for giving too much leeway for national differences to stall progress.[75] In fact, Bolton's criticism was based on a mis-taken view of the facilitators' role. Whilst Bolton argued that each facilita-tor was assigned a discrete part of the text and was charged with finding a consensus, in actuality they worked together on all parts of the draft.[76] Ping anticipated that a final draft would be prepared and agreed upon by the end of August 2005, well before the summit itself. In the end, the summit nego-tiations proved more protracted and divisive than Ping or Annan had imag-ined. They were only concluded at the last minute, when it seemed that the whole reform agenda would collapse. In the diplomatic maelstrom, the R2P made it into the summit declaration in spite of last-ditch attempts to have it removed, but the outcome was a R2P principle which was very different from the one envisaged by the ICISS.

Once the negotiations started, it was expected that the R2P would be controversial on account of its association with humanitarian intervention. There was, however, broad support for setting a high 'just cause' threshold and for the principle that the host state had primary responsibility. The P5 states remained solidly against the 'code of conduct', as they had been throughout – a position increasingly supported by the wider UN member-ship, which saw the veto as an important barrier against western interven-tionism. As a result, not even the HLP's revised 'code' survived long in the negotiations.

Disagreement remained on several critical issues. First, there was the question of whether the Security Council had exclusive or only primary authority to authorise armed intervention. The US and UK continued to argue that unauthorised intervention could not be expressly ruled out, but the majority of states held that, if the R2P was to *constrain* western inter-ventionism – a core component of Canadian and ICISS advocacy – then the absolute primacy of the Security Council had to be reaffirmed. Second, there was profound disagreement about criteria. Whereas several African states, the HLP and Annan endorsed the view that these were essential in making the Security Council's decisions more transparent, accountable to the wider membership and hence legitimate, the US, China and Russia opposed them – although for very different reasons: the US, because it believed that criteria would limit its freedom of action; the others, because they feared that criteria might be abused and might legitimise interventions not authorised by the Security Council. There were also ambiguities to be resolved, not least the question of the point at which the responsibility to protect transferred from the host state to international society; the nature of international society's obligation in such cases; and the relationship between the UN and regional organisations. Finally, several states, notably India (see above), maintained that the R2P was an intervener's charter, designed to legitimise Western interference in the domestic affairs of developing states. This view was publicly expressed by only a few states, but Canada's regional consultations had revealed that this was a significant underlying concern in many parts of the world, especially Asia. These states were joined by others in arguing that a commitment to the R2P was only feasible once agreement had been reached on development assistance and Security Council reform. After 'In larger freedom', for example, the G77 insisted that 'priority attention be given to the issue of development' and that development could not be narrowly associated with security and terrorism.[77]

Between March and August 2005, steady progress was made on the outcome document. Western states made significant concessions on development, but without securing clear commitments on their priority issues such as terrorism, UN secretariat reform and a new Human Rights Council. The G77 was also reluctant to commit to the R2P, though insiders reported that so long as they believed there to be movement on development they were happy to find compromises on other issues, including R2P.[78] By 5 August, this careful diplomacy had produced a comprehensive draft outcome document which included commitment to R2P and some of its core components.

The draft document emphasised that the R2P 'lies first and foremost' with the host state and it maintained that this responsibility was taken up by external actors when the host government proved itself 'unable or unwilling' to fulfil its responsibilities.[79] It also included a request that the P5 refrain from using their veto in cases of genocide, war crimes, ethnic cleansing and crimes against humanity, and it recognised an international 'obligation' to use all diplomatic, humanitarian and other peaceful means to help protect populations – which translated into a 'shared responsibility' to take collective action through the Security Council when necessary.[80] The HLP's suggestion that the Security Council should be empowered to act in anticipation of a humanitarian crisis had been sidelined by Annan and then omitted at an early stage, at the insistence of Russia and China. The negotiations also revealed little support for Annan's suggestion that the R2P created an 'obligation' to take collective action when the 'just causes' thresholds were breached – the US was identified as being responsible for killing off the language of obligation in that regard.[81] Instead, the document resolved simply that international society had a 'responsibility' in such circumstances.

It was clear from the outset that creative ambiguity would be the order of the day in relation to authority. On the one hand, the G77 would not accept a form of words which implied a 'right of intervention' without Security Council approval. On the other hand, the US would not accept a form of words which expressly precluded it. In order to bridge this divide, the draft document followed ICISS in emphasising shared responsibilities. It stated that the UN membership recognised its 'shared responsibility to take collective action, in a timely and decisive manner, through the Security Council, in accordance with the Charter . . . should peaceful means fail' – leaving for another day the question of what should happen in cases where the council failed to agree, but not expressly prohibiting unilateralism. In order to address concerns raised by China and India that the R2P would legitimise the use of force outside the council framework, Ping and his aides maintained the textual separation between 'R2P' and 'Use of Force' proposed by Annan. The recommendation for criteria was watered down into a commitment to continue discussing criteria, in order to keep on board the Americans (who thought that criteria would be constraining), some G77 members, and China and Russia (who thought they would be too enabling and open to subjective interpretation).[82] Ultimately, however, it was broadly recognised that criteria would be a 'bridge too far' for the Americans, and they were never seriously put on the table.[83] Thus a broad consensus about the phrasing of the world's commitment to the R2P had begun to emerge in early August. On 3 August, however, John Bolton – a renowned anti-UN hawk – took up position as America's ambassador to the UN and set about tearing this consensus apart. Indeed, he believed that no such consensus existed – and suggested that Australia's John Dauth shared his own scepticism both about the text's substance and about the process, a suggestion that Dauth himself rejects.[84]

When Bolton arrived at the UN, he announced his intention to begin renegotiating the summit document from scratch. Starting on 29 August – less than three weeks before the summit – he began issuing a series of communiqués (referred to as 'Dear Colleague' letters) calling for the redrafting of hundreds of paragraphs (including the R2P paragraphs) and for the deletion of many others. Although Bolton was no fan of the principle, describing it as 'a moveable feast of an idea that was the High Minded *cause du jour*', his problems with the R2P itself were relatively minor.[85] He argued that it was necessary to redraft the R2P paragraphs so as to take account of three important considerations. First, whilst the US accepted that host states had the primary responsibility to protect and international society had a responsibility to act when the host state permitted or perpetrated atrocities, it was important to recognise that 'the responsibility of the other countries in the international community is not of the same character as the responsibility of the host, and we thus want to avoid formulations that suggest that the other countries are inheriting the same responsibility as the host state has'.[86] He argued that the Security Council was not *legally* obliged to protect endangered populations, whereas host states were. Bolton also counselled against continuing the discussion about criteria, arguing that the Security Council must have the freedom to decide the most appropriate course of action on a case-by-case basis. Finally, Bolton shared the UK's view that commitment to the R2P 'should not preclude the possibility of action absent authorization by the Security Council'.[87]

None of these propositions was remarkable in itself. They reflected long-standing American views which had already been accounted for by Ping and could have been resolved relatively easily, albeit at the expense of further weakening commitment to the R2P. The sting in the tail came in Bolton's proposed amendments to the wider UN reform project. Taking umbrage at a draft passage that welcomed the fact that many developed states had made progress towards committing 0.7 per cent of their GDP to international aid, the US ambassador insisted that the outcome document should remove all references to the Millennium Development Goals (MDGs), the 'right to development' and the goal of debt reduction. Although Bolton was right to argue that the US had always distinguished between the goals themselves, agreed to in 2000, and the quantifiable targets (such as the 0.7 percent of GDP) set out by the UN secretariat in 2001, none of these passages had been found objectionable by the US before and it was quite a leap of logic to go from objecting to references to specific targets to requesting that all references to the MDGs be removed from the text.[88] He also rejected references to disarmament and the control of small arms, and he even called for radical reform to the proposed Peacebuilding Commission, which the Bush administration had publicly supported.[89] The effect of all this – especially the inexplicably hard line on development – was to destroy consensus on the Ping document. Bolton's intervention declared open season for other spoilers to reopen contentious issues. As John Dauth, Ping's Australian facilitator, put it in late August, 'everyone is trying to reopen issues' that had been agreed over the previous month.[90] The R2P was among them.

In late August, China signalled its change of heart on the R2P and announced 'deep reservations'. Two months earlier, China had indicated its acceptance of the R2P, with the provisos that the primary responsibility lay with the host state and that any military response to massive humanitarian crises should be sanctioned by the Security Council, both of which had been incorporated into the Ping draft.[91] At the World Summit itself, however, Chinese President Hu Jintao defended a traditional understanding of the UN Charter, insisting that 'the purposes and principles of the UN Charter are crucial to safeguarding world peace and security. They have been widely recognized as the basic norms governing international relations and must be complied with in real earnest. As the special agency of the UN responsible for maintaining world peace and security, the Security Council must be given the authority to carry out its mandate.' Alluding to the R2P, Hu insisted that 'we should all oppose acts of encroachment on other countries' sovereignty, forceful interference in a country's internal affairs, and willful use or threat of military force'.[92] Nonetheless, negotiators on the UN side believed that, whatever their reservations, the Chinese would not make the R2P a 'deal breaker'.[93]

Russia, which had earlier shared China's view that no action should be taken without Security Council approval but had otherwise tolerated the R2P, followed suit and began arguing against the R2P itself. Russian diplomats maintained that the UN was already equipped to deal with humanitarian crises and suggested that, by countenancing unauthorised intervention, the R2P risked undermining the Charter.[94] The Russian delegation's legal adviser proved particularly difficult, raising a steady stream of technical problems with the R2P paragraphs and airing new – flimsy – concerns at every turn. In the end, Canada's Allan Rock approached the Russian permanent representative directly, intending to ascertain whether Russia had any deep-seated political or philosophical problems with the R2P. When the legal expert failed to mount a convincing case against the R2P, the permanent representative indicated that Russia had no objections of principle and would cease its obstructionism.[95]

Russia and China were joined by several G77 and NAM states which had made concessions on the R2P and the Human Rights Council in return for the commitment to the MDGs which Bolton was now challenging. A short time earlier, the NAM Coordinating Bureau had restated its rejection of the 'so-called right' of humanitarian intervention, ominously observing that there were 'similarities' between 'the new expression [of] responsibility to protect and humanitarian intervention'. NAM ministers requested the bureau to reconsider the R2P, focusing on its implications for the principles of non-interference, non-intervention, territorial integrity and national sovereignty.[96] Algeria argued that the R2P was incompatible with international law, while Egypt disputed both the assertion that international society had a responsibility to protect civilians (arguing that there was no shared responsibility beyond a state's responsibility to its citizens) and the notion that the protection of civilians should trump sovereignty.[97]

Most dangerous, though, was the eleventh-hour attack launched by India – an influential member of the G77/NAM. Although India had expressed long-standing concerns about the R2P, it had been somewhat less vocal than other states, producing something of a surprise with its last-minute opposition. In one of the many meetings designed to help bridge the ever-widening chasms on the Outcome Document, India's Ambassador Nirupem Sen launched a broadside against the R2P, challenging its legal status and moral foundations. The very label 'R2P', he argued, was patronising and offensive. Through protracted negotiations, in which Canada's Ambassador Allan Rock used influential third parties, Sen's resistance was whittled down to opposition to the label. In response, Canada developed four or five alternative labels it could live with, but Sen held out, refusing to respond to Rock's proposals. Rock then asked Canadian Prime Minister Paul Martin to take up the matter directly with India's Prime Minister Manmohan Singh.[98] However, Singh was en route to Washington DC prior to his attendance at New York and hence unavailable. In the end, the brackets were simply removed from the R2P paragraphs, without India granting its support. Ultimately Sen had overplayed his hand, because Singh was not prepared to scuttle the summit by rejecting the R2P paragraphs at the last moment.[99]

On the other side of the ledger, the R2P won vocal support from some influential states in the developing world. South Africa maintained that, although it was important to incorporate safeguards against abuse, the R2P was essential for dealing with Africa's myriad problems.[100] Both Tanzania and Rwanda also supported R2P, publicly challenging the NAM's position and lending moral weight to the advocates of R2P.[101] Both were encouraged by the Canadian government, with Allan Rock, Canada's ambassador to the UN, providing advice to the Rwandans on how to frame their support for the R2P. The relationship between Canada and Rwanda began in 2004, when their respective permanent delegations in New York co-hosted a commemoration of the Rwandan genocide. It helped to spearhead an important relationship with sub-Saharan Africa which proved to be crucially important in the final days of the negotiations. Rwanda told G77 sceptics that the R2P might provide real protection against future genocides, whilst South Africa told an open G77 session on R2P that 'we're not likely to respond to threats of genocide in London, Rome or San Francisco . . . this is all about us, in our countries, on our continent'.[102]

With less than three days to go, the negotiations were in disarray and the R2P had been struck from the list of issues agreed in principle. In fact, there was agreement on only three issues: management reform, the Human Rights Council (but no agreement on what it would look like), and a vaguely worded commitment to tackling terrorism. The UK, now playing a leading role in the negotiations, argued that it would not consider including development unless the G77 gave ground on other issues. Bolton, meanwhile, had become entirely isolated, partly because of his refusal to adopt common positions with like-minded states like Britain and partly because of his seemingly outrageous negotiating position. Things got so bad that few diplomats were willing to associate with Bolton. The British reportedly expressed 'dismay' over the scope and direction of Bolton's proposed amendments and its permanent representative, Emyr Jones Parry, reportedly told his EU colleagues that 'Bolton is playing his own game' and receiving his instructions from neo-conservatives in the US administration such as Cheney and Rumsfeld, rather than from his boss, Secretary of State Condoleeza Rice.[103] Meanwhile the South Africans labelled his approach 'filibustering'.[104] Bolton himself was unconcerned, having 'little interest' in developing common positions with American allies.[105] In his memoirs, Bolton recounts that, if he had been given a choice between taking the World Summit agreement or leaving it, he would have happily 'left it in a heartbeat'.[106]

As is now well known, at the eleventh hour Jean Ping and the UN leadership pulled a diplomatic sleight of hand. Ping and a small group of senior UN officials, principally Robert Orr – an American who had formerly worked for Bill Clinton's UN Ambassador Richard Holbrooke – had continued to work on the original document, making amendments so as to take the ebb and flow of debate into account, but without going back to first principles, as Bolton had demanded. This parallel document was a closely guarded secret and was finished in final 'clean' form (without parentheses) only on the night of 12 September (the conference being due to start on 14

September).[107] From the outset of the negotiations, Annan had believed both that UN reform required a consensus at the level of heads of state or government and that the permanent delegations in New York would rather commit to a sub-optimum declaration than be forced to greet their political masters with the news that there was no declaration for them to sign. After alerting Nicholas Burns and Secretary of State Condoleeza Rice to the existence of the parallel document and gaining their approval to move forward with it, Ping outmanoeuvred Bolton and the other spoilers by releasing it to the permanent delegations. Bolton maintained his opposition but was overruled by Rice.[108]

This final version included the R2P paragraphs, but in revised form. Some states continued to argue against the paragraphs, forcing the R2P's supporters to drop some of the substantive components of the R2P declaration in order to secure the World Summit's endorsement. As John Dauth explained, the final text was agreed at the very last minute in the 'North's Delegates Room' and 'reflected only an absolute determination on our side to have the concept included, at the cost of dropping everything else'.[109] Although key states like India had not indicated their consent, the brackets around the R2P paragraphs were simply removed by Annan and Ping – along with many other brackets – as world leaders began arriving at New York's airports on 14 September.[110]

The last-minute changes to the R2P paragraphs and to associated paragraphs on the use of force were minor but important; they reinforced the transformation of the R2P described earlier. To appease the US and G77, the threshold at which the responsibility for dealing with genocide and mass atrocities passed from the host state to international society was altered. Initially the host state had to prove itself 'unable or unwilling' to protect civilians from mass killing and ethnic cleansing. That was subsequently altered to a 'manifest failure' to protect civilians – a significantly higher threshold. Bolton also won a watering-down of the scope of the Security Council's responsibility. Where in Ping's original drafts (5 and 10 August) the UN membership recognised its 'shared responsibility' (see above), the revised version carefully omitted to mention anything extending beyond the responsibility to use peaceful means (para. 139). Thus UN member states recognised their responsibility to protect their own citizens but *did not* recognise a *responsibility to act* beyond using peaceful means in cases of mass killing, genocide and ethnic cleansing. Instead, they simply reaffirmed their *preparedness* to use other measures if they saw fit – a significantly lower standard.

The final wording on authority placed the R2P's coercive components firmly within the ambit of the Security Council, although the relevant paragraphs could be read as implying that concerned states *may* also choose to work through alternative arrangements. Paragraphs 77–80, on the use of force, left open the possibility of unauthorised intervention by reiterating the obligation of states to refrain from the threat or use of force in *any manner inconsistent* with the UN Charter; by insisting that states 'strictly abide' by the Charter; by reaffirming the Security Council's authority to mandate coercive action; and by asserting its 'primary responsibility' for international peace and security. By forbidding the use of force in a manner inconsistent with the Charter, the Outcome Document left open the possibility of unauthorised intervention aimed either at upholding the UN's humanitarian principles outlined in Article 1 of the Charter or at acting on the 'implied authorisation' of past Security Council resolutions.[111] In short, the R2P which emerged from the World Summit amounted to an important formal recognition of the responsibility of sovereigns to their own citizens, a reaffirmation of the idea that the Security Council has the authority to intervene if it sees fit to do so – an idea established by practice a decade or so earlier and formally declared by the Council in Resolution 1265, some six years earlier (1999), and – perhaps most significantly for practical purposes – a commitment to develop the institutional capacities and behaviours necessary to prevent genocide and mass atrocities, to assist states in the fulfilment of their responsibilities and to improve the effectiveness of non-coercive measures. True, this was much less than had been envisaged by the ICISS, but it marked an important milestone in the normative development of international society and it pointed towards a weighty policy agenda for international institutions, regional organisations and individual states. This policy agenda is set out and analysed in greater detail in the second half of this book.

After the Summit

The World Summit's declaration on R2P received a mixed reception. Todd Lindberg viewed it as a 'revolution in consciousness in international affairs'.[112] Prominent international lawyer Simon Chesterman agreed, arguing that 'it's a lot more than I would have expected a couple of years back . . . what we're seeing is a progressive redefinition of sovereignty in a way that would have been outrageous sixty years ago'.[113] Others were more equivocal. Another international lawyer, Michael Byers, argued that the declaration had watered down the R2P to such an extent that it would not afford protection to threatened populations and might even limit the Security Council's ability to respond decisively to humanitarian disasters.[114]

Gingrich and Mitchell, architects of the American task force on UN reform, expressed 'dismay' at the summit's outcomes, noting that it 'fell significantly short' of their recommendations.[115] For his part, John Bolton said of the document: 'I plan never to read it again. I doubt many others will either'.[116] The ICISS commissioners themselves were also initially divided on the summit's outcome. Ramesh Thakur welcomed it, noting that the R2P was one of the few human rights initiatives to survive the negotiations. Gareth Evans, however, reportedly expressed 'deep disappointment' with the summit. Describing it as a whole as a 'huge wasted opportunity', Evans argued that 'it needed to be a big leap forward. It wasn't – it was a slow, small crawl and I don't think we've got any great optimism that we're going to get better than that for a very long time to come'.[117]

Judgements about whether the summit declaration furthered or hindered the progress of the R2P depend on what that declaration is compared with.[118] Compared to the ICISS report, the HLP report or Annan's 'In larger freedom', the outcome document might be considered a step back, because fundamental recommendations – most notably the criteria for intervention, the P5 'code of conduct' and the question of authority – were absent. Nor was there explicit recognition that the R2P implied a continuum of measures from prevention to rebuilding. Compared, however, to what was on the table immediately before the summit, the declaration represented a significant step forward. John Dauth, the Australian ambassador to the UN who had served as one of Ping's 'facilitators', remarked that it was an important achievement to have any reference at all to the R2P, but expressed disappointment at the content of the document because it was much reduced from what the draft text had been for much of 2005.[119] That disappointment was echoed by the International Service for Human Rights (ISHR) which argued that the human rights promise of the World Summit had been 'scuttled by international politics'.[120]

Whatever its flaws, the Outcome Document indicated a profound shift in the meaning of sovereignty. As Annan put it, a month after the summit: 'Consider that thought. Human life, human dignity, human rights raised above even the entrenched concept of state sovereignty. Global recognition that sovereignty in the twenty-first century entails the responsibility to protect people from fear and want'.[121] According to William Pace and Nicole Deller then – leading figures in the R2P–CS programme – the summit reconciled the rights of individuals and sovereigns, established a 'basis for accountability' and codified international society's responsibility to prevent, as well as to react to, large-scale killing and ethnic cleansing.[122] Moreover, although the summit's specific dealing with the R2P was short and narrow, it was dense in content and its potential mandate was strong; besides, among the summit's other reforms were a whole range of initiatives with the potential to contribute directly to the realisation of the vision set out by the ICISS. Much of this will be detailed in the following three chapters.

The advocacy effort did not end at the World Summit. Attention now turned to attempts to persuade the Security Council to reaffirm the R2P (see Chapter 5); to operationalise the R2P within the UN system through the appointment of a Special Adviser to the Secretary-General (see Chapter 4); and to advance the shaky consensus forged at the World Summit. New civil society groups dedicated to R2P advocacy and research sprang up around the world. In Africa, the WFM–IPG worked with FEMNET in Mali and the West African Civil Society Forum (WACSOF) in Nigeria, to organise workshops in 2006 for promoting discussion of the R2P and for generating ideas about how NGOs and governments might operationalise the principle. Among their suggestions was a proposal to establish a regional network of NGOs that would, among other things, provide early warning of potential crises and coordinate R2P advocacy.[123] A similar programme was also initiated in south-east Asia.

Among the most notable of these civil society initiatives was the R2P Coalition, based in Chicago. The R2P Coalition persuaded the Illinois State Assembly to adopt a bipartisan resolution reaffirming the R2P and calling upon the US government effectively to implement measures 'to ensure that the responsibility to protect populations has both credible meaning and effect, and that the United States is in the forefront of its domestic and global application'.[124] The city councils of Chicago and San Francisco soon followed suit.

To help spearhead these efforts, in 2007 Gareth Evans proposed the creation of a 'Global Centre' for R2P, with five key priorities: advancing and consolidating the World Summit consensus; protecting the concept's integrity by preventing its use in issue areas not directly related to large-scale killing and ethnic cleansing; clarifying when 'non-consensual military force' can be used in a manner consistent with the R2P; building capacity in international organisations, states, and NGOs; and developing strategies for effective responses to crises.[125] The centre was established in 2008, along with four regional associates – NUPI in Norway, FRIDE in Spain, the Kofi Annan International Peacekeeping Training Centre in Ghana and the Asia–Pacific Centre for the Responsibility to Protect, which has offices in Australia and Indonesia.

However, the painful summit negotiations held portents of future difficulties. Most importantly, many in the General Assembly felt that

Annan had ceded too much ground to the Americans. They worried that potential improvements to the UN's institutional capacity in areas such as conflict prevention, human rights, peace operations, and post-conflict reconstruction (signalled at the summit) might increase America's influence and its ability to use the UN to interfere in the domestic affairs of others. As will become clearer in the following three chapters, these concerns helped to create a set of relatively weak institutional reforms and persisted after the summit, manifesting themselves in a pronounced reluctance to grant the UN the resources needed to operationalise R2P. As Stephen Stedman, one of Annan's senior advisers charged with implementing the reform agenda, put it: 'Faced with the choice between having a more effective UN that furthered American interests and continuing with an ineffective UN, many countries chose an ineffective UN'.[126] This struggle provides the underlying political context for much of the debate about operationalising the R2P which is covered in the remainder of this book.

It is worth ending this chapter by noting two trends made evident by the summit negotiations. First, the ICISS was correct to insist on distancing the R2P from 'humanitarian intervention'. It is clear that there is significant hostility to 'intervention' and that the association of the R2P with intervention was a key barrier to consensus.[127] What is more, there was a clear consensus on the centrality of prevention in particular. The new language of R2P helped to illuminate a broad constituency of states and civil society actors prepared to acknowledge that sovereignty entails certain responsibilities and that it is legitimate for international society to assist states in fulfilling their responsibilities, even if this sometimes requires non-consensual measures authorised by the Security Council. Questions of who has the authority to take such decisions and in what circumstances remained controversial enough to derail the commitment to the R2P, but it is significant that so many states were prepared to endorse the principle of sovereignty as responsibility.

Second, the negotiating process revealed a relatively small group of states such as Venezuela, Algeria, Belarus, Pakistan, Cuba and India which were adamantly opposed to the R2P and able to secure considerable support for their views. The concept has many more supporters than downright opponents, and many of those supporters – including South Africa, Rwanda, Zambia, Ghana, Chile, Guatemala, Mexico and Argentina – are members of the NAM/G77 blocs, which have typically sought to limit endorsements of the R2P. A majority of states, and most NAM/G77 members, sat somewhere between these two positions. They did not reject the R2P in principle, and indeed they accepted that states have responsibilities to their citizens and that international society also has a role to play. But they remained concerned about the potential for the R2P to be abused by great powers, opposed to efforts which may weaken the rules governing recourse to force, and sceptical about the West's commitment to the R2P continuum, especially prevention. In some regions (most notably south-east Asia and Africa), these concerns translated into the view that the R2P is best administered by host states and relevant regional organisations paying due respect to regional norms and cultures.[128]

Conclusion

The adoption of the R2P by the 2005 World Summit transformed the principle, from a commission proposal actively supported by a relatively small number of like-minded states, into an international principle endorsed by the entire UN membership. R2P's international life had an inauspicious start and was kept alive only by the determined advocacy of the Canadian government, by prominent commissioners such as Evans and Thakur and by civil society activists. The task confronting these advocates was made still more difficult by the 2003 invasion of Iraq. It was clear almost from the outset that there was little chance of building consensus around the vision of the R2P set out by the ICISS. For example, the P5 were almost unanimous in their rejection of the idea of criteria to guide their decision-making on the use of force. However, protracted consultations also revealed that consensus might be possible around the basic concept; and some of the less controversial ideas relating to prevention, capacity building and coercive measures sanctioned by the Security Council. The R2P, as was argued by Canada and Thakur especially in the wake of Iraq, could inhibit unjust interventions as well as enable collective responses to genocide and mass atrocities.

If the Canadians and key advocates kept the concept alive, it was Kofi Annan's decision to adopt the R2P that secured its place on the international agenda in 2005. There can be little doubt that, without Annan's support, the R2P would not have been part of global discussions about the reform of the UN and governments would not have been forced to position themselves in relation to the protection of their citizens against genocide and mass atrocities. Annan put the R2P on the agenda the moment he invited Gareth Evans – the concept's most active advocate – to serve on the High-Level Panel. Evans persuaded the HLP to endorse the R2P and Annan adopted that proposal. As we have seen earlier, changes in American attitudes and the AU's endorsement of the R2P created a broad constituency of support which made the summit declaration possible.

International consensus required making some important changes to the R2P – not least, the idea of criteria was rejected; there was little support for a code of conduct for the use of the veto; and there was no support either for anything that might appear to sanction coercive measures not authorised by the Security Council. The threshold regarding when the R2P transferred from the host state to international society was lifted from the host state proving itself to be 'unable and unwilling' to it 'manifestly failing' in its responsibility to protect its own citizens. Finally, the idea that the R2P implied responsibilities – even obligations – on the part of international society, and especially on the part of the Security Council – an idea emphasised by Annan and critical to giving the R2P a role in preventing future Rwandas – was weakened, the council being committed only to 'standing ready' to act when necessary. Of course, prudence dictated a 'case-by-case' approach, but the insertion of words to that effect was a deliberate attempt to water down the Security Council's responsibility to protect.

But we should not succumb to the view that the R2P which emerged from the 2005 World Summit was too weak or insubstantial to make a difference. On the one hand, the declaration of principle itself – by every member of the international society – makes the R2P an active policy agenda with real clout. It can be used by diplomats in debates about how best to respond to crises; by mediators brokering agreements (as Kofi Annan himself did in Kenya in 2008); and by international officials going about their work in relation to human rights, peace operations and genocide prevention. It also enabled the creation of a Special Adviser to the Secretary-General, given the task of translating the commitment to the R2P into concrete proposals for institutional reform and behavioural change (see Chapter 4). On the other hand, careful reading of the Summit Document reveals the potential for a substantial policy agenda – aimed at preventing genocide and mass atrocities, at bringing outbreaks to a more rapid end and at ameliorating their worst effects. This agenda is studied in the following three chapters, but it is worth concluding this chapter by setting out the three pillars of the World Summit's commitment to the R2P. If we understand the R2P post-2005 as those elements that international society has signed up to, the principle refers to the following main points:

1   The responsibility of the state to protect its own population from genocide, war crimes, ethnic cleansing and crimes against humanity, and from their incitement.

2   The commitment of the international community to assist states in meeting these obligations.

3   The responsibility of United Nations Member States to respond in a timely and decisive manner, using Chapters VI (Pacific Settlement of Disputes), VII (Action with Respect to Threats to the Peace) and VIII (Regional Arrangements) of the UN Charter as appropriate, when a state is manifestly failing to provide such protection.

The remainder of this book focuses on what is being done, and what can be done, to translate the commitment made by world leaders in 2005 into a more effective system, to end genocide and mass atrocities.

4

Prevention

The inclusion of prevention in the R2P framework was widely applauded (see Chapters 2 and 3) and prevention figured prominently in the 2005 World Summit's endorsement of the R2P (see Chapter 3). Situating armed intervention within a continuum of measures which included prevention was a crucial part of reconceptualising the relationship between sovereignty and human rights. The inclusion of prevention also reflected the R2P's focus on the victims' point of view, emphasising the saving of lives over and above the rights of the interveners in cases where lives had already been lost on a massive scale. The 'responsibility to prevent' therefore helped to persuade sceptics that the R2P principle was not an 'intervener's' charter' and opened the door to the potential operationalisation of a range of preventive measures. If successful, the responsibility to prevent will reduce the frequency with which world leaders are confronted with a choice between 'sending in the Marines' and standing aside in the face of humanitarian emergencies.[1] But its inclusion has also stoked a major problem: should the 'responsibility to prevent' address the direct and structural prevention of armed conflict itself, as suggested by the ICISS, or should it focus only on the prevention of genocide and mass atrocities, to remain consistent with the rest of the R2P agenda?

The Dilemma of Comprehensiveness

According to Edward Luck, a leading American scholar who was appointed special adviser to the UN Secretary-General on matters relating to R2P in 2008, the 'dilemma of comprehensiveness' refers to the problem, inherent in conflict prevention, that 'it appears as if the advocates of prevention have tried to make it be all things to all people; but in the process it could end up meaning very little to anybody'.[2] But it is not so much that the advocates of prevention have made it *appear* amorphous; rather, policy makers and scholars have been made to realise that, because there exists a bewildering range of structural and direct *causes* to violent conflict – one report identified fifty root causes of war – comprehensive conflict prevention entails a bewildering range of policies and a potentially vast political and economic commitment.[3] Whilst advocates of conflict prevention point, with some merit, to the argument that even structural prevention is far cheaper than reaction, they have – to date – been unable to resolve several associated problems.[4] Not least important among these is the problem that prevention requires governments to ask their citizens to commit resources to regions not yet in conflict and, if violence is averted, it leaves them open to the accusation that they have wasted precious resources averting non-existent crises.

Even more importantly, there is no agreement about just how comprehensive the 'responsibility to prevent' needs to be. For diplomats, conflict prevention tends to be associated with early warning, preventive diplomacy and crisis management – the 'direct preventers' or tools aimed at tackling the immediate causes of conflict. Even here, though, engagement with conflict prevention can involve processes which cover a wide range of options, from mediation to coercive diplomacy, economic considerations such as sanctions, trade, humanitarian and financial aid, military measures such as deterrence, embargoes, peacekeeping and a variety of legal measures.[5] It is commonly agreed, however, that, although these more immediate concerns might reduce the chances that a dispute would result in violent conflict, they will not prevent the emergence of disputes in the first place, and they are unlikely to succeed in all cases. Meeting this challenge requires a deeper commitment to 'structural prevention'. Structural prevention is prefaced on the view that the root causes of violent conflict are systemic and involve economic inequality, under-development and poor governance – among other things. Structural prevention encompasses measures to facilitate economic development and poverty reduction.[6] Its advocates point to good governance, human and minority rights, environmental protection, security sector reform, and judicial reform as crucial components – among others – of conflict prevention.[7]

The problem here for R2P advocates is fourfold. First, given the sheer range of policy areas, it is difficult to discern measures which are directed specifically at the prevention of genocide, war crimes, crimes against humanity and ethnic cleansing (those crimes that are relevant to the R2P), measures which relate more broadly to conflict prevention in general and measures only indirectly related to violence.[8] Second, the absence of discernible limits provokes concerns among states keen not to commit themselves publicly to additional costs without tangible benefits. Third, this also raises concerns among the states likely to be on the receiving end of preventive measures who fear that an expanded prevention agenda might lead to additional encroachments on their sovereignty. Finally, there is a 'turf' issue, because – whereas direct prevention is typically the domain of diplomats – structural prevention has become chiefly connected with development. It is therefore unclear what sorts of agencies should take the lead.

The ICISS attempted to ameliorate this situation by setting out four areas – political/diplomatic, economic, legal and military – which run through every aspect of the responsibility to prevent (see Chapter 2). However, it was less than clear on what it was that governments had a responsibility to prevent. The commission's list of 'basic principles' described the 'problem' as consisting of cases where 'a population is suffering serious harm, as a result of internal war, insurgency, repression or state failure'. Its description of prevention covers 'the root causes and direct causes of internal conflict and other man-made crises putting populations at risk'. And, most famously, its 'just cause' thresholds for the use of force focused on large-scale loss of life and ethnic cleansing (see Chapter 2). These are three different standards which imply different emphases when it comes to prevention. In practice, the first two ways of describing the 'problem' have been eschewed in favour of the third, with the World Summit couching the R2P in terms of genocide, war crimes, ethnic cleansing crimes against humanity (see Chapter 3). The problem, of course, is that the commission's treatment of prevention was directed towards a broader interest in the prevention of 'internal wars' and 'other man-made crises', and not exclusively towards the prevention of the four types of crime singled out by the World Summit. As such, operationalising the responsibility to prevent will require a departure from the commission's recommendations.

It is important to understand that associating a comprehensive account of conflict prevention with the R2P is likely to dilute the principle, making it less able to marshal the necessary international commitment to protect endangered populations. A broad understanding of structural prevention leads directly to wider debates about the 'right of development' and the nature and scope of human security. It also implies that, of all the UN's organs and agencies, the UN Development Programme (UNDP) is best placed to lead prevention efforts. As we have noted in the previous chapter, several G77 states defended the priority of development over the R2P, maintaining that consensus could only be reached on the latter if progress was made on the former. This position was inspired by a mixture of genuine concerns about development and cynical diplomatic manoeuvring aimed at keeping the R2P off the agenda by making it conditional on 'northern' concessions on development. If the 'responsibility to prevent' is understood as including structural prevention, it is a short walk from there to maintaining that R2P includes a 'right to development'. Widening the R2P in this way would have two consequences. First, it would overwhelm the R2P agenda with human security, political, economic, social and cultural agendas linked to the right to development, diverting attention from the prevention of genocide and mass atrocities. Second, it would diminish the global consensus on the R2P broached at the 2005 World Summit by, on the one hand, raising concerns among the R2P's 'Western' supporters, who – despite having moved a significant way on economic development in the past decade – remain sceptical about calls for a 'right of development' and, on the other hand, feeding the doubts of the states which are hostile to expanding the scope of R2P's potential interference with the domestic affairs of sovereigns.

There are therefore good reasons for thinking that a narrow but deep approach, focusing only on the prevention of genocide, war crimes, ethnic cleansing and crimes against humanity is preferable in the first instance. It is more likely that a consensus can be built around a narrowly focused system of prevention directed at those crimes, already identified as related to the R2P by the General Assembly. Taking a broader approach would probably mire the R2P in protracted debates about economic development and national sovereignty which would do little to provide protection in the immediate term. A narrowly focused conception of prevention is more likely to generate concrete measures to protect endangered populations.

If it is not narrowly understood, prevention has the potential to widen and dilute the R2P by situating it within policy arenas it was not intended for, such as economic development and human security. It is also important that the R2P add value rather than simply replicate pre-existing policy agendas. This problem is perhaps most acute in relation to prevention because the concept is so amorphous and because the 'responsibility to prevent' spoke to a pre-existing UN interest in the prevention of armed conflict which is significantly wider in application than the R2P. Unfortunately, this problem was left unexplored by ICISS, creating a contradiction in its report. On the one hand, the R2P itself applied only to the actual or apprehended large-scale killing and ethnic cleansing of civilians. In other words, the R2P was concerned with a quite narrow range of human ills. On the other hand, accepting the historical fact that such atrocities tend to occur during armed conflict, the commission articulated an unoriginal conception of prevention, which included both the direct and the structural measures relating to all forms of armed conflict. As laudable as this was, there was a tension between the R2P's ostensibly narrow focus on a limited number of human ills and the insistence that it implies a commitment to tackling 'economic deprivation' as part of the responsibility to prevent. It is clear, therefore, that the ICISS left much conceptual work to be done on prevention. If, as Evans, the Canadian government and others assert, global consensus on the R2P depends upon a narrow interpretation of the principle, the commission's embrace of a wide account of prevention presents a major problem.[9]

It should be stressed that this is an argument for decoupling the preventive aspects of the R2P from broader initiatives relating to the prevention of armed conflict, which, properly considered, should include a focus on structural prevention and economic development. It is *not* an argument for narrowing the scope of conflict prevention per se. The R2P deals only with a particular type of human suffering and, to be plausible and effective, R2P measures should be narrowly focused on preventing the particular ills which concern it. It goes without saying that 'narrow' R2P prevention and the 'wider' prevention of armed conflict are not mutually exclusive.

To make good on the responsibility to prevent, much work is needed to reconcile prevention with the R2P and to identify the measures necessary to fulfil the former. In the remainder of this chapter, I defend the argument that the responsibility to prevent should be reframed so as to focus specifically on those measures designed to have a direct impact on the prevention of genocide and mass atrocities in the first instance. I will do this in two instalments. First, I will briefly highlight the UN's on-going interest in prevention – which is much wider than the responsibility to prevent – before highlighting the place of prevention in the HLP, 2005 World Summit and in subsequent UN initiatives. The purpose of this discussion is to show that the ICISS' conception of prevention drew from a broader policy debate. After this, the second part of the chapter will put forth a narrower understanding of the responsibility to prevent and analyse four sets of initiatives which will facilitate the translation of the responsibility to prevent from words to deeds: early warning, preventive diplomacy, ending impunity and preventive deployments.

Making Prevention Work

The prevention of deadly conflict is one of the fundamental goals of the UN. The preamble to the UN Charter commits the organisation to 'saving future generations' from the 'scourge of war'. In his 1955 report to the General Assembly, Dag Hammarskjöld identified the prevention and solving of conflicts as the organisation's most significant function.[10] UN peacekeeping itself grew out of the Secretary-General's belief that the world organisation's primary role was to prevent and resolve conflict. The case for conflict prevention was strengthened in 1997, when the Carnegie Commission on Preventing Deadly Conflict estimated that even a maximal commitment to broadly defined prevention would cost less than half the price of intervention and rebuilding.[11] Nevertheless, the UN's conflict prevention function developed in an ad hoc fashion and was based mainly on the Secretary-General's preventive diplomacy and on the proliferation of social, economic, cultural and humanitarian organisations under the UN umbrella – none of which was integrated into a *system* of conflict prevention.[12] Importantly, however, regional organisations have developed their own mechanisms for preventing armed conflict. These included the AU's Continental Early Warning System, the OSCE's preventive missions in the Baltic, Balkans, Caucasus and Central Asia and the EU's 'Conflict Prevention Assessment Missions'.[13]

Efforts to develop a conflict prevention system at the UN began in earnest under the secretary-generalship of Pérez de Cuéllar, who established the short-lived Office for Research and Collection of Information (ORCI), designed to provide him with information, advice and early warning on emerging crises. Although responsible for ORCI's closure (see below), Boutros-Ghali placed prevention centre-stage in his 1992 'Agenda for peace' and established an Interdepartmental Working Group to encourage the UN's major departments to coordinate conflict prevention strategies.[14] In his 2001 report on the 'Prevention of armed conflict', Kofi Annan urged the secretariat and the member states to foster a 'culture of conflict prevention', wherein the UN's key agencies and departments would each develop expertise in prevention and would coordinate their responses to particular crises.[15] The phrase 'culture of prevention' was first developed in the late 1990s by Michael Lund, as a way of elevating structural prevention.[16]

The 'culture of prevention', Annan argued, should be based on ten broad principles, including the notions that 'preventive action should be initiated at the earliest possible stage of a conflict cycle'; that 'an effective preventive strategy requires a comprehensive approach that encompasses . . . political, diplomatic, humanitarian, human rights, developmental, institutional and other measures'; and that 'conflict prevention and sustainable and equitable development are mutually reinforcing activities'.[17] In response, the Security Council passed Resolution 1366 (30 August 2001) affirming the centrality of conflict prevention to the council's work, welcoming the creation of a central fund for the provision of conflict prevention training for UN staff, calling for the development of regional conflict prevention capacity and promising to 'employ all appropriate means' to prevent violent conflict. In his 2003 follow-up report, Annan noted that, although practically every arm of the UN had adopted a conflict prevention 'lens', more work was needed in order to 'agree on practical measures to integrate conflict prevention further into its activities, to build a more structured link between political and socio-economic strategies and to ensure that the prevention of armed conflicts becomes a deliberate component in the planning and coordination arrangements of development programmes'.[18] Three years later, Annan noted an 'unacceptable gap between rhetoric and reality' on conflict prevention.[19]

Annan's High-Level Panel (HLP) endorsed an even broader conception of prevention, one which located the prevention of mass atrocities together with the prevention of armed conflict, humanitarian catastrophes and a range of other ills, including environmental calamities, poverty, WMD proliferation and infectious disease. When it came to prevention, the HLP overlooked the ICISS' recommendations almost entirely. This was in part, no doubt, a product of the fact that the commission had offered few innovative proposals on prevention and had failed to tie prevention clearly either to the R2P itself or to its criteria for non-consensual force. The HLP therefore followed Annan in associating the wider aspects of root cause prevention with economic development.[20]

Running against this tendency towards a focus on structural prevention was the creation of the important UN Office of the Special Adviser on the Prevention of Genocide in 2004 (see below) – inspired, Annan maintained, by ICISS and HLP recommendations.[21] This new post offers the potential for the UN to take the lead in institutionalising the responsibility to prevent genocide and mass atrocities, and it found support in the US. The Mitchell-Gingrich report (see Chapter 3) recommended that the US Administration assess what bilateral measures might enhance the capabilities of regional and international organisations to prevent genocide, mass killing and massive human rights violations. It also endorsed the office of the special advisor and called for it to receive significantly greater resources, which might enable it to play an important role in early warning.[22] Other groups of states, for instance the NAM and the AU, indicated their support for the special adviser position on the grounds that the interference in sovereign affairs implied by the post would be limited to grave emergencies such as genocide – though the NAM also argued that prevention strategies must include a commitment to economic development.[23] The NAM maintained that 'any effort to transform the UN into an effective instrument for preventing conflict should take into account the need for states to respect international law and the importance of sustainable development'.[24]

Some states adopted a different approach altogether, calling for conflict prevention to be placed squarely under the rubric of economic development or maintenance of traditional sovereignty. Pakistan argued that conflict prevention was best supported through the recognition of a state's 'right to develop'.[25] China meanwhile insisted that the key to conflict prevention lay in the recognition of 'the basic norms guiding state-to-state relations' – a thinly veiled reference to sovereignty and non-intervention.[26]

From this brief survey it is clear that Edward Luck is right to argue that the politics of conflict prevention is caught in the dilemma of comprehensiveness. The key problem for the R2P is that the ICISS commissioners themselves maintained – not without reason – that the prevention of armed conflict itself reduces the likelihood of genocide and mass atrocities. As a result, they adopted the key tenets of conflict prevention theory – including the endorsement of both structural/root cause prevention and direct prevention. This opened the door for states to argue that positive movement on the R2P should be related to similar progress towards the right to development. The right of development is a laudable proposition in itself, but it places the R2P advocates in a double bind. Promoting Annan's prevention agenda, including the focus on root causes endorsed by the ICISS, would involve forging consensus on a broad range of development and governance issues. Not only is consensus on these issues difficult – not least because of very different ideas about what development entails and requires – but the ICISS' commitment to the 'primacy of prevention' created an opportunity for R2P sceptics to stall progress on the principle, namely by situating it within debates about economic inequality. Nor is there a necessary causal link between economic development and the commission of genocide and mass atrocities. On the other hand, advocating the dissociation of R2P from wider conflict prevention runs the risk of shattering the 2005 consensus and the R2P's image as a realistic – and better – alternative to 'humanitarian intervention'. This dilemma was partially overcome by the World Summit's Outcome Document. The first step was to dissociate the R2P from the UN's wider prevention of armed conflict agenda, something which was accomplished by the World Summit through its clear identification of prevention as a core part of the R2P, distinct from and additional to the UN's broader commitment to conflict prevention (see Chapter 3). The second step is to set out carefully the scope of the responsibility to prevent by identifying those measures which contribute directly to its realisation. That is the purpose of the remainder of this chapter.

Realising the Responsibility to Prevent

This section identifies a range of measures directed at the prevention of genocide, war crimes, ethnic cleansing and crimes against humanity. Although individual governments (especially the UK, with its 'Conflict prevention pool', and Canada, whose Institute of Applied Negotiation has established an 'Early response unit'), NGOs, regional organisations and global bodies apart from the UN engage in a wide range of preventive activities, I will focus mainly on initiatives related to the UN, as this is the organisation vested with primary responsibility for international peace and security. The four areas of prevention discussed below are: early warning, preventive diplomacy, ending impunity and preventive deployments. This is by no means an exhaustive list.

Early warning

The first part of a prevention system is its early warning mechanism. According to James Sutterlin, effective early warning mechanisms must have three components: access to information, analysis capabilities, and a communication channel to decision-makers capable of authorising effective measures.[27] The need to see early warning as encompassing more than simply the acquisition of information is made clear by the fact that some of the worst recent atrocities, such as the war in Bosnia and the genocide in Rwanda, were predicted – the former by the CIA, in reports that were only made public after the war had begun, and the latter, with startling clarity, by the commander of the UN's mission in Rwanda, General Romeo Dallaire. The problem in both cases was that the warnings were issued on an ad hoc basis to institutions which were not specifically assigned the task of preventing atrocities. The US government chose not to share the CIA's advice with others, and Dallaire was advised by the UN Department of Peacekeeping Operations (DPKO) that preventive measures such as the disarmament of militia groups were beyond the scope of UNAMIR's mandate.

There are also problems related to the specificity of early warning. Although it is relatively straightforward to identify countries at risk of political turmoil or humanitarian disaster, it is much more difficult to predict precisely when conflicts will escalate into genocide. Crises involving the R2P's four crimes can develop very quickly and, whilst warning mechanisms might identify dozens of 'at risk' countries, those risks are only likely to manifest themselves in outbreaks of genocide and mass atrocities in one or two cases.[28] This has prompted at least one prominent critic – Stephen Stedman, a key architect of Annan's UN reform agenda – to argue that, as policy makers do not have 'crystal balls', we should not be too optimistic about the prospect of effective early warning.[29] The danger is that a cavalier approach to early warning (sounding the alarm whenever a country is deemed at risk) is likely to generate false alarms, making it more difficult to engage political will and attracting opposition from countries which might be subject to these false alarms. It is not surprising therefore that many governments expressed concern that the 'culture of prevention' might undermine the principles of sovereignty and territorial integrity by legitimising external interference in a wider number of cases. At a Security Council debate in November 1999, several states argued that preventive action should never violate sovereignty.[30] Sovereignty concerns also explain why it took two years for the General Assembly to negotiate a resolution endorsing Annan's 2001 report on prevention.[31] In addition, concerns have been raised to the effect that precipitate intervention could make matters worse by encouraging rebel groups to take up arms in order to attract international attention.[32]

There are many early warning systems which, when taken together, can provide accurate warning of impeding crises. These systems are run by individual government departments (such as USAID), regional organisations (EU, OSCE, AU), global organisations (the UN), and NGOs (International Crisis Group, FEWER, and Swisspeace). There are broadly three types of system: those focusing on political crises; those which predict impending humanitarian crises; and – less relevant to the R2P and therefore not discussed here – those which provide early warning of natural disasters.

Many organisations are engaged in the early warning of political crises. Perhaps the most comprehensive are the International Crisis Group's (ICG) Crisis Watch programme and Swisspeace's FAST early warning system. Crisis Watch uses the ICG's global network of researchers to provide a monthly survey of country-by-country analyses, identifying countries at risk and conflict trends. The monthly reports issue 'conflict risk alerts' and identify 'conflict resolution opportunities'. Swisspeace's FAST initiative produces a similar type of reports. Using quantitative methodology, FAST researchers identify those events that are considered relevant to conflict development and assign them a numeric value according to the type and significance of the event and its place in the conflict cycle. As with Crisis Watch, data is collected by field researchers who build local information-gathering networks which are then coded and analysed by country coordinators.

Among regional organisations, the OSCE has an advanced early warning mechanism comprising field missions which provide ongoing reporting on current or potential crises to the organisation's permanent council and scrutinise the members' compliance with human rights standards. OSCE field missions have been credited with helping several former Soviet states, especially Estonia, Latvia and Ukraine, to avoid potential ethnic conflict between the majority nationalities and significant Russian minorities.[33] In Africa, the Intergovernmental Authority on Development (IGAD) established its own early warning and response mechanism (CEWARN) in 1995. The mechanism focuses on the prevention of pastoral conflicts on the borders of Ethiopia, Kenya and Uganda.

In the non-governmental sector there is a range of NGOs and private risk assessment businesses which provide early warning of impending political crises. Much work has been conducted by American universities. Among the most prominent is the University of Maryland's Minorities at Risk programme, overseen by Ted Robert Gurr. This programme provides model-based risk assessments of potential ethnopolitical conflicts based on open source secondary material. In a separate project led by Barbara Harff, the University of Maryland (in conjunction with the US Naval Academy) also assesses and models conflict accelerators and inhibitors, developing 'sequential models' for anticipating genocide and large-scale loss of life. Under the leadership of Barnett Rubin, the US Council on Foreign Relations occasionally dispatches teams of researchers to write field reports on imminent conflicts and to suggest preventive measures. The Mershon Centre at Ohio State University has developed a World Handbook of conflict indicators, including indices of conflict intensity and durability. Meanwhile, Harvard University's Institute for the Study of Genocide has developed a model which gives early warning of genocide. In the business sector, early warning services are provided by *The Economist*'s intelligence unit, which provides twice a year political and economic risk assessments based on in-country reporting and data modelling – a service also offered in the US by Evidence Based Research Incorporated (Washington DC).[34]

There is an equally wealthy supply of early warning about impending humanitarian crises. These include the Humanitarian Early Warning System (HEWS), the EU backed RESPOND, and USAID's food security alert mechanism. HEWS was originally created by the UN's Office for the Coordination of Humanitarian Affairs (OCHA) in 1995. It had a small staff (three or four people) and had the task to use computer modelling to track potential humanitarian crises in over 100 countries. The system was soon overwhelmed by the sheer volume of data and overtaken by the free availability of information on the internet. It was discontinued in 1998 in order to permit the reallocation of resources, having failed to issue even one 'early warning'.[35] Subsequently, UN agencies including the World Food Program, UNICEF, UNDP, OCHA, UNHCR and the World Health Organization joined forces with prominent NGOs like the ICRC, ICG and International Organization of Migration (IOM), to resuscitate HEWS as a free-standing entity outside the UN. Drawing information from open sources as well as from the specialised sources of partner organisations like the US Geological Survey, HEWS provides advance warning of natural phenomena like droughts, storms, floods, earthquakes and volcano eruptions which are likely to cause humanitarian crises. RESPOND, an initiative primarily funded by the European Commission, is an alliance of NGOs and international organisations which uses mapping, satellite imagery and geographic information to provide early warning of humanitarian emergencies and ongoing information to agencies in the field. The American government's development agency, USAID, provides a Famine Early Warning System (FEWS), which uses modelling to predict food shortages. The UN's Food and Agricultural Organization (FAO), based in Rome, has a Global Information Early Warning System which provides global monitoring of food demand and supply and uses open source material to generate early warning alerts. The UNHCR issues assessments of situations which are likely to generate refugee flows, and has tried to produce a dynamic model for charting and predicting refugee flows.

This brief overview demonstrates the significant amount of work being done on early warning. The problem, as the UN's experience with HEWS suggests, is not an absence of information but the absence of consolidated analysis and advocacy. It has long been argued that the UN is best placed to house an early warning system in one form or another, and we noted in Chapter 2 the ICISS proposal to establish an office for receiving and analysing relevant information in order to guide the Secretary-General. After all, Article 99 of the UN Charter gives the Secretary-General a responsibility to alert the Security Council to situations which may endanger international peace and security. However, the HLP chose not to make specific proposals for strengthening the organisation's early warning capabilities.[36]

Given the wide range of early warning systems available today, relatively minor reforms could have a significant effect on the world's capacity to produce specific early warning of genocide and mass atrocities and to turn those signals into comprehensive plans for preventive action. One way of operationalising the responsibility to prevent would be to centralise early warning in the UN Department of Political Affairs (DPA) by giving it the capacity to receive, analyse and disseminate information to the Secretary-General and to the Security Council. The DPA could receive reports and raw data from the organisations mentioned above and many more besides; it could analyse that data and provide regular briefings. It could also supply the Secretary-General with immediate alerts to be brought to the council's attention, which would give him the capacity to act on the duties set out in Article 99. The DPA need only collate and analyse already available data, especially data collected by UN agencies, perhaps augmenting what is available to the general public with the specialised intelligence information alluded to by the ICISS, risk analysis reports from private early warning companies. The unit need not imply the creation of an independent intelligence-gathering capability.[37]

It is not particularly novel to argue that the DPA should have a dedicated capacity for early warning. In 1981, a report written by Prince Sadrunnin for the Human Rights Commission called for the creation of just such an office.[38] Six years later, Javier Pérez de Cuéllar created ORCI, housed within the office of the Secretary-General (forerunner to the DPA), to endow the organisation's security and humanitarian arms with information about the potential causes of conflict and with notification of emerging warning signs.[39] ORCI was to use computer modelling and a database in order to give early warning and to foster the development of research which should identify conflict trends. Sadly, several key states were concerned by what they saw as the development of an independent intelligence-gathering capacity by the UN. Conservatives in the US Congress viewed it as inconsistent with the UN's role as a neutral body, some even describing ORCI as a 'communist conspiracy'. Soviet ire was stirred when it was discovered that ORCI's interests included signs of political conflict in the Baltic.[40] Although both American and Soviet attitudes improved, neither state was prepared to support the dedication of new resources to the initiative. This compounded ORCI's other problems. At the time, there was a freezing of new appointments at the UN, which forced de Cuéllar to find staff for his new office by moving them from other departments. This caused delays and inter-departmental resistance – creating the impression that the office was unable to fulfil its ambitious mandate.[41] There were no mechanisms for the sharing of information between UN agencies either, and many of them were hostile to cooperating with UN headquarters in such an overtly 'political' enterprise, in some cases because their mandates prevented them from reporting on political matters.[42] In addition, UN representatives in the field worried that early warning indicators might jeopardise their relations with the local authorities.[43] Shortly after taking over as Secretary-General,

Boutros-Ghali closed ORCI down as part of a broader programme of staff cuts forced on the UN by its major donors.[44]

Since then, there have been various efforts to improve the organisation's early warning capabilities, including through recommendations for the re-establishment of a unit not dissimilar to ORCI. In 1995, a Ford Foundation report appealed for the creation an early warning and threat assessment capability within the Secretary-General's office.[45] In the same year, a UN Joint Inspection Unit (JIU) called for the creation of a specialised unit within DPA, to identify emerging crises and to coordinate the 'anticipatory planning' of 'appropriate actions' by the Secretary-General.[46] In one of his first reports to the General Assembly as Secretary-General, Annan criticised the JIU for underestimating the sovereignty concerns of member states, pointing out that a majority of UN members had rejected his prede-cessor's efforts to create integrated UN offices on the grounds that this was an attempt to 'obtain political reporting on Member States' internal affairs'. Annan also criticised the JIU's expansive understanding of preven-tion, which included root causes and economic development, arguing instead that conflict prevention was an 'essentially political' activity.[47] Unsurprisingly, the General Assembly chose not to adopt the JIU's recom-mendation. Nonetheless, some UN officials continued to press the case. One of the many reports on the Rwandan disaster identified the absence of an early warning system as a contributing factor, noting that there was no way of channelling evidence gathered by UN agencies in the field to the key decision-makers.[48] Likewise, Marrack Goulding, former head of UN peace-keeping, pressed the case for consolidated early warning analysis and policy development.[49] The high-profile and well-regarded Brahimi report on peace operations (2000) proposed the consolidation of various departmental units into a single entity designed to gather, analyse and disseminate information – the Information and Strategic Analysis Secretariat for the Executive Committee for Peace and Security (EISAS).[50] Finally, the HLP recom-mended that the proposed Peacebuilding Commission should serve as a focal point for conflict prevention, including early warning (see Chapter 6).

DPA officials have tended to be concerned to avoid repeating the per-ceived failings of centralisation evinced by the ORCI and UN HEWS initiatives. Moreover, officials outside the DPA were openly hostile to centralisation under the DPA. In 2000, for example, Mark Malloch Brown – the UNDP Administrator who would go on to be Kofi Annan's influential chief advisor and then a member of the British House of Lords – pointedly maintained that 'when we talk prevention we mean using existing, acknowledged tools [of development policy] in transparent accepted ways:

for example, helping developing countries make use of . . . poverty action plans to identify and respond to potential social problems such as growing inequality'.[51] As Andrew Mack and Kathryn Furlong rightly point out, Malloch Brown's position was clearly at odds with Annan's view that prevention was 'essentially political'.[52]

In the face of concerted opposition from large UN agencies and many member states, Annan backtracked and advocated the diffusion of prevention expertise throughout the whole organisation – the system-wide 'culture of prevention' mentioned earlier. This change of position suited the G77's preference for seeing prevention in terms of economic development by turning the focus to structural prevention. Under this rubric, in 1998 the UN Staff College in Turin developed an Early Warning and Preventive Measures Project aimed at training UN officials and members of its field missions in early warning. Meanwhile, the DPA focused on encouraging a culture of prevention across the whole UN system, fostering the broad-ranging proposals identified earlier. In 1998, Under-Secretary-General for Political Affairs Kieran Prendergast established a Policy Planning Unit and gave it the task of developing a comprehensive plan for an early warning and prevention system across the whole UN. In the DPA, this involved the creation of 'prevention teams'. Each of the DPA's four regional divisions was required to provide the Secretary-General with early warning of emerging crises in their area on the basis of information gathered from open sources and other UN departments and agencies.[53] More recently, the DPA has cooperated with UNDP and the Department for Humanitarian Affairs in putting together country-specific prevention packages on an ad hoc basis. Seen in this context, the 'culture of prevention' set out in Annan's 2001 report can be seen as a partial triumph for the expansive 'prevention-as-development' view endorsed by the UNDP and G77.

However, Annan has oscillated somewhat between the 'culture of prevention' and the lingering ideas of centralisation, lending support to centralisation by creating the position of special adviser on the prevention of genocide, for instance. Moreover, whilst in the main his 2006 report on the UN's efforts on conflict prevention testifies to the diffusion model, being replete with an annex demonstrating the organisation's prevention efforts across its departments and agencies, Annan also alluded to centralisation briefly, asking member states to 'support a strengthening of its [the UN's] capacity for analysing conflicts'.[54]

The diffusion model remains largely ad hoc in its capacity to analyse and in its ability to shape preventive action, and it fails to utilise fully the vast wealth of global early warning indicators described earlier. A small early warning unit in the DPA has some significant advantages. By collating and analysing material already in the public realm, a DPA early warning unit would have the capacity to issue comprehensive and specific early warning reports and to enhance the Secretary-General's ability to discharge his or her Article 99 duties. This model clearly comes with two major problems. There are concerns among member states about the development of an independent intelligence-gathering capability and potential interference in domestic political affairs.[55] There are also fears that a revived centralised approach would simply repeat the organisational failures of ORCI and UN HEWS and cause turf battles between different departments and agencies. The first problem could be partially resolved by limiting the unit's intelligence-gathering to open-source information. Ideally, the Secretary-General would be empowered to send high-level fact-finding missions to augment this endeavour, but it is important to note that both the Security Council and the Human Rights Council already have mandates to despatch such missions. The turf issue is perhaps less easily resolved, though it is worth mentioning that the UN is today much more tightly integrated than it was when ORCI and UN HEWS were created.

It may be, however, that these obstacles are too great to surmount. If that proves to be the case, it might be worth sacrificing political location on the part of interested actors by establishing an R2P early warning organisation outside the UN system. In a discussion paper on ways of strengthening the special adviser on the prevention of genocide (on which see below), Bertrand Ramcharan suggested the creation and maintenance, outside the UN system, of a database of potential risk situations. 'This is best done outside the UN', Ramcharan argued, 'as its existence and maintenance within the UN are likely to engender leaks and diplomatic protests in an environment in which developing countries in particular are already sensitive to intrusions into their internal affairs.' There is obvious merit to Ramcharan's recommendations, which are well grounded in first-hand experience of ORCI; but it could be argued that Crisis Watch and Swisspeace already perform this function and that this approach cannot secure the access to decision-makers needed in order to translate information and analysis into effective action.[56]

Preventive diplomacy

Traditionally, the UN's principal role in conflict prevention has been in the field of preventive diplomacy. First conceptualised by Dag Hammarskjöld, preventive diplomacy typically refers to the Secretary-General's efforts to broker agreements between conflicting parties. In his 1992 'Agenda for peace', Boutros-Ghali presented preventive diplomacy as the UN's principal contribution to conflict prevention, describing it as a range of measures designed to 'create confidence' between potential belligerents. Preventive diplomacy, he maintained, used traditional instruments such as mediation, conciliation and the provision of good offices and more intrusive measures such as 'preventive deployments and, in some situations, demilitarized zones'.[57] Between 1990 and 2002, the UN significantly increased its role in this area. The number of preventive diplomacy initiatives rose from one to six, and the organisation's good offices programmes rose from four to fifteen. According to the 2005 Human Security report, these efforts helped to prevent a number of potential conflicts from erupting into violence and accounted for a significant number of peace agreements bringing violent conflict to an end.[58]

The ICISS noted calls for the strengthening of the UN's capacity in this area, called on member states and regional organisations to issue reports to the UN about their preventive efforts – creating a repository of best practice – and recommended greater cooperation between the UN and its financial institutions, the World Bank and IMF.[59] It also advocated setting aside funds for the use of the Secretary-General on preventive diplomacy and improvements to the UN's capacity to respond quickly to emerging crises. The HLP noted the increasing demand for good offices and the organisation's 'minimal' capacity to deliver, and called for more resources to be given the Secretary-General to improve the UN's 'capacity for mediation and good offices', with the DPA serving as the organisation's centre of expertise in mediation services. These recommendations were endorsed by the World Summit, spurring efforts to improve the DPA's capacity and to strengthen the Office of the Special Adviser on the Prevention of Genocide, made evident by the office's upgrading to the status of 'Special Representative' of the UN Secretary-General.[60]

In 2006, the DPA managed over thirty good-offices missions, carried out by fewer country-desk officers than the International Crisis Group.[61] Recent efforts to strengthen the DPA's preventive diplomacy have focused on three initiatives. The first involves changing the department's recruitment and work ethos. On the one hand, the DPA has concentrated on recruiting experienced envoys, mediators and support specialists. On the other, it has begun to emphasise mobility. Ibrahim Gambari, then Under-Secretary-General for Political Affairs and head of the DPA, maintained that 'we need to get officials away from their desks in New York and out into the field so they can expand their contacts, take the pulse more frequently and deepen their understanding of the complex dynamics of conflicts'.[62]

The second initiative involved the creation of the Mediation Support Unit in 2006. The unit, funded by modest voluntary donations from a handful of members, will act as the repository of best practice and of the lessons learned on peacemaking, as it was envisaged by the ICISS and HLP. It will also recruit and maintain lists of experienced envoys, who can be called upon by the Secretary-General at short notice. In addition, the unit will conduct training for envoys and mediators to disseminate best practice, as well as providing ongoing advice and support for them.[63] In 2007, Ban Ki-moon announced the appointment of Kofi Annan's humanitarian chief, Jan Egeland, as special envoy at Under-Secretary-General level, who was to lead the UN's efforts in this area. Egeland's role would be to coordinate a stand-by team which could be deployed at short notice to assist the UN's peace envoys.

The third initiative is the UN Peacemaker programme, which involves the creation and maintenance of a website to provide practical guidance to envoys and mediators. The website (www.unpeacemaker.org) is designed to be a repository of information on best practice and lessons learned for those engaged in preventive diplomacy and conflict management. As Gambari explained, 'with a laptop and satellite phone, an envoy meeting with insurgents in some jungle will now be only a mouse-click away from a wealth of information that could further his or her discussions'.[64]

These are relatively modest initiatives; but, if they evolved into a capacity for the UN to deploy high-profile envoys like Egeland or Annan, at short notice, with professional staff in support, they would significantly improve the UN's capacity to use diplomatic means so as to prevent genocide and mass atrocities. There are, however, significant obstacles which need to be overcome. Political concerns about measures aimed at strengthening the UN Secretariat's capacity and a more general lack of will to provide the necessary resources has translated into a funding shortfall. The HLP singled out the 'deliberate chronic underresourcing' of the DPA as a major impediment to the UN's preventive diplomacy capacity, and the World Summit made a commitment to redress this situation. However, actual contributions have fallen well short of what is needed for that to happen.

DPA funding comes from two sources: the regular UN budget, set by the General Assembly, and voluntary donations into trust funds. The DPA's regular budget for the two years 2004–5 was around $59 million, and it was not significantly increased despite the World Summit pledge. In addition, the DPA has two trust funds, one for Preventive Action and the other for Special Missions And Other Activities Related To Preventive Diplomacy And Peacemaking, both of which were established in 1997. Money from these trust funds has been used to fund a range of DPA activities, including the resolution of disputes between states and the HLP itself. Given the General Assembly's reluctance to increase the DPA's regular budget significantly, the trust funds will be a crucial component in funding the modest initiatives described above. Between 1997 and 2005, however, the funds received a mere $33 million in donations from some thirty-five donors. In response, after identifying the 'unacceptable gap between rhetoric and reality' when it comes to conflict prevention, Annan used his 2006 report to the General Assembly to 'encourage Member States to consider seriously the recommendations of the Office of Internal Oversight Services evaluation, which found the Department of Political Affairs to be in need of substantial additional resources'.[65] Without those additional resources, the DPA's ability to turn the aforementioned activities into an effective program of diplomacy to prevent genocide and mass atrocities will be limited.

In addition to strengthening the DPA's capacity to orchestrate effective preventive diplomacy, in 2004 Kofi Annan created the position of Special Adviser on the Prevention of Genocide as part of his five-point plan for preventing genocide. This position was assigned the following tasks: (1) collecting information on massive and systematic violations of human rights which, if not prevented or halted, might lead to genocide; (2) acting as an early warning mechanism for the Secretary-General; (3) making recommendations on actions for the prevention of genocide; and (4) liaising with the UN system on measures to prevent genocide. The special adviser was not, however, in the business of determining whether particular crises constituted genocide. In recent years, the UN has tended to defer this judgement to competent judicial tribunals, a position reiterated by the Security Council's special commission on Darfur (see below).

The appointment was broadly welcomed, the first Special Adviser Juan Méndez reporting that he had received 'clear signs of support' for the development of an early warning capability in relation to genocide.[66] However, because of funding restrictions Méndez was appointed only on a part-time and year-by-year basis – which limited severely the extent to which he could do more than act as a vocal figurehead. Méndez set to work quickly, contributing to the Secretary-General's plan for preventing genocide, which was announced in April 2005. The plan called for the following: prevention of armed conflict in general – because war usually provides the context for genocide; protection of civilians; ending of impunity through international criminal proceedings; early warning; and swift and decisive responses, including the use of force as a last resort. Méndez explored the early warning indicators that might point to impending genocide and consulted with NGOs to identify four clusters of indicators – namely the existence of groups at risk; the violations of human rights; hate speech; and histories of genocide.[67] Indeed, Méndez himself described his role as 'com[ing] up with ideas for early action that are relatively less costly, but also produces a result'.[68]

Méndez devoted much of his attention to Darfur, but he also wrote notes to the Secretary-General on Côte D'Ivoire and DRC and made his concerns known on the situations in Colombia, Myanmar, West Papua, Togo, northern Uganda and Somalia. He visited Darfur several times, criticising governments for their 'insufficient' response to the suffering there and describing this response as 'very eerily reminiscent' of the world's reaction to the Rwandan genocide. Méndez also provided the Secretary-General with policy recommendations which focused on the physical protection of vulnerable populations through the deployment of peacekeepers, through the provision of humanitarian assistance and legal accountability, and through efforts to advance the peace process.

After Méndez retired in March 2007, three NGOs – Amnesty International, Human Rights Watch and WFM–IGP – expressed concerns at reports that UN Secretary-General Ban Ki-moon planned either to downgrade the appointment or to merge it out of existence by tying it to a new advisory position on the R2P.[69] There is some evidence that Ban did indeed come under pressure to alter the position of special adviser. The head of the US aid agency (USAID), Andrew Natsios, indicated his disquiet with using the term 'genocide' in the position title of a UN official and a UN official informally let it out that concerns had been raised about the title of 'special adviser' on account of the fact that states had expressed a reluctance to permit the adviser to visit. As the official explained, 'who would want to let into their country an office with genocide in the title?'[70] However, Ban Ki-moon confounded the NGOs' expectations by appointing the highly regarded Francis Deng to the position, by elevating it from 'special adviser' to 'special representative' status, by making it a full-time position and by increasing the staff under its office. Ban also slightly altered the title, adding 'mass atrocities' to 'genocide': in this way he made it reflect more clearly the mandate handed down by Annan.[71] Deng's position was augmented through the appointment of Edward Luck as Special Adviser on the R2P. Sharing Deng's office, the Special Adviser was given the role of bringing forward recommendations for translating the R2P from words to deeds within the UN system. This involved identifying what is required in order to operationalise the commitment made in the World Summit Outcome Document and deepen international consensus on the R2P. Luck began his work in 2008 with a round of global consultations with governments and with the creation of an inter-agency working group within the UN.[72]

Unfortunately, both positions ran into difficulty when the General Assembly came to endorse them and to assign funds. Several NAM members objected to the widening of Deng's job title and insisted that 'mass atrocities' should be dropped. This was not altogether surprising, given the difficulties associated with defining 'mass atrocities' in precise legal terms. The position's expansion to cover 'mass atrocities' was later dropped after coming under fire from states concerned that the enlargement of Deng's mandate represented an affront to sovereignty. Concerns were also expressed about Luck's remit on the – rather bizarre – grounds that the World Summit had only committed the General Assembly to some further discussion of the R2P or to a general principle of civilian protection, rather than to the R2P itself.[73] In the end, Ban Ki-moon and Edward Luck persuaded the General Assembly to endorse the new special adviser's job description in return for removing the phrase 'R2P' from Luck's job title. Luck regarded this as a good deal, which allowed him to get on with his work on substantive issues, whilst Gareth Evans argued that the compromise indicated that the position lacked a 'job description of much prospect of tenure longevity'.[74] Although these protracted discussions certainly highlight continuing unease about the commitments made in 2005, the fact that the two positions were endorsed and funded suggests that some small progress had been made. As mentioned earlier, Deng and Luck were located in the same office – Deng focusing on responding to emergent crises and Luck on addressing longer-term policy and reform challenges.[75]

There have therefore been significant, if modest, efforts to improve the UN's capacity to use diplomatic measures for the prevention of genocide and mass atrocities. As with early warning, however, the UN's efforts in this area require a careful balancing of political hurdles. Member states remain wary of strengthening the Secretary-General's capacity for independent action and reluctant to provide the necessary resources. In addition, many states remain sensitive to the possibility of interference in domestic politics.

Ending impunity

The third way in which the world could strengthen its capacity to prevent the commission of genocide and mass atrocities is through measures designed to end impunity through international criminal law or human rights diplomacy. On the one hand, the development of international criminal law through the International Criminal Court (ICC), ad hoc tribunals such as those created in relation to Rwanda and Yugoslavia (ICTR, ICTY), and 'hybrid' courts organised by national authorities but overseen by the international community (such as that in Sierra Leone) offer a judicial deterrent to mass atrocities. On the other hand, the disbanding of the discredited UN Human Rights Commission and its replacement by the Human Rights Council has the potential to offer a new avenue for the international community to keep watch over human rights and to take early consensual measures to prevent the abuse of human rights developing into the commission of mass atrocities. Although there is much potential in both avenues, progress has been painfully slow. Four years after its creation, the ICC has begun to play a significant role in prosecuting and indicting individuals like former Liberian President Charles Taylor and Stephen Kony, leader of the murderous Lord's Resistance Army (LRA) in Uganda. However, the early signs from the Human Rights Council (HRC) are that, despite the best efforts of some of its members, this body is unlikely to avoid the politicisation which undermined its predecessor. I will briefly explore the ICC and HRC in turn.

The idea that some crimes are so heinous that they fall under universal jurisdiction is not new. Immediately after the Nuremberg and Tokyo trials at the end of the Second World War, which were tainted somewhat by the appearance of 'victor's justice', the UN established the International Law Commission (ILC), charged, among other things, with laying the groundwork for a global war crimes court. This idea fell victim to the Cold War, but states were prepared to formalise the laws of war through the 1949 Geneva Conventions and subsequent Protocols (1977) and to develop international humanitarian law, not least through the 1948 Convention on the Prevention and Punishment of Genocide. The problem, however, was that this emerging body of law lacked the necessary institutions and authority for their enforcement – a situation which enabled the emergence of a 'culture of impunity'.

The first tentative steps to end this culture came in the mid-1990s, when the Security Council established ad hoc tribunals to prosecute the perpetrators of grave crimes in Bosnia and Rwanda. However, governments were initially reluctant to provide the tribunals with the necessary resources, and some expressed concern that criminal proceedings would make it harder for interlocutors to broker political settlements. As a result, both tribunals got off to very slow starts. In 1994, the General Assembly granted the ICTY a mere $5.4 million to cover its expenses – a figure which increased to $94 million once NATO became actively interested in the tribunal's workings during its 1999 intervention in Kosovo.[76] There were also accusations of obstructionism by Security Council members who refused to release documents and other information necessary for investigations.[77] The Kosovo experience helped to reverse the West's neglect, and both political will and resources were poured especially into the ICTY; this delivered the indictment and trial of Slobodan Milošević and the arrest of Radovan Karadzić in 2008. What is more, in 1999 the British Law Lords, ruling on the case of Augusto Pinochet, found that sovereigns did not enjoy immunity from prosecution for crimes committed during their rule and that some crimes were so heinous as to fall under universal jurisdiction.

All of these initiatives suffered from the problem of selectivity. If the international community was serious about ending the culture of impunity, many argued, it would have to create an authoritative, independent and universal judicial instrument. From the mid-1990s, the effort to build an ICC was driven by a group of 'like-minded' states such as Canada and (after the Conservatives were swept from power in 1997 by Tony Blair) the UK. By April 1998, when a draft court statute was presented to Kofi Annan, the document had grown from the sixty or so articles of the original text proposed by the ILC to 116 articles. This included 478 bracketed passages, which were identified as areas of dispute.[78]

161 states sent delegations to a 1998 International Summit in Rome to work on the final statute, though not all of them had the intention of making a positive contribution. Indicative of the American attitude at Rome, for instance, were remarks by the head of a Senate delegation attached to the negotiating team: 'this court is truly a monster', he opined, 'and it is a monster that must be slain'.[79] The US delegation refused to budge on relatively minor issues, even when confronted with a huge majority which included its closest allies.

In general, positions on the ICC divided into three camps. The 'like-minded' group of over sixty states – including Canada, the entire EU except France, New Zealand, Argentina, South Korea and South Africa – advocated a strong and independent court, invested with authority to launch investigations wherever it saw fit. A second group comprised the permanent members of the Security Council except the UK and insisted that the ICC should be controlled by the council. In the end, Russia and France were satisfied enough with the Rome Statute to vote for it, whilst the US and China ultimately voted against. The third group, in which the US had at least one foot, were obstructionists and included Libya, Iran and Saddam's Iraq. In the end, 120 states voted in favour of the final statute and only seven (including the US, Israel, China, Iran, Iraq and Libya) voted against. The identity of the seventh state remains unknown.

The Rome Statute held that ICC jurisdiction could be invoked when a state proved unwilling or unable to investigate evidence pointing to the commission of widespread and systematic war crimes, crimes against humanity and genocide. The ICC prosecutor could initiate proceedings in cases where he/she was able to persuade a panel of judges that a case fell under the court's jurisdiction, where a complaint was made by a signatory state, or where a case was referred to the prosecutor by the Security Council. The Security Council also reserved the right to postpone investigations by one year.

As in 2005, the US found itself with some strange bedfellows in opposing the court. Syria argued that the court's jurisdiction should not cover internal conflicts; this would make governments immune from prosecution in case they massively abused their populations. China opposed clauses dealing with forced sterilisation. Israel opposed wording prohibiting enforced population transfers. America's main bone of contention was that, if the ICC could act independently of the Security Council, it might launch 'politicised' prosecutions against Americans. The US argued that the ICC threatened to sit in judgement of national laws and that this represented a grave attack on sovereignty. American justice, it argued, was superior to international justice.[80]

Of the court's opponents, none has done more to undermine the ICC than the US. It argued that peacekeepers should be given immunity from the Rome Statute, and it threatened to block the renewal of peacekeeping mandates until it got its own way. In mid-2002, it acted on its threat and vetoed the routine extension of the UN mission in Bosnia. Thankfully for Bosnia, the EU was on hand to take up the baton, but the American intention was clear: to hold UN peacekeeping to ransom in return for immunity from the ICC. The Security Council buckled under American pressure and in 2002 passed Resolution 1422, granting UN peacekeepers twelve months' immunity from ICC prosecution. This immunity was extended in June 2003 by the US-introduced Resolution 1487, passed by twelve votes with three abstentions (France, Germany and Syria). France and Germany argued that the resolution misused Chapter VII, since the council had not identified a threat to international peace and security; that it was based on a wrong interpretation of the ICC statute; and that it exhibited unsubstantiated fears about the court's politicisation.[81] Nevertheless, the two states maintained that the council had to balance its responsibility for managing peace operations with the majority's support for the court.

Resolutions 1422 and 1487 represented compromises designed to assuage US concerns about the ICC and to prevent further disruption to the UN's peace operations.

As a result of American hostility to the ICC, the Security Council has, to date, referred only one matter to the court: suspected crimes committed in Darfur. The US acquiesced in this only grudgingly. On 25 January 2005, a UN Commission of Inquiry concluded that, while the Sudanese government did not have a discernible policy of genocide in Darfur, where government forces and *Janjaweed* militia had unleashed a reign of terror on the civilian population which led to the death of some 250,000 and to the displacement of over two million, it was implicated in war crimes and crimes against humanity. Moreover, '[i]n some instances individuals, including government officials, may commit acts with genocidal intent'.[82] However, the commission maintained that only a competent court would be able to determine whether specific crimes were genocidal. The report sparked a heated debate about the appropriate venue for the prosecution of accused war criminals. EU members argued that the Security Council should refer the matter to the ICC. The British ambassador to the UN insisted that the ICC referral was 'non-negotiable'.[83] The US, keen not to lend credence to the ICC, argued that the Security Council should create a special tribunal in Arusha to indict and prosecute war criminals, and Nigeria offered a compromise in the form of an AU tribunal. EU members rejected the Nigerian proposal, fearing that any compromise would fatally undermine the ICC and that a regional alternative would be less thorough and authoritative than the global court.[84] For more than two months, as the killing in Darfur continued, the debate hamstrung international diplomacy.

The deadlock was broken on 31 March, when the council passed Resolution 1593 referring Darfur to the ICC. Explaining its decision to abstain, the US reaffirmed its opposition to the ICC – which, it claimed, 'strikes at the essence of the nature of sovereignty' – but noted the importance of a unified response to Darfur and the need to end impunity in the region.[85] The US had very few options regarding Darfur, and was ultimately forced to accept the ICC referral as the only alternative to inaction or unilateralism. In June 2006, ICC Prosecutor Luis Moreno-Ocampo briefed the Security Council on the collection of evidence of massacres, thousands of 'slow deaths' from forced displacement and the destruction of foodstocks, and hundreds of reported rapes (the overwhelming majority of rapes went unreported). The problem for the prosecutor is that the Security Council has remained reluctant to use coercion in order to force the Khartoum government to stop obstructing the ICC's investigations and to hand over suspected criminals.[86]

We should avoid the temptation of thinking that American acquiescence to Resolution 1593 implies a softening of its position on the ICC. This was an exceptional move, driven by a combination of deep interest in being seen to be acting so as to ameliorate a crisis it had described as genocide, and the determined diplomacy of the UK in particular. When it came to incorporating the ICC into the Security Council's commitment to R2P, the US remained steadfast in its opposition (see Chapter 5). For their part, European and Canadian advocates of the court have developed their own ad hoc strategy of seeking to insert references to the court wherever possible and of utilising the court in relatively uncontroversial but important cases (Kony is a good example) in order to get the US used to a world with an ICC.

However, it is clear that the court will add a new layer of complexity to international society's engagement with genocide and mass atrocities because it involves balancing the pursuit of justice and the pursuit of peace. Efforts to end the conflict in northern Uganda faltered because Kony's LRA insisted that the charges against their leader should be dropped as part of any agreement. This prompted the Ugandan government to ask the ICC prosecutor to drop charges against Kony, which the prosecutor is unable to do. A similar problem was created in July 2008, when Moreno-Ocampo moved to lay charges against the President of Sudan, Oman al-Bashir, for crimes committed in Darfur. Many fear that this proposed indictment could jeopardise efforts to deploy AU/UN peacekeepers in Darfur and to negotiate a peaceful settlement to the conflict, whilst supporters of the indictment argue that it is essential for ending impunity and might aid the cause of peace by delegitimising Bashir in the eyes of other Sudanese leaders. It is too early to tell the ICC's impact on the conflicts in northern Uganda and Darfur, but it is important to note the potential tensions between the pursuit of peace and the pursuit of justice.

The second main component of the effort to end impunity involves diplomatic rather than judicial tools. Among the achievements of the 2005 World Summit was the agreement to replace the discredited Human Rights Commission with a new Human Rights Council and with a strengthened office of High Commissioner for Human Rights. The council was named this way to reflect the ambition that, over time, it would evolve into one of the principal organs of the UN. Between them, the Human Rights Council and the office of High Commissioner have the potential to provide early warning and preventive action by monitoring human rights and by fostering collective measures to assist states to protect the rights of their citizens. This level of early international engagement may prevent the deterioration of human rights crises into genocide and mass atrocities by turning the lights of the world's attention onto emerging problems. Additionally, by encouraging collective consensual measures, the council and the high commissioner might facilitate preventive initiatives.

Unfortunately, the World Summit was unable to agree on what the new council should look like; it settled instead for a commitment to discuss the matter further. The West was more or less united in advocating a small and robust council comprising states of good standing in relation to human rights – a view endorsed by Kofi Annan. The key problem with the former commission, they argued – and with good reason – was that it had allowed some of the world's worst abusers to sit in judgement of their peers. So politicised, the commission focused its resolutions on a few select causes favoured by the G77 (especially apartheid in South Africa and the Palestinian situation), while ignoring the massive abuse of human rights elsewhere. In addition, the commission's size (fifty-three members from an original membership of eighteen) and consensus requirements made it ineffectual. The G77 had a different view. They only reluctantly accepted the need to replace the commission and did so, by and large, only in return for Western concessions on development. They argued that the council needed to be broad and representative and that, granted that members should have good human rights records, it should be for the General Assembly to make judgements in this regard. The two sides also disagreed about what the HRC should do. The West wanted a robust mandate which included the *protection* of human rights. The G77 preferred a consultative mandate which should focus on the *promotion* of human rights.

Negotiations dragged on for months after the World Summit, but agreement was reached in March 2006. Through sheer weight of numbers, the G77 got most of what it wanted: the HRC mandate focused on promotion more than on protection; the council would have forty-seven members; and election to the HRC was entirely at the discretion of the General Assembly and would be by simple majority rather than by the two-thirds majority sought by the Secretary-General. The West did win some important concessions. Council members would be obliged to expose themselves to scrutiny of their human rights record, which would deter the worst human rights abusers from seeking membership. In addition, the council would significantly expand its workload, sitting for three ten-week periods each year.[87] In the end, the Europeans and Canada decided that this was the best they could hope for and voted in favour of the council. The US and

Australia voted against the proposal, arguing that this format was too similar to that of its predecessor. The HRC's early record in relation to Darfur suggests that the sceptics might have had a point.

In April 2004, the Human Rights Commission had dispatched a fact-finding team to Darfur. The team found 'a disturbing pattern of disregard for basic principles of human rights and humanitarian law, which is taking place in Darfur for which the armed forces of the Sudan and the *Janjaweed* are responsible'.[88] It concluded that 'it is clear that there is a reign of terror in Darfur' and that the Sudanese government and its proxies were almost certainly guilty of widespread crimes.[89] Before the commission could vote on a resolution, the report was leaked to the press. Pakistan and Sudan condemned the leak and called for an immediate inquiry.[90] Unwilling to force the issue and concerned that a strongly worded resolution would be rejected by the commission's African and Asian members, the EU members watered down a draft resolution they were preparing. The redrafted resolution neither condemned Sudan nor mentioned its crimes. It was passed with fifty votes in favour and only three against (United States, Australia, Ukraine).[91]

After months of difficult negotiations, on 11 December 2006, the new HRC dispatched a High-Level Mission (HLM) to Darfur, to assess the human rights situation there. This decision was widely applauded as a signal of the members' willingness to compromise in order to make the HRC work. Almost immediately, however, the HLM ran into difficulties. The Sudanese government refused to grant access to the HLM because one of its members, Bertrand Ramcharan, had earlier criticised its behaviour in Darfur. The head of the mission, Nobel Laureate Jody Williams, decided that Ramcharan would remain a member of the mission and that the HLM would conduct its work without entering Darfur if the Sudanese government did not change its mind. Earlier missions conducted under the auspices of the commission had done likewise when they were denied visas by apartheid South Africa and Israel. However, the HLM's Asian representative, Indonesian Ambassador to the UN in Geneva Makarim Wibisono, pulled out, arguing that without access to Darfur the HLM would be unable to fulfil its mandate.[92] Wibisono took no part in writing the HLM's report, opening the door for states to challenge its legitimacy on procedural grounds.

Significantly, the HLM report used the R2P to evaluate the Sudanese government's performance. It argued that the R2P was an appropriate framework because the World Summit declaration created a mandate, as Sudan was one of those countries which had accepted its R2P and pledged 'to act in accordance with it'.[93] The Mission's findings were conclusive and damning: 'The Mission further concludes that the Government of the Sudan has manifestly failed to protect the population of Darfur from large-scale international crimes, and has itself orchestrated and perpetuated those crimes. As such, the solemn obligation of the international community to exercise its *responsibility to protect* has become evident and urgent.'[94] This was a landmark finding. For the first time, a UN commissioned report had applied the R2P framework as set out at the 2005 World Summit and found that a state had 'manifestly failed' to protect its citizens. The HRC was thus presented with an opportunity to operationalise the R2P into its human rights diplomacy.

Sadly, the opportunity was not seized. Sudan and the representatives of the Arab Group, Asia Group and Organization of Islamic Conferences (OIC) launched an assault on the report's legitimacy, in an effort to prevent deliberation on its findings. Speaking for Sudan, Mohammed Ali Elmardi argued that the report was nothing more than a 'conspiracy' against his government, maintaining that the HLM's failure to visit Sudan rendered its findings 'faulty' and 'illegitimate'. Speaking on behalf of the Arab Group, Lazhar Soualem (Algeria) argued that the report was illegitimate and should not be discussed because it was not written by the full mission. Speaking for the OIC, Tehima Janjua (Pakistan) endorsed Algeria's position and criticised the HLM's use of the R2P. As the HRC had not written the R2P into its mandate, he argued, the HLM had no right to comment on the R2P. Moreover, Pakistan maintained that, because the R2P involved political and security matters, it fell outside the mandate of the HRC itself. These views were endorsed by Sri Lanka representing the Asian Group, Indonesia, Egypt and Bangladesh, which described the report as 'illegitimate'. China concurred, arguing that the report should not be considered because the HLM's mandate had not been 'faithfully implemented'. Russia was somewhat less forthright in its criticism, but it too questioned the report's status.

Standing against this barrage of criticism were Europe, Canada, Australia, Japan, some South American states and – significantly – sub-Saharan Africa. Both the UK and France endorsed Jody Williams' use of the R2P in her report. Zambia argued that the critics were wrong to maintain that a mission's inability to visit a country impaired its legitimacy. As a former frontline state in the struggle against apartheid in South Africa, its ambassador argued, Zambia had first-hand experience of the UN accepting reports in cases where a mission had been denied access. Zambia insisted that the HRC should focus on the protection of human rights, not on political and bureaucratic technicalities, warning that, if the council failed to pay attention to the report and allowed technicalities to divert its attention away from the systematic abuse of human rights in Darfur, it would discredit itself, as its predecessor had done. These sentiments were shared by Ghana, which insisted that the report would make the world take the HRC seriously and that its substance was entirely appropriate. Likewise, Nigeria endorsed the report, argued that it should serve as the basis for further action and maintained that the council should focus on the protection of human rights instead of procedural technicalities.

In the end, the council agreed to discuss the report, but convened a group of seven 'mandate holders' to work with the government of Sudan in developing recommendations for further action. In consultation with Sudan, the group of experts pieced together a list of forty-four recommendations for improving human rights, complete with timeframes and 'performance indicators'.[95] It is too early to tell the impact of this work. For some, the recommendations constitute an important attempt to use the HRC to make a genuine difference to human rights through cooperation with the host government. There are, however, good grounds for scepticism. The follow-up report made no mention of the R2P and failed to recognise Sudan's poor track record on human rights. Worse still, close scrutiny of the recommendations reveals that few would make much practical difference to the situation in Darfur, whilst others might actually make matters worse. For example, recommending that Sudanese forces should conduct 'regular police patrols' to refugee and IDP camps (1.1.5) and should take 'all necessary measures' to prevent attacks on civilians (1.1.3) effectively gives a green light for government forces to continue the counter-insurgency activities which have caused so much civilian suffering. Likewise, making government authorities responsible for protecting women and girls from rape – when it is often those very authorities that have either stood aside and permitted rape or perpetrated it – constitutes wishful-thinking at best. Most recommendations require only the delivery of plans, instructions and statements; scant regard is given to concrete human rights protection. Some call for a handful of officials to be given human rights training, as if that would change the culture of impunity so evident in Darfur. Clearly, these recommendations are unlikely to protect human rights in Darfur.

To summarise: there are moves afoot to end the culture of impunity which has so often enabled the commission of mass atrocities, but progress is painfully slow. If their potential is realised, the ICC and HRC might make important contributions to the prevention of genocide and mass atrocities. Progress, however, is hard won, and there are many actors who would gladly see both institutions decay into irrelevance. Fulfilling the promise will therefore depend on the persistent activism of these institutions' supporters.

Preventive deployments

A fourth strategy for operationalising the responsibility to prevent is the deployment of preventive peace operations. The preventive deployment of peacekeepers is intended to build confidence between potential belligerents, to monitor human rights and to prevent the outbreak of violence. First raised in the Palme report (1982) on measures for addressing international security problems, the idea of preventive deployments was set out by Boutros-Ghali in 'Agenda for peace', largely at the instigation of one the report's main authors, James Sutterlin.[96] The Secretary-General was reportedly sceptical at the outset but was turned around by the force of Sutterlin's case and by other key figures such as Bertrand Ramcharan.[97] To this day, the only dedicated preventive peace operation was the UN's Preventive Deployment in Macedonia (UNPREDEP), though the EU's two missions in support of MONUC in the DRC had important preventive components. Significantly, all three were deployed with the consent of the host state and mandated by the Security Council. This means that, although each has provoked its own form of controversy, the general concept of preventive UN peacekeeping has proven relatively uncontroversial.

UNPREDEP is widely considered a successful example of preventive peacekeeping.[98] The mission was first deployed under the auspices of UNPROFOR at the request of Macedonian President Kiro Gligorov, who feared that the conflict engulfing Bosnia would spread southwards. UNPROFOR's Macedonian component comprised 700 soldiers from Scandinavia and the US. Security Council Resolution 795 (11 December 1992) gave the peacekeepers three main tasks: to establish a presence on Macedonia's borders; to monitor and report on developments which could threaten stability; and to deter violence. UNPROFOR's Macedonia Command was replaced by UNPREDEP in 1995, and the new mission was given a wider mandate which included building confidence between the Slav Macedonian and the Albanian communities, assisting humanitarian agencies and helping the government and local NGOs to improve the country's infrastructure. UNPREDEP made an important contribution to Macedonia's relatively peaceful transition from Yugoslav rule to independence and democracy. According to one commentator, there was 'a direct causal relationship . . . between the presence of UNPREDEP and other preventive initiatives . . . and the sustained relative stability in the region'.[99]

Sadly, a trade deal between Macedonia and Taiwan infuriated the Chinese, prompting them to block the mission's extension and to force its premature withdrawal in early 1999. Shortly afterwards, limited violence erupted between Albanian nationalists and the Macedonian army, though concerted efforts by the EU, OSCE and NATO helped to prevent the outbreak of generalised violence.

If UNPREDEP shows the extent to which preventive peacekeeping might preclude the outbreak or the spreading of armed conflict itself, the EU's two engagements with the MONUC mission in the DRC shows how the temporary deployment of a limited number of troops can prevent the commission of atrocities – though they also expose some of the weaknesses of this approach.

'Operation Artemis' was a French-led operation comprising 1,500 troops (drawn from 13 EU and 3 non-EU states) deployed to the town of Bunia in the eastern Democratic Republic of Congo (DRC) between early June and 1 September 2003.[100] The mission aimed to put an end to the periodic killing of civilians in Bunia, to protect the 5,000–8,000 civilians who sought refuge near the UN compound and to prevent widely anticipated mass atrocities. The deployment of well-armed Western (mainly French) troops with air support had a rapid impact on the security situation in Bunia, granting greater freedom of movement to humanitarian agencies and 'severely weakening' the Union of Congolese Patriots (UPC), who, it was feared, was planning a massive wave of ethnic killing and forced displacement. However, because the mission was limited temporally ('Artemis' was only a three-month deployment) and geographically (its mandate extended only to the town of Bunia), its contribution to saving lives in the wider Ituri district was 'minimal'.[101] The killing of civilians continued in the countryside around Bunia and persisted after the operation's withdrawal. In February 2005, for example, Bangladeshi peacekeepers were ambushed in the Ituri district and nine were killed and mutilated.[102] Throughout 2005–6, UN forces were engaged in enforcement operations – including 'Operation Ember' – conducted alongside government forces of the DRC. The key points here are that the rapid deployment of a short-term robust preventive mission prevented the commission of some mass atrocities, but, when such deployments are spatially and temporally limited, their preventive effect will also be limited in these ways.

In April 2006, the Security Council authorised the deployment of a European Reserve Deployment (Eufor RD) to the DRC, to assist MONUC and the Kinshasa government during elections. Eufor RD's mandate, set out in Security Council Resolution 1671 (25 April 2006), included the protection of civilians, the provision of security at Kinshasa's airport, and limited operations aimed at extracting key individuals associated with the elections if their security was threatened. In other words, Eufor RD was to provide additional support to MONUC in order to prevent the outbreak or escalation of violence during national elections and immediately after. The mission was limited to a four-month mandate and, although Resolution 1671 did not set geographic limits, Eufor RD mainly operated around Kinshasa. The mission comprised a modest-size 'advanced deployment' of approximately 400–500 peacekeepers to Kinshasa and a larger, battalion-size deployment (around 1,500 troops) on stand-by outside the DRC in Gabon. After the first round of voting, in late October 2006, an additional 300 troops from the stand-by force were deployed. Eufor RD was formally concluded on 30 November 2006. Observers agree that, although there was some violence in the aftermath of the second round of voting, Eufor RD made an important contribution to preventing the escalation of violence against civilians.[103]

Short-term and geographically focused deployments like 'Artemis' and Eufor RD have the potential to prevent specific outbreaks of genocidal violence and mass atrocities. Evidence that larger missions like UNPREDEP help to prevent the escalation of violence against civilians is more conclusive. The problem with missions like 'Artemis' and Eufor RD is that there is a fine line between directing deployments where they are most needed through tight temporal and geographic limits and weakening the deployment's ability to protect civilians by constraining it too much. The two EU missions are cases in point. There is little doubt that both saved lives and that 'Artemis' especially helped to ward off potential genocide in Bunia. Neither, however, provided comprehensive protection to civilians or dealt with the underlying threats.

Conclusion

Much work remains to be done on clarifying the responsibility to prevent, on identifying the measures required to realise that responsibility, and on persuading world governments to take effective and timely action. The first, and perhaps most important, task is to identify precisely what it is that the responsibility to prevent is seeking to prevent and what measures are necessary to achieve that goal. The ICISS adopted a broad conception of prevention, almost identical to that developed by the UN's thematic interest in the prevention of armed conflict. This broad conception is based on the view that, because mass atrocities tend to take place during armed conflict, the

R2P should contribute to the prevention of conflict in general. This implies in turn a concern for tackling the 'root causes' of violent conflict, for instance economic inequality. This approach raises the 'dilemma of comprehensiveness': it implies a broad range of preventive strategies without clearly stipulating which ones are essential for the prevention of genocide and mass atrocities. Whilst on the one hand this broad approach has the advantage of appealing to governments in the global South, which are understandably preoccupied with economic development, it runs the risk of diluting the responsibility to prevent and of reducing the likelihood that governments and international organisations will be able to operationalise measures designed to prevent the four crimes relating to the R2P.

In this chapter I have advocated a narrower understanding of the responsibility to prevent as referring only to the prevention of genocide, war crimes, ethnic cleansing and crimes against humanity. In order to improve the world's capacity to prevent genocide and mass atrocities, I have identified four areas – early warning, preventive diplomacy, ending impunity and preventive deployments – where concrete measures have already had an impact and where there is real scope for the building of further capacity. However, the fact that even modest reforms in these areas, for instance the creation of a small early warning unit within the DPA, have proven deeply controversial suggests that it is not possible to separate 'norm building' from 'operationalisation', because the building of real capacity depends on agreement about the desirability of committing the necessary resources and political will. The UN Secretary-General's Special Adviser, Edward Luck, and the UN Special Representative on the Prevention of Genocide, Francis Deng, have important roles to play in this regard. On the one hand, they need to clarify the scope and content of proposals which aim to improve the UN's capacity for the prevention of genocide and mass atrocities. On the other hand, they need to consult with member states in order to build consensus around their proposals.

5

Reaction

The 'reaction' component of the R2P is typically understood as referring to the use of non-consensual military force. Indeed, the R2P has often been portrayed by senior figures such as Stephen Stedman – Kofi Annan's special adviser on UN reform – as primarily, or even solely, concerned with the use of military force.[1] It is certainly the case that some situations are so dire that only the use of force will protect endangered populations. Historically, genocides end either with the military defeat of the perpetrators or with the annihilation of the victims. Only military force can directly prevent ethnic cleansing, stand between the warlords and their intended victims, and protect the delivery of humanitarian aid. But the use of military force is inherently dangerous. Its impact is difficult to predict, and force might sometimes inflame rather than improve situations, as in Somalia in the early 1990s. It is also easy to think of cases where the non-consensual deployment of military force could be expected to do more harm than good – the hypothetical despatch of peacekeepers to Chechnya against the will of the Russian government is an oft-cited case in point.

We also need to be realistic about what force can and cannot achieve. Properly used, force can offer physical protection to civilians in immediate danger. Soldiers can stand guard over vulnerable people, encourage militia groups to disarm, coerce political leaders and compel spoilers. They can assist in the building of infrastructure and of the indigenous security sector. But they cannot compel the parties to build sustainable peace, rebuild shattered governments, economies and societies, protect civilians in the long-term, or provide comprehensive security.

The R2P points to a range of different options for reacting to grave humanitarian crises. As Lee Feinstein argued, all too often policy options in such circumstances are portrayed as a choice between 'sending in the Marines' and doing nothing.[2] One of the ICISS' main innovations was to provide a continuum of measures designed to reduce the number of times governments will be faced with this choice. Before tackling questions relating to non-consensual force and practical questions about the modalities of civilian protection, I will therefore consider a range of measures – short of force – identified by the ICISS. Some of those measures were canvassed in the previous chapter and others will be dealt with in the following chapter, so the present one will focus on the use of sanctions. Before that, however, we should situate the question of how best to protect civilians in immediate danger within the Security Council's ongoing thematic interest in civilian protection, which led to the reaffirmation of the R2P by the Security Council in 2006.

Security Council Resolution 1674

After six months of intense debate, on 28 April 2006, the Security Council unanimously adopted Resolution 1674 on the protection of civilians in armed conflict. The resolution 'reaffirmed' the World Summit's provisions 'regarding the responsibility to protect populations from genocide, war crimes, ethnic cleansing and crimes against humanity' and the Security Council's 'readiness' to adopt appropriate steps 'where necessary'. Although Resolution 1674 amounted to much less than the ICISS had wanted from the Security Council (see Chapter 2), it was nevertheless a significant statement of support, which has tied the R2P to the UN's efforts to protect civilians.

The Security Council's interest in civilian protection can be traced to April 1998, when Kofi Annan used a council dialogue on armed conflict in Africa to identify the protection of civilians as a 'humanitarian imperative'.[3] Canada persuaded the council to adopt a Presidential Statement requesting that the Secretary-General should submit a report on how the UN might improve the protection of civilians and pledging periodic council reviews of the issue (12 February 1999). The council informally agreed to hold two open debates on the protection of civilians each year, in June and December. In September 1999, the council unanimously adopted the landmark Resolution 1265, which pre-empted the R2P by expressing the council's 'willingness' to 'respond to situations of armed conflict where civilians are being targeted or where humanitarian assistance to civilians is being deliberately obstructed' and by binding it to consider adopting 'appropriate measures'. It also called on states to ratify key human rights treaties and prosecute those responsible for genocide, crimes against humanity and 'serious violations of international humanitarian law'. Finally, the council expressed its willingness to explore how peacekeeping mandates might be reframed to afford better protection to civilians.

The resolution enjoyed broad support within the council. China limited itself to criticising western 'selectivity' and called for a renewed focus on the root causes of conflict.[4] However, several prominent General Assembly members launched a stinging attack both on the draft resolution and on the Secretary-General's report that preceded it. Egypt argued that efforts to protect civilians should not 'compel us to flout the [UN] Charter' and criticised Annan for advocating preventive measures without stressing the necessity for host state consent. This, the Egyptians argued, 'flouts the sacrosanct Charter principle of the sovereignty of states'.[5] This view was supported by India, which issued a point-by-point rebuttal of the more than a dozen recommendations proposed by Annan. India maintained that Annan ignored relevant legal instruments by stretching the competence of the Security Council beyond its 'narrowly defined' remit; questioned the council's authority to engage itself in matters not directly related to military security; cast doubt on the legitimacy of ad hoc tribunals; criticised the council's engagement with IDPs, seeing this as a matter for the internal jurisdiction of states (see below); denounced the supposed 'right of humanitarian access' implied by the council's demands in that area and the use of sanctions as a 'blunt instrument'; and pointed to numerous instances where Annan and the council should have deferred to sovereignty.[6]

This concerted attack prompted the council to shift its focus from broad issues and principles towards UN peace operations. In April 2000, Annan's report on civilian protection was greeted with a further UK-sponsored resolution (Resolution 1296, 19 April 2000) focusing on operational matters designed to improve the capacity of UN peace operations to protect civilians. This avenue produced an *Aide Mémoire* on civilian protection, issued as an annexe to a Security Council Presidential Statement (15 March 2002) and updated by the Office for the Coordination of Humanitarian Affairs (OCHA) in 2004.[7] The *Aide* identified a range of measures necessary in order to realise each of the council's civilian protection objectives. For example, in relation to the council's demand that belligerents should grant safe and unimpeded humanitarian access to the civilian population, the *Aide* identified five specific issues for consideration and action:

1 the provision of appropriate security arrangements (e.g. role of multinational forces, safe corridors, protected areas, armed escorts)
2 engagement in dialogue with belligerents
3 facilitation of delivery of humanitarian assistance
4 safety and security of humanitarian personnel
5 compliance with international legal obligations.

The document covered fifteen related topics in this way and has since been used to guide and frame council briefings on civilian protection.

The opening of the Security Council's deliberations on civilian protection and the R2P in December 2005 was prompted by the release of another periodic report by the Secretary-General. Annan recommended that the council endorse the R2P and its commitment to protect civilians in war, take measures to facilitate the delivery of humanitarian aid, continue to clarify the place of civilian protection in peacekeeping mandates and develop systems for monitoring compliance.[8] The UK drafted a resolution containing an operative paragraph which 'recalled' the World Summit's Outcome Document and '*underlined*' the importance of its provisions relating to the R2P. It also reiterated calls for states to ratify relevant human rights instruments, to prosecute war criminals and to afford protection to refugees and IDPs; and it reaffirmed the civilian protection duties of peace operations and the importance of safe and unimpeded humanitarian access.[9]

The proposed reaffirmation of the R2P proved highly controversial. Russia, China and three non-permanent members (Algeria, the Philippines and Brazil) argued that it was premature to bring the R2P to the council because the World Summit had merely committed the General Assembly to further deliberation on the principle.[10] Algeria sounded a strong note of caution about the R2P, insisting that 'we recall that the September summit mandated the General Assembly to continue the debate on that concept [R2P] – a concept about which there is still no unanimity within the international community and whose parameters still need to be rigorously defined'.[11] Likewise, Brazil argued that, although the R2P 'does merit an adequate place in our system', the UN was not created to impose its will on member states; and the World Summit stressed that the General Assembly 'should examine the responsibility to protect populations' and 'assess all its ramifications, bearing in mind the United Nations Charter'.[12] In the council's open debate, Egypt maintained that the Security Council was constitutionally required to limit its interest in the protection of civilians to individual cases of armed conflict. Egypt's ambassador also expressed disquiet at the potential for the Security Council to 'legislate' on the R2P, noting that the General Assembly had been mandated by the World Summit to continue considering the concept and that this process had not yet begun.[13]

On the other side of the debate, the EU supported adoption of the R2P – a position shared by Canada, Japan, South Korea and other 'Westerners'. Once again, several sub-Saharan African states joined the West in defending the R2P. Rwanda insisted on the necessity of a collective R2P. Benin signalled its 'full support' for the reaffirmation of the R2P – something done 'more easily when we recognize that the same collective responsibility to protect is the basis of the creation of the African Union'.[14] Tanzania maintained that 'when governments fail or are unable to offer such protection, we should have a collective responsibility to protect humanity' – a view shared by South Africa. The R2P received support from other regions too. Qatar (indirectly), Peru and Nepal – all endorsed the concept. Peru, for instance, argued that 'the United Nations has a responsibility to protect populations from serious and systematic violations of international humanitarian law' and that the R2P should be seen as 'a concept that guarantees the achievement of the ultimate goal of State sovereignty'.

The greatest barrier to the affirmation of the R2P by the Security Council was the opposition of two permanent members: China and, more trenchantly, Russia. Resolution 1674 was secured only when British negotiators developed a compromise with the Chinese which isolated Russia, forcing it to acquiesce. At the beginning of the debate, in December 2005, Russia's Ambassador Rogachev offered strident support to the Egyptian and Indian position:

> We were struck by the report's [Annan's report on the protection of civilians] finding with regard to the responsibility to protect. We believe that it is clearly premature to advance that concept in Security Council documents. We all remember well the complex compromise that was required to reflect that issue in the 2005 Summit Outcome document. In that connection – and the outcome document states this – we need to have a detailed discussion in the General Assembly of the issue of the responsibility to protect before we can discuss its implementation.[15]

Although China privately indicated its support for the view that the R2P should return to the General Assembly for further deliberation, its public position was more nuanced – as it had been in the World Summit negotiations. China argued that 'all activities pertaining to protection' be performed with due respect for the Charter; affirmed the council's 'primary responsibility' for peace and security; and called for 'further comprehensive and in-depth discussions', noting that 'the outcome document went on to develop the concept at length, owing to the sensitivity and complexity of the issue'.[16] Significantly, China stopped short of publicly insisting that deliberation in the General Assembly was a necessary precursor to the endorsement of the R2P by the Security Council.

There were other problems too. The Europeans (UK, France and Denmark) wanted the resolution to refer to the ICC, but the US objected.

This time the British were not prepared to make the ICC into a deal breaker and agreed to drop the references. Negotiations also focused on the difficult question of humanitarian access – the target of earlier criticism from Egypt and India. The resolution's sponsors favoured the reaffirmation of the robust language used in Resolution 1265. Others preferred the weaker and less specific language endorsed by the World Summit. Another key element in the debate related to a paragraph condemning torture, which was seen as potentially problematic in view of the American record in the war on terror.[17]

The change in the non-permanent membership of the Security Council at the end of 2005 had a profound impact on these negotiations. Of the five non-permanent members stepping down in 2005, two (Algeria and Brazil) had openly declared their hostility to the R2P and another (the Philippines) had tended to side with the sceptics. Among the new members were Slovakia, Qatar and Peru, who had voiced support for the R2P in the December debate, Ghana, who had not participated in that debate but was also an R2P supporter, and Congo, who in June 2006 informed the council of its 'strong support' for the principle.[18]

Undeterred, Russia continued to argue that the inclusion of the R2P was premature, and it strongly advocated a paragraph condemning torture in occupied territories – a move largely designed to draw American opposition. In addition to torture and the ICC, the US also worried that reaffirming the R2P might create pressure on the council to act in a greater number of cases. For its part, China took a more pragmatic view, dropping its earlier private support for General Assembly primacy in favour of luke-warm support for council endorsement of the R2P on the condition that it used language identical to that adopted by the World Summit.[19]

In an effort to overcome the impasse, the UK released a revised draft resolution on 13 April 2006. Reportedly in an effort to isolate Russia, the UK had already discussed and agreed the revised draft with China in private before circulating it to the full council membership. The 13 April draft retained the reference to the R2P in an operative paragraph but toned down the endorsement, limiting the council simply to reaffirming the relevant paragraphs of the World Summit document – in line with Chinese requests. Other compromises were designed to satisfy the US. Explicit references to the ICC were removed and, although a reference to torture remained, it was limited to the 'condemnation' of torture and other prohibited activities without the specific reference to 'occupied territories' advocated by Russia. Finally, the Secretary-General's next progress report would not come for another eighteen months: this reflected a sentiment in favour of slowing down the pace of the reform. Other key parts of the resolution remained more or less intact. The robust demand for humanitarian access was retained, as was the reaffirmation of the council's willingness (expressed in Resolution 1296) to take action in cases where civilians were deliberately targeted and the host state proved itself unwilling or unable to protect them – and retained in spite of American concerns that this provision might lead to expectations of 'automaticity'.[20] Within two weeks, the draft became Resolution 1674 – which was endorsed unanimously by the Security Council.

This was an important milestone. Resolution 1674 identified a number of concrete measures the council could take to realise the R2P and reinforced global support for the principle. Significantly, China has since consistently referred to the resolution as providing the appropriate 'legal framework' for the protection of civilians in armed conflict.[21] But the protracted negotiations also revealed just how deeply divided the world was. Since the passage of Resolution 1674, the council's focus returned to implementation issues such as the protection of journalists (Resolution 1738, 23 December 2006). Meanwhile, key advocates of the R2P and of the council's thematic interest in civilian protection – especially the UK, France and Belgium – became reluctant to propose the further use of the R2P by the council because of the political difficulties exposed by the Resolution 1674 negotiations.[22] This experience helped to persuade the R2P advocates in the Security Council that progress is more likely without specific references to the R2P.

These concerns were borne out by the council's June 2007 debate on the protection of civilians. Several states – including the European states, Canada (which also spoke on behalf of Australia and New Zealand), Panama, Peru, Ghana and Congo – called for concrete steps to realise the R2P. On the other hand, Qatar, Russia and China argued for a narrowing and slowing down of the R2P. Qatar embraced the principle, but cautioned against its 'exploitation' or 'abuse'. Russia argued that the council should strictly adhere to the R2P parameters set out in the World Summit. As such, Russia's ambassador argued, the question of IDPs should not be linked to the R2P. For its part, China returned in 2007 to the position first adopted by R2P sceptics in the wake of the World Summit. 'At present', it argued, 'there are still differing understandings and interpretations of this concept among Member States. The Security Council should therefore refrain from invoking the concept of the responsibility to protect. Still less should the concept be misused. The Security Council should respect and support the General Assembly in continuing to discuss the concept in order to reach broad consensus.'[23] In response, in his first report on the protection of civilians, new Secretary-General Ban Ki-moon made a series of recommendations for future measures, including further measures in dealing with humanitarian access and the creation of a working group to explore avenues for translating the council's rhetorical commitment to protection into tangible outcomes for endangered populations.[24]

It has therefore proved very difficult to build consensus around the idea that the Security Council should advance the R2P in cases where civilian populations are deliberately targeted. But a shaky consensus has emerged nonetheless, and in the process the council has developed a broad thematic interest in civilian protection. But how do these political debates translate into practical measures designed to protect civilians? It is important to note from the outset that the ICISS' research team, led by Thomas Weiss and Don Hubert, identified an important distinction between two types of measures. The first consists in measures aimed at 'compelling compliance'. That is, measures to protect civilians indirectly by changing their potential tormentor's calculations of costs and benefits. The second type involves measures aimed at 'providing protection' directly.[25] The remainder of this chapter will focus on the development of these different types of measures, starting with measures which stop short of force.

Non-Military Aspects of Reaction

According to the ICISS, the failure of prevention to 'stave off or contain a humanitarian crisis or conflict does not mean that military action is necessarily required'.[26] When the time and the circumstance permit, or where prudence dictates, decision-makers should consider non-military measures – such as economic sanctions and arms embargoes to protect the victims of war. As an illustration, this section will briefly evaluate recent developments in relation to targeted sanctions, which are perhaps the most common non-military means for coercing compliance.

The failure of comprehensive sanctions

Sanctions are coercive because they seek to persuade their targets to change behaviour through a reconfiguring of the balance of costs and benefits associated with particular courses of action. In theory, sanctions are less costly and risky than military action, but they promise only indirect protection; it may take years before they have the desired effect; and they can inflict serious harm on the civilian population. The likelihood of 'success' is also rather limited. According to one study, only 34 per cent of sanctions regimes changed the target's behaviour, and the success rate is only 24 per cent for regimes after 1973.[27] Later studies have either confirmed these findings or concluded that the success rate is even lower.[28] However, because sanctions impose very few costs on those who apply them and can produce positive effects a quarter of the time without imposing the heavy costs associated with military deployment, they are a potentially valuable policy tool.

Sanctions were imposed by the Security Council only twice during the Cold War, against white African governments in Rhodesia and South Africa. That situation began to change in the 1990s, starting with the imposition of comprehensive sanctions against Iraq in response to its August 1990 invasion of Kuwait. Under Resolution 661, the council imposed comprehensive sanctions, banning all trade, international flights and financial transactions, and freezing Iraqi assets.[29] Soon afterwards, the council imposed similarly broad measures against Yugoslavia, partial economic sanctions against Haiti and Libya and a range of embargoes on Somalia, Libya, Haiti, UNITA/Angola and Rwanda. In relation to Yugoslavia, successive envoys reported that the sanctions played a key role in motivating the Serb leader, Slobodan Milošević, to engage in peace talks; but neither the arms embargo nor economic sanctions delivered protection to vulnerable populations, and it was ultimately the use of force that secured Serb acquiescence to a peace agreement in 1995. Moreover, sanctions had negative humanitarian and social effects: Serbia's health-care system was shattered and infant mortality increased; the sanctions enabled the flourishing of organised crime, supporting various militia leaders; and economic hardships only strengthened Milošević's grip on the economy.[30]

Yet this was just the tip of the iceberg. Comprehensive sanctions against Iraq inflicted massive harm on civilians without having any discernible impact on Iraq's leadership. In 1995, the FAO reported that infant mortality had more than doubled and that sanctions were responsible for 567,000 child deaths in Iraq. In 1996, UNICEF reported that 4,500 children under the age of five were dying each month from preventable hunger and disease. An independent study conducted at Columbia University found that 'excess' deaths of children under five in Iraq was somewhere between 100,000 and 227,000 and that three quarters of them were attributable to the sanctions.[31] Kofi Annan reported malnourishment of one third of all the children under the age of five and of a quarter of all the Iraqi men and women under the age of twenty-six. Annan called attention to the serious degradation of the Iraqi health-care system, the inadequate supplies and storage facilities, the interrupted and unclean water supplies, the unreliable electricity supplies and broken sewage systems as reasons for the spiralling death toll.[32] By causing this suffering, the sanctions undermined the UN's credibility as a humanitarian organisation.[33]

By the mid-1990s it had become clear that comprehensive economic sanctions caused massive civilian suffering without bringing tangible results. Annan recognised this problem in his Millennium report, arguing that:

> When robust and comprehensive economic sanctions are directed against authoritarian regimes, a different problem is encountered. Then it is usually the people who suffer, not the political elites who[se] behaviour triggered the sanctions in the first place. Indeed, those in power, perversely, often benefit from such sanctions by their ability to control and profit from black market activity, and by exploiting them as a pretext for eliminating domestic sources of political opposition.[34]

This discovery was supported by research which found a mere 2 per cent success rate for economic sanctions against 'authoritarian regimes'.[35] In response, the British Parliament's International Development Committee concluded in 2000 that 'we find it difficult . . . to believe that there will be a case in the future where the UN would be justified in imposing comprehensive economic sanctions on a country'.[36] In the same year, a paper prepared for the UN Human Rights Commission argued that comprehensive sanctions violated human rights.[37] The ICISS shared these sentiments, arguing that blanket sanctions were 'blunt instruments' and indiscriminate. What was needed, it argued, were sanctions which targeted the source of the problem directly.

Targeted sanctions

The development of 'smart' or 'targeted' sanctions was spearheaded by the 'Interlaken process' sponsored by Switzerland, by the 'Bonn–Berlin process' sponsored by Germany and the 'Stockholm process on the implementation of targeted sanctions' (SPITS). Together, these initiatives responded to valid criticisms of earlier sanctions regimes by advancing two basic principles: (1) that sanctions must be carefully targeted against those whose behaviour has to change in order to satisfy the will of international society; and (2) that sanctions must contain humanitarian exemptions, in order to ensure that the basic needs of the civilian population are met.[38]

The 'Interlaken process' (1998–9), organised by the Swiss Federal Office for Foreign Economic Affairs, involved representatives from governments, the finance sector, the UN and other interested organisations, and focused on improved ways of targeting financial sector sanctions. The first meeting addressed the need for a clear understanding of the target's vulnerabilities and characteristics. The second meeting focused on the technical requirements for operationalising targeted financial sanctions.[39] The 'Bonn–Berlin process' initiated by the German government had three main objectives: to identify deficiencies in past UN sanctions regimes; to develop proposals for the improvement of the effectiveness of arms embargoes and travel bans; and to identify other measures requiring more detailed study.

Indicative of the sorts of studies commissioned by these processes was a report on arms embargoes which found them to be 'seriously flawed' thanks largely to problems of implementation. The report found that 'frequent breaches conspire to reduce potentially powerful instruments to mere pronouncements of intent'. Worse still, poorly implemented embargoes enabled the flourishing of an illegal trade in small arms conducted by transnational criminal networks specialised in trafficking arms, conflict goods and people. These flaws were caused by three factors. First, most states had no domestic legislation empowering the authorities to prosecute nationals engaged in the illegal shipment of arms to countries subject to UN arms embargoes, and they were reluctant to enact such legislation. Second, states were reluctant to provide the UN with the necessary resources for policing arms embargoes efficiently. Third, the UN lacked the necessary institutional capacity to oversee arms embargoes. Whilst the Security Council's Sanctions Committees were invested with the authority to monitor and implement sanctions, they had little administrative support and lacked the capacity to conduct independent fact-finding.[40]

To bring a remedy, the report articulated its support for the creation of a designated unit, meant to supervise the implementation of all UN arms embargoes – an idea first touted by Human Rights Watch and supported by the Netherlands during its term on the Security Council. The Netherlands used its September 1999 presidency of the Security Council to push the proposal but, although it succeeded in persuading the council to commit itself to working towards an improved effectiveness of arms embargoes, it ultimately failed to make the council establish a designated unit. The report identified other measures designed to tighten embargo regimes. These included clear and specific mandates; the creation of sanctions offices in neighbouring states so as to oversee implementation; the provision of expertise and resources for the improvement of the capacity of customs offices; and consideration by the council of mandating the deployment of civilian observers to investigate embargo violations.[41]

The next step was SPITS, funded by the Swedish government in 2002. SPITS provided a consolidated report written by the programme's director, Peter Wallensteen. The report was presented to the UN in 2003 and contained hundreds of specific recommendations. Those recommendations included calls for measures designed to improve the Security Council's capacity to monitor, enforce and refine sanctions regimes; measures designed to enhance reporting procedures by member states; and actions designed to develop ways of responding to the measures taken by the targets of the sanctions so as to mitigate the effects or profit from the sanctions regime. Although there is no space here to explore the proposals in detail, it is worth mentioning some of the generic recommendations highlighted by Wallensteen and his team:

- Sanctions mandates should be drafted with implementation in mind and should clearly specify how the sanctions will be administered.
- Sanctions should maintain public support by, among other things, minimising humanitarian impact.
- Regimes should have the capacity to monitor compliance, to follow up and to improve the measures.
- The capacity of the UN Secretariat should be strengthened through the creation of a database containing information on current sanctions and lessons learned. Member states should also consider the appointment of a special adviser on sanctions.
- Lessons (such as the value of creating designated contact points among member states, or the value of an obligatory reporting of the activities undertaken by member states pursuant to Security Council resolutions) can be learned from the UN Counter-Terrorism Committee.
- The UN and other agencies should consider ways of strengthening the capacity of member states to enforce sanctions. Owing to the diverse nature of the targeted sanctions regimes, this involves the development of a range of specialised capacities.
- Accuracy is a vital component of targeted sanctions and this fact heightens the need for constant reviews in order to ensure that the sanctions affect only the intended targets. Consideration should be given to unintended consequences and especially to the effects of sanctions regimes on Third World states .

The Wallensteen report was presented to the Security Council on 25 February 2003 and was warmly welcomed by most members. This being said, Bulgaria and Pakistan argued that sanctions regimes should compensate third parties for unintended harm, while Cameroon pointed to 'differences of opinion' among council members about the scope and length of sanctions regimes. But these were relatively minor concerns.[42]

Between them, the three processes had a profound impact on UN sanctions. Not since 1994 has the Security Council imposed comprehensive sanctions, preferring targeted sanctions instead. Of those, the most often used are targeted financial sanctions, arms embargoes, travel bans and associated aviation restrictions, and embargoes on particular trades (diamonds and timber in Liberia; diamonds in Angola; oil in Libya, Angola and Sierra Leone). In addition, the council has gradually begun to adopt measures for improving the effectiveness of sanctions regimes – most notably by appointing expert panels to monitor compliance and by creating an informal working group to identify measures for increasing effectiveness (see below).[43]

But are targeted sanctions an effective way of reacting to crises characterised by genocide, war crimes, ethnic cleansing and crimes against humanity? It is certainly true that – properly implemented – targeted sanctions are much more effective than their predecessors. Perhaps the clearest example of this is the sanctions regime imposed on the UNITA rebels in Angola. Jonas Savimbi's UNITA was primarily responsible for the continuation of Angola's civil war into the 1990s.[44] Starting with Resolution 864 in 1993, the Security Council took steps to prohibit the sale and supply of weapons and military assistance to UNITA. For the first few years, however, these measures were ineffective because member states did little to enforce them. The situation began to change with the imposition of travel bans in 1997 and of an embargo on the sale or export of diamonds in 1998. Under the leadership of Robert Fowler – the Canadian ambassador to the UN who assumed the chair of the Angola sanctions committee in 1999 – the UN adopted measures to improve the regime's effectiveness. Fowler sought to increase awareness of the embargo through consultations with neighbouring states and regional organisations. He built alliances by lobbying key stakeholders in the diamond industry, by working with key international agencies such as Interpol and by supporting British- and American-led initiatives to persuade the G8 to tighten its regulatory framework on diamonds. Finally, Fowler pioneered the creation of instruments designed to give effect to the embargo, prompting the Security Council to set up an expert panel in order to monitor violations and advise the council.[45]

The main product of these endeavours was a March 2000 report to the Security Council by the panel of experts which identified violations of the sanctions by Savimbi. The report marked a watershed in that it adopted a 'naming and shaming' strategy – identifying those governments, agencies and individuals who had directly or indirectly violated the sanctions – and it raised the level of Security Council engagement by identifying four factors contributory to the ineffectiveness of sanctions. These were as follows: the readiness of Zaire (DRC), Togo and Burkina Faso to provide end-user certificates facilitating the passage of arms to UNITA; the readiness of some arms manufacturing countries – especially Bulgaria – to sell weapons without regard for where they would end up; the readiness of arms brokers and transport companies to act as intermediaries between UNITA and arms suppliers; and UNITA's capacity to pay.[46] Thus armed, the Security Council advanced measures to strengthen the sanctions regime and used diplomacy to persuade governments to cease sanctions-busting activities. Gradually this policy starved UNITA of the resources and finances it needed to continue the war and isolated it internationally, contributing to its military defeat by the Angolan government in February 2002 and hence to the establishment of a more sustainable peace.

This feat was repeated in relation to sanctions against the RUF in Sierra Leone. Once again, a panel of experts identified embargo breakers (Liberia, Burkina Faso, Niger, Côte D'Ivoire), thereby facilitating Security Council action. In this case, the Security Council imposed tighter sanctions, including an arms embargo on Charles Taylor's Liberia which was a punishment for its violation of sanctions in Sierra Leone (Security Council Resolution 1343, 2001). As in Angola, the strengthened sanctions reduced the RUF's ability to translate the control over natural resources into money and weapons, contributing to its defeat and laying the foundations for peace.[47] More recently, a similar framework was used to oversee an arms embargo on Côte D'Ivoire which helped to stymie the descent into civil war there. These targeted sanctions had much less of a humanitarian component than their comprehensive counterparts, and in none of these cases was there evidence of targeted sanctions having a negative impact on the civilian population.

Quiet progress has been made towards formalising some of these arrangements. As mentioned earlier, in April 2000 the council established an informal working group, designed to examine issues relating to the effectiveness of sanctions regimes. Progress on a consolidated report was slow, because the parties were deadlocked on the question of the duration and termination of sanctions regimes – some arguing that regimes should only be terminated when their objectives were met, whilst others maintained that regimes should always have fixed timeframes.[48] Not until 2006 did the working group finally adopt a report. Although stopping well short of endorsing the Dutch proposal for a special unit to manage sanctions – which was rejected in part because of concerns among the P5 that this would limit their flexibility – the report recommended that the council should adopt credible mechanisms to monitor the implementation of sanctions, and called upon the secretariat to pool for, and make better use of, existing expertise and thus enhance the ability of the Security Council Subsidiary Organs Branch (the entity responsible for administering sanctions committees) to advise on the implementation and design of sanctions and on their monitoring, enforcement and humanitarian impact.[49]

Despite these advances, there remain some serious problems connected with the use of sanctions as a non-military means of coercing compliance. Used in this capacity, sanctions provide only indirect protection and can take years to work. In both Sierra Leone and Côte D'Ivoire, targeted sanctions were accompanied by the deployment of large UN peace operations. In the absence of such operations, even precisely targeted and rigidly enforced sanctions can do little to protect endangered populations. In addition, it would be foolhardy to believe that it is any easier to build international consensus on the imposition of sanctions than it is to forge consensus on military deployments. Typically, sanctions are not a politically cheap alternative available in cases where the Security Council is divided on how to respond to genocide and mass atrocities. The world's reaction to the crisis in Darfur provides ample evidence of this. In the first three years of the crisis, the council failed to agree on anything other than limited travel bans against a small number of individuals. Proposals for sanctions targeting the political elite's foreign assets and oil revenues were repeatedly blocked by China, Russia and some non-permanent members – which significantly reduced the amount of pressure brought to bear on the Khartoum government.[50]

Other problems are of a more technical nature. There are still no clear guidelines for how individuals become targets of UN sanctions and, despite gradual moves towards improving the UN secretariat's capacity for managing sanctions regimes, the system remains ad hoc.[51] There are therefore good grounds for arguing that the Secretary-General and the Security Council should revisit the Dutch proposal for a designated unit; but this seems unlikely given the difficulties encountered by the informal working group, which, having issued a report, was wound up and declared a 'success'.

When to Use Force

When non-military ways are unable to protect endangered civilians, and when it is prudent to do so, the R2P calls for the deployment of military force. Military force can be used either to protect populations from attack or to coerce or compel compliance by targeting those responsible for attacks on civilians. But little tangible progress has been made on the question of how to make decisions about the use of force for R2P purposes – nor is future progress likely. In relation to the employment of military means for protection purposes, the R2P has had much more impact on the conduct of operations. Before discussing these operational issues, however, we should consider two other sets of issues, relating to the decision to deploy military force. The first set is connected to the fact that the overwhelming majority of military deployments for R2P purposes enjoys the consent of the host state. This type of operation normally involves the use of military means to protect endangered populations. The second set relates more specifically to the use of the R2P in decision-making about the deployment of non-consensual force. Importantly, the use of force in this fashion is normally coercive rather than protective, in that it aims to coerce or compel recalcitrant belligerents to cease attacks on civilians and to permit their protection by peacekeepers.

Consensual deployments

The advent of the R2P corresponded with a renaissance of peace operations. In early 2008, the UN had seventeen operations and around 80,000 personnel deployed around the world (set to rise to 100,000). In addition, a range of regional organisations and 'coalitions of the willing' have undertaken their own peace operations. In most cases, military deployments are undertaken with the consent of the host government. The prevalence of host state consent points to the spread of the idea that international assistance aims to support governments in the fulfilment of their responsibilities and hence in realising their sovereignty. The UN missions in East Timor, Haiti, Côte D'Ivoire, DRC, Central African Republic/Chad and Liberia and the non-UN missions in the Solomon Islands and Afghanistan are primarily concerned with the restoration of state authority, capacity building, political reconciliation and with economic reconstruction. The DPKO's 'capstone doctrine' for peacekeeping confirms this view, reminding us that 'one of the principal functions of the UN's multi-dimensional peacekeeping operations is to help build the foundations of a functioning state in countries emerging from protracted internal conflict'.[52]

Sometimes consent is not freely given and may have to be coerced by a variety of non-military means, including threats of punitive action. One of the most obvious cases of coerced consent was the 1999 intervention in

East Timor. In mid-1999, Indonesian-backed militia reacted to a UN-sponsored referendum in favour of independence with a wave of mass murder and forced displacement. The need for international intervention was widely recognised, but pivotal states such as Australia maintained that it would be politically unfeasible and militarily dangerous to intervene without Indonesia's consent. The Indonesian government was reluctant to grant consent to what some prominent figures saw as an unwarranted international interference in its domestic affairs. To break the deadlock, the US threatened to veto the extension of World Bank loans to Indonesia unless it relented. In the wake of the Asian financial crisis (1997), the denial of loans would have crippled the Indonesian economy. The Indonesian government yielded and consented to the deployment of the Australian-led INTERFET force.[53]

Occasionally, consent might be granted by governments with questionable legitimacy, causing additional problems. The 2002 French intervention in Côte D'Ivoire, which paved the way for the subsequent deployment of UNOCI, provides a good example. Côte D'Ivoire's President Gbagbo seized power in a 1993 coup and then legitimised his rule through flawed elections. Once in government, Gbagbo favoured political allies, discriminated against whole regions, and silenced political dissent. In 2002, a combination of political disenchantment, the return of Côte D'Ivoirians from the war in neighbouring Sierra Leone and Liberia, and the infiltration of illegal trade networks led to a revolt against Gbagbo's rule. France responded swiftly to the president's request for intervention, establishing a buffer zone between the belligerents.[54]

Although military deployments for R2P purposes benefit from host state consent, once they are in place they should prioritise civilian protection over the need to maintain host government support in cases where one cannot be established except at the expense of the other. The role of UNOCI in Côte D'Ivoire provides a good example of a mission which has done precisely this. Initially deployed at Gbagbo's request, the UN mission refused to be a government puppet and set about fulfilling its mandate without prejudice towards the rebels. Building a sustainable peace required the peacekeepers to refuse to do the government's bidding and to institute reconciliation and political reform instead. Unsurprisingly, this attracted opposition from Gbagbo, and government forces engaged in sporadic attacks on French and UN forces. The international response was swift and decisive. The French conducted airstrikes, destroying the Côte D'Ivoirian air force and, within twenty-four hours of a French request, the Security Council imposed an arms embargo – preventing both the government and rebels from augmenting their military stockpiles. Although the political process remains weak and disjointed, it is ongoing. Moreover, the continuing presence of international forces has prevented conflict escalation, protecting endangered populations.[55] Thus far, international engagement has helped Côte D'Ivoire to avoid the worst of the mass atrocities that afflicted its West African neighbours.

Host state consent eases sovereignty concerns and makes it easier for peacekeepers to go about their duties; but, in addition to issues of dealing with illegitimate regimes, there are two further problems. First, if a genocidal regime grants consent, are the interveners entitled to act only in ways consented to – for instance by delivering aid but not using force to protect civilians? The R2P answer to this question is clearly 'no'. In cases where the limits of consent prevent the interveners from fulfilling their human protection role, the scope of consent should be overridden. The second problem is that governments might have non-humanitarian motives for requesting assistance, as in the cases of Yugoslavia's request for an arms embargo in 1991 and of Gbagbo's request for help in suppressing the rebels. Thus, whilst host government consent confers legal legitimacy and practical assistance, it is not enough to render the deployment of military force legitimate or illegitimate – a point recognised by the ICISS. This brings us to the question of when it is legitimate for states to resort to non-consensual force for human protection purposes through Chapter VII of the UN Charter.

Non-consensual force: The Darfur debate

According to many commentators, the crisis in Darfur posed the first real test of whether the R2P can guide international debate over the best way to respond to humanitarian emergencies. According to Lee Feinstein, 'if Darfur is the first "test case" of the responsibility to protect, there is no point in denying that the world has failed the entry exam'.[56] Or, as Nick Grono put it, 'until this first ethnic cleansing campaign of the twenty-first century is reversed, R2P will remain aspirational, not operational, and "never again" will be "yet again" once again'.[57]

The R2P has certainly played a role in the debate. Some states invoked the R2P to prod the Security Council into action. In July 2004, the Philippines argued that Sudan has failed in its duty to protect its citizens and that international action was warranted. The reference to the R2P could not have been clearer: 'Sovereignty also entails the responsibility of a State to protect its people. If it is unable or unwilling to do so, the international community has the responsibility to help that State achieve such capacity and such will and, in extreme necessity, to assume such responsibility itself.'[58] Others, however, used R2P logic to argue against sanctions and military intervention. The UK expressed concern about proposed sanctions on the grounds that the Sudanese government had the primary responsibility to protect the civilians of Darfur, whereas sanctions would not help it in this task. A similar view was aired by states such as China, Russia and Pakistan – states who argued against Security Council activism on the grounds that the primary responsibility lies with the government of Sudan, working in cooperation with the AU. This view was endorsed by some senior UN officials. Jan Pronk argued that, 'if the government is unable to fully protect its citizens by itself', it should 'request and accept assistance from the international community'.[59] The underlying problem here is that, in the hands of skilled diplomats, R2P language may be used to justify a range of different proposals, inhibiting consensus over collective action in response to genuine humanitarian emergencies as much as enabling such consensus. Nor is it likely that the criteria proposed by the ICISS but rejected by world leaders would have helped. As we have noted in Chapter 2, agreement on criteria does not necessarily produce agreement on how to proceed in particular cases. The best that criteria can hope to achieve is to guide debate and to focus attention on the needs of the victims. As adopted by world leaders in 2005, the R2P principle succeeded inasmuch as states agreed that the Security Council ought to be involved in the protection of Darfuri civilians but disagreed on the best way to achieve that goal. It is unlikely that the ICISS criteria would have helped break the deadlock in the council because, when it comes to using the criteria in specific cases, even individuals and groups which share a deep commitment to the R2P and interpret its requirements in similar ways can exhibit profound differences of opinion.

Gareth Evans, the International Crisis Group, Ramesh Thakur and Francis Deng all argued against non-consensual military force in Darfur on the grounds that it would do more harm than good. They were supported in this by a leading commentator on African affairs, Alex de Waal – whose own position on the deployment of peacekeepers actually changed between 2004 and 2006. Initially, he argued that foreign troops could make a 'formidable difference' to the lives of Darfuri civilians, writing in July 2004 that:

> The immediate life and death needs of Darfur's people cannot wait for these negotiations to mature. A British brigade could make a formidable difference to the situation. It could escort aid supplies into rebel-held areas, and provide aerial surveillance, logistics and back-up to ceasefire monitoring, helping to give Darfurian villagers the confidence to return to their homes and pick up their lives.[60]

Soon after, de Waal was invited to help the AU in its efforts to broker a political settlement, but the negotiators failed to persuade all but one of the rebel groups to sign the Darfur Peace Agreement. The experience of coming 'agonisingly close' to a political settlement no doubt contributed to de Waal's change of heart on the potential of non-consensual force. In 2006 he wrote:

> The knock-down argument against humanitarian invasion is that it won't work. The idea of foreign troops fighting their way into Darfur and disarming the *Janjaweed* militia by force is sheer fantasy. Practicality dictates that a peacekeeping force in Darfur cannot enforce its will on any resisting armed groups without entering into a protracted and unwinnable counter-insurgency in which casualties are inevitable. The only way peacekeeping works is with consent: the agreement of the Sudan government and the support of the majority of the Darfurian populace . . . Without this, UN troops will not only fail but will make the plight of Darfurians even worse.[61]

Later, de Waal maintained that, 'however attractive it might be from a distance, actually providing physical protection for Darfurians with international troops is not feasible'.[62] Which version is more accurate – that foreign forces could make a 'formidable difference' to Darfuri civilians or that this position was 'sheer fantasy'? Francis Deng supported de Waal's 2006 opinion. Non-consensual intervention, he concluded, would 'complicate and aggravate' the crisis by increasing the level of violence and by undermining the potential for cooperation from the Sudanese government.[63]

In October 2006, the ICG issued a report where it applied to Darfur the ICISS criteria on the use of force.[64] The report found that the Darfur crisis had crossed the 'just cause' threshold, so that intervention would satisfy the 'proper purpose' criterion and would be proportionate. On two grounds, however, the ICG found that non-consensual intervention would fail the ICISS test. First of all, it would fail the last resort test. The ICG concluded that 'much more still can and should be done by the international community before non-consensual military intervention is considered', pointing to targeted sanctions against government and *Janjaweed* figures; to the provision of support for the AU mission in Darfur; to the imposition of a no-fly zone; and to the deployment of a rapid reaction force to Chad to prevent the conflict's spread.

The second reason for rejecting non-consensual force was the 'balance of consequences', which requires that more good than harm must be anticipated. The ICG argued that 'a non-consensual deployment would be desperately difficult . . . and the overall security situation for civilians in the region could well worsen'. The group identified five key reasons for this:

1   Logistics would be problematic because of Darfur's geographic location and of the need for goods to be shipped across the country from Port Sudan.

2   The risk to civilians would increase prior to the deployment of forces – civilians would be left 'hostage' to their tormentors during this period.

3   There would be an 'inevitable collapse of humanitarian relief operations'.

4   Non-consensual intervention would jeopardise the Naivasha peace in the south and undermine UNMIS.

5   Intervention might provoke an Iraq-style insurgency, called for by al Qaeda.

For these reasons, the ICG argued that the world's response to the Darfur tragedy should involve non-military measures, in order to persuade the Sudanese government to consent to a UN/AU hybrid peace operation (UNAMID).

How apt are these arguments? The first thing to note is that the ICG quite rightly pointed out that no governments were calling for non-consensual intervention and that it would have proved impossible to build support in the Security Council for non-consensual intervention. The same argument, of course, could apply to some of the ICG's recommendations. For example, the US spent two years trying to persuade the council to adopt key proposals supported by the ICG such as targeted sanctions and a no-fly zone – and to no avail. Moreover, the problem with the last resort criterion is that it provides no clear guidance on when non-military means are exhausted. How long should non-military measures be attempted or applied without effect before military measures are contemplated? Theoretically, there are *always* non-violent alternatives – just not always effective ones.[65] Finally, Justin Morris and Nicholas Wheeler have argued that, had a group of western states sought a mandate for force from the Security Council, China and Russia might have been shamed into acquiescing.[66] Even if this is perhaps a little too optimistic, it is worth remembering in this regard that UNAMID was authorised under Chapter VII of the Charter after the Security Council identified the situation in Darfur as a continuing threat to international peace and security, was mandated to use force to protect civilians, its own personnel and humanitarian workers, and assigned a mandate to be the largest to date of the UN's twenty-first century peace operations (Resolution 1769, 31 July 2007). Although it reaffirmed the international society's support for Sudan's territorial integrity and it indicated a strong preference for cooperation with the government, nowhere did Resolution 1769 *require* the consent of the Sudanese government.

But what of the argument that non-consensual intervention would have done more harm than good? This question gets to the very heart of the limits of what criteria can achieve; for, even when shorn of political interests, answers to this question can only ever be predictive judgements, based on past experiences and interpretations of the relevant situation and of what is proposed. To illustrate the problem, I will set out an equally plausible case for non-consensual intervention by reference to the issues raised by the ICG on the basis of alternative assessments of the situation and likely consequences. I should stress that I am using these points only to demonstrate the limits of criteria and not to argue the case for non-consensual intervention.

Logistics

The ICG rightly pointed out that the bulk of humanitarian aid was shipped through Port Sudan. It went on to assume that this port would be made unavailable in the event of a non-consensual intervention and that the use of ports in southern Sudan would be 'expensive' and would endanger the Naivasha peace. These assumptions are not necessarily well founded. The World Food Programme, for example, delivered food aid to Darfur not through Port Sudan, but through Tripoli in Libya.[67] In 2004, UNHCR launched a major emergency relief effort which used aircraft flying out of Chad – thus by-passing the Port Sudan supply route altogether. It is also worth noting that in 2007, when France suggested the deployment of forces to open a humanitarian corridor, it envisaged the movement of humanitarian supplies eastwards from Chad into Darfur, not through Port Sudan. Therefore good grounds exist for thinking that there are viable alternatives to the use of Port Sudan, were the Sudanese government to close that route.

Immediate risk to civilians

It is not clear why there would be an immediate risk to civilians prior to deployment. The civilian population was already hostage to their tormentors. It could be argued that, if anything, the impending arrival of a robust force empowered to apprehend individuals indicted by the ICC would deter rather than accelerate attacks. Moreover, a well-equipped non-consensual intervention could have rapidly deployed forward elements and provided immediate air coverage, deterring such attacks even further.

Collapse of humanitarian relief operations
Again, no reason is given as to why non-consensual intervention would collapse humanitarian relief operations. By 2007 there were approximately 11,000 aid workers operating in and around Darfur.[68] The main problem they confronted was not a shortage of supplies, but an insecure and unstable environment, which made it difficult to move around and transport relief to where it was most needed. In the first few months of 2008, for example, forty-five trucks conveying humanitarian aid were hijacked and twenty-three drivers remained unaccounted for.[69] As de Waal argued in 2004, a military deployment could have protected aid workers and opened humanitarian corridors.

Jeopardise Naivasha
Several governments were concerned that efforts to coerce the Sudanese government would impair the implementation of the peace agreement with the south. This was a real possibility, but not an inevitability. International society could have used a variety of sticks and carrots to persuade Khartoum not to pursue this course of action, targeting its oil revenue for instance. Moreover, Khartoum's overt non-compliance would have increased the likelihood of the south's eventual separation from Sudan – which is provided for by Naivasha. In addition, the Naivasha peace is overseen by a large UN force – UNMIS – and this fact seriously limits Khartoum's ability to act as spoiler.

Insurgency
The ICG was right to point out that al Qaeda, the Khartoum government and various militia all threatened to wage a bloody insurgency against foreign interveners. This threat was made apparent by the October 2007 rebel attack on the AU peacekeepers based at Haskanita – an attack which left ten peacekeepers dead – and by the July 2008 attack by *Janjaweed* militia on AU/UN peacekeepers, which left seven dead. However, little assessment has been done to ascertain the seriousness of the overall threat and to establish what measures the interveners could take to prevent this from happening. In the case of both attacks described above, AU/UN peacekeepers had insufficient firepower and no air support. It is not unusual for perpetrators of mass atrocities to threaten those who come to stop them – Kosovo Serbs, pro-Indonesian militia in East Timor and 'West Side Boys' in Sierra Leone threatened dire consequences for potential interveners. Intervention always involves risks and costs. There is no solid evidence to suggest a higher risk in Darfur than in other places where

peacekeepers come under attack (e.g. DRC), nor is it clear that a well-equipped force would be unable to deal with the risk effectively.

It is also possible to put forth equally plausible 'last resort' and 'balance of consequences' arguments in favour of non-consensual intervention. In terms of last resort, the ICG report came two and a half years into the crisis. At that time the Security Council failed to take measures to protect Darfuri civilians, and the measures it did adopt had little positive effect on the ground. Of course, the ICG was right to argue that non-military options must remain open, but none of the options it recommended promised protection for Darfur's civilians. Ultimately, the UN was able to persuade the government of Sudan to give its consent to a hybrid peace operation in 2007, but how many Darfuri civilians were killed in the interim? If the R2P starts from the victim's perspective, it is not too hard to conclude that the 'last resort' was reached a long time before October 2006. What, though, of the balance of consequences? If we only accept that the worst-case scenario set out by the ICG is unlikely to happen, or that a large and well-equipped force could manage the risks effectively, then it could be argued that the balance of consequences tilts decisively in favour of non-consensual intervention.

From this perspective, if the Security Council had authorised intervention to protect civilians, this would have satisfied the criteria set out by ICISS. It is hard to envision the ICG opposing an intervention in such circumstances, especially one that has succeeded. My main point here, though, is not to argue the case one way or the other, but to show that even among supporters of the R2P there remains the possibility of profound disagreements on the best way to act in particular crises. Thus, despite the headline-grabbing qualities of criteria for intervention decisions, they are of limited utility in practice.

When it comes to the use of force, the R2P has a much more pronounced role to play in shaping the way military forces go about their business once deployed. This involves the use of military force for civilian protection purposes, as opposed to the use of force to coerce compliance.

How to Act

The past five years have seen a dramatic transformation in the place of civilian protection in peace operations. Traditionally, peacekeepers were to remain impartial and neutral and were entitled to use force only in self-defence. All too often – as the fate of UNAMIR in Rwanda attests – peacekeepers lacked the wherewithal to defend themselves, let alone the civilian population. Only infrequently was the protection of civilians considered to be a core part of the peacekeepers' mandate. What came to be described as a 'culture of impartiality' led UN peacekeepers in Rwanda and Bosnia to treat the aggressors and the victims as moral equals and to place concerns about force protection and diplomatic interests ahead of civilian protection.[70] Troops operating in the UN 'safe areas' in Bosnia, for instance, were – not unambiguously – mandated to use force in order to protect the civilians, and they were chronically under-resourced. When the Security Council first began debating safe areas in 1993, the secretariat advised that around 34,000 new troops were necessary to police them. The US, the UK and France considered this estimate to be 'excessive', and the Security Council chose instead to authorise an extra 7,000 troops. In the event, the UK and France refused to extend their contribution to UNPROFOR and Spain, the US, Norway, Sweden, Russia and Canada all refused requests to contribute troops for the safe areas. In the end only around 2,000 new soldiers arrived to protect the safe areas. That the safe areas policy failed so badly in 1995, resulting in the massacre of 7,600 men and boys in Srebrenica, was predominantly due to an unworkable mandate and to chronic under-resourcing.[71] The UN's subsequent report on the genocide in Srebrenica issued a call for the organisation to take a stand by rethinking the concept of impartiality. The report found that 'the cardinal lesson of Srebrenica is that a deliberate and systematic attempt to terrorise, expel or murder an entire people must be met decisively with all necessary means', and that the use of force is sometimes required 'to bring a halt to the planned and systematic killing and expulsion of civilians'.[72]

A year later, the Brahimi report concluded that, once the UN Security Council was committed to deploying a peace operation, it had a responsibility to ensure that the mission was properly authorised and staffed, if it was to implement the mandate successfully and protect both UN personnel and the civilians in its care. As the Brahimi panel put it, UN peace operations must be capable of projecting 'credible force' in order 'to confront the lingering forces of war and violence, with the ability and determination to defeat them'.[73] This stance raised two fundamental challenges for the UN: first, confronting the 'forces of war and violence' involved abandoning the organisation's 'culture of impartiality'. Second, widening the scope of peace operations in this way raised practical questions about what is needed to protect vulnerable populations. I will briefly address each question in turn.[74]

In order to protect civilians, the UN needs to be able to identify the sources of threat and to understand whether those actors might be brought into the peace process by non-violent means (and, if so, how) before it can begin to design appropriate tactics for using force against persistent spoilers and to calibrate the limited use of force with the wider peacebuilding effort. The Brahimi report took an important step towards all this by redefining the meaning of 'impartiality' in peace operations. 'Impartiality for United Nations operations', the report argued,

> must therefore mean adherence to the principles of the Charter: where one party to a peace agreement clearly and incontrovertibly is violating its terms, continued equal treatment of all parties by the United Nations can in the best case result in ineffectiveness and in the worst may amount to complicity with evil.[75]

In other words, impartiality should be understood, not as a form of neutrality – as it has been in the past – but as a commitment to treating all parties equally in relation to their compliance with the relevant mandates and peace agreements. Read this way, impartiality does not involve reluctance to use force in order to protect civilians, but a readiness to do so irrespective of the source of the threat. The cultural shift from blind neutrality to identifying the sources of threat was helped by the advent of the ICC and by the use of expert panels in relation to targeted sanctions – both of which have forced the Security Council to begin identifying and naming specific individuals and groups responsible for attacks on civilians.

However, traditional sovereignty concerns have made it typically easier to identify non-state threats than to identify threats emanating from governments. To date, the Security Council's targeting of Charles Taylor and of the Taliban regime after September 11, and the use of force by the French against government forces in Côte D'Ivoire, provide the few clear existing cases of the UN and its peacekeepers identifying governments as troublemakers and taking action against them. These cases should be contrasted with the reluctance of many world leaders to identify the Sudanese government as complicit in the killing in Darfur. On the other hand, the Security Council has been much quicker to identify threats to the civilian population emanating from non-state actors such as the Lord's Resistance Army in Uganda, UNITA in Angola, the RUF and the West Side Boys in Sierra Leone, and the Democratic Forces for Liberation of the Congo (FDLR), Allied Democratic Forces (ADF) and Union of Congolese Patriots (UPC) in the DRC and to develop comprehensive strategies for dealing with them. In Sierra Leone and the DRC, those strategies involved the extensive use of force against militia groups guilty of targeting civilians and disrupting the peace.

The second challenge is the practical one of developing concrete measures to protect civilians. Although much work remains to be done, there have been significant strides in the past few years that provide us with a clearer picture of what is required – though much less work has been done on how these requirements might be met. We noted earlier that in 2002 the Security Council issued an *Aide Mémoire* identifying measures necessary to protect civilians which has been used to guide mission reporting. Two years later, the Stimson Centre organised a series of workshops to identify what was required for civilian protection, as a preliminary to identifying the sorts of capacities needed. The workshops identified twenty-five tasks such as securing safe corridors and the passage of convoys; establishing safe havens; preventing mob violence; disarmament and demobilisation; coercive disarmament; de-mining; enforcing curfews; protecting VIPs; eliminating special threats; stopping hate media; training local security forces; and the direct use of force against killers.[76] A year later, UN officials began calling for deeper consideration of how civilian protection might be realised. In his June 2005 briefing to the Security Council, Under-Secretary-General for Humanitarian Affairs Jan Egeland, argued as follows:

> We must provide better physical security. Humanitarian presence is not enough. The creation of a secure environment for displaced populations should be a primary objective of peacekeeping operations. We need strategic deployment around camps to provide area security for the displaced, we need it in areas of unrest to prevent new displacement, and in areas of origin to facilitate voluntary and safe return.

He concluded that 'the provision of protection against violence needs to be incorporated into the concept of peacekeeping operations and clear guidance developed'.[77]

Building the capacity to achieve this goal requires developments in three interrelated areas: unambiguous mandating; the political will to provide the necessary resources; and civilian protection doctrine. The connection between these three elements was recognised by Boutros-Ghali in the early 1990s, when he identified a 'chasm' between 'the tasks entrusted to the organisation' and the means provided to it. 'Nothing is more dangerous for a peacekeeping operation', the Secretary-General argued, 'than to ask it to use force when its existing composition, armament, logistic support and deployment deny it the capacity to do so.'[78]

The Brahimi report recognised the important connection between mandates and resources. Whilst insisting that peacekeepers who witness violence against civilians should 'be presumed to be authorised to stop it, within their means', the report also cautioned against the granting of 'blanket mandates' which might be unachievable, given the scale of the threat and the limited resources of the peacekeepers. In order to bridge this gap, Brahimi advised that missions should only be given specific civilian protection mandates when the council is prepared to provide the resources necessary to fulfil that mandate, and that in other cases the place of civilian protection should be carefully limited. The report made the following observation:

> The potentially large mismatch between desired objective and resources available to meet it raises the prospect of continuing disappointment with United Nations follow-through in this area. If an operation is given a mandate to protect civilians, therefore, it must be given the specific resources needed to carry out that mandate.[79]

The Security Council has taken heed of this advice in two ways. In the past few years, peace operations have tended to be larger than their predecessors. Missions in Sierra Leone, Liberia, DRC, Sudan and Darfur all – at one stage or another – had more than 10,000 soldiers. Furthermore, the combination of better coordination between the Security Council and the troop contributing nations, the UN's stand-by forces arrangements, and closer cooperation between the UN and regional organisations has produced a progressive bridging of the gap between the number of troops mandated by the Security Council and the number actually deployed. This additional capacity has permitted UN forces to engage in limited enforcement operations against groups involved in attacks on civilians in the DRC, Sierra Leone and Haiti.

Taking heed of the fact that it is never likely either to authorise or to generate large enough forces to provide comprehensive security for civilians, the Security Council has also been careful to limit the scope of its civilian protection mandates, though there are signs that the council has begun to roll back these limits when necessary. Typically, when drafting civilian protection mandates, the council has demonstrated a distinct preference for limiting their scope by including various caveats. Examples of these limitations can be found in the mandates for the missions in Sudan (UNMIS), Liberia (UNMIL) and Côte D'Ivoire (UNOCI). UNMIS was mandated 'to facilitate and coordinate, within its capabilities and in its areas of deployment, the voluntary return of refugees and internally displacement persons, and humanitarian assistance, *inter alia*, by helping to establish the necessary security' (Resolution 1590, 24 March 2005). The civilian protection man-dates handed down to UNMIL and UNOCI were more or less identical: 'to protect civilians under immediate threat of physical violence, within its capabilities' (Resolution 1509, 19 September 2003; Resolution 1528, 27 February 2004).

By contrast, the MONUC mission in DRC was originally given a narrow civilian protection mandate, which was gradually extended. Initially, MONUC was originally authorised to

> facilitate humanitarian assistance and human rights monitoring, with particular attention to vulnerable groups including women, children and demobilized child soldiers, as MONUC deems within its capabilities and under acceptable security condition . . . MONUC may take necessary action, in the areas of deployment of its infantry battalions and as it deems it within its capabilities, to protect United Nations and co-located JMC personnel, facilities, installations and equipment, ensure the security and freedom of movement of its personnel, and protect civilians under imminent threat of physical violence (Resolution 1291, 24 February 2000)

This limiting tendency was reinforced by the council mandate handed down to the French-led intervention in the eastern DRC town of Bunia. Resolution 1484 (30 May 2003) authorised the deployment of troops to protect the airport, IDPs housed in camps in Bunia and, 'if the situation requires it', to 'contribute to the safety of the civilian population'. In the face of continuing violence against civilians, however, the limits on MONUC's civilian protection role were dropped in 2004. Tripling the size of the UN's military presence in the DRC, Resolution 1565 (1 October 2004) authorised the force to 'ensure the protection of civilians, including humanitarian personnel, under imminent threat of physical violence' without any limiting clause. The UN's mission in Burundi was given a wide protection mandate from the outset, Resolution 1545 granting ONUB a mandate to protect civilians without the usual limits.[80]

These resolutions exhibit a preference for limiting the role of civilian protection to regions covered by the mandate and the capabilities of the peacekeepers, though the council has occasionally waived these limits, as in DRC and Burundi. It is, of course, sensible to match mandate and means, but the Brahimi panel called for missions with civilian protection mandates to be given 'the specific resources needed'. This is not the same as the Security Council devising mandates with the assumption of under-resourcing built in.[81] In practice, it means that, although the council has adopted the principle that civilian protection ought to be a core function of peace operations, it has often shied away from efforts to actualise it, choosing instead to limit the geographic scope of civilian protection. This creates three further problems, identified by Ian Johnstone. First, peace operations are unlikely to fulfil local expectations of protection, which undermines their legitimacy. Second, geographically limited mandates can encourage population displacement, as civilians move to seek UN protection. Third, protecting civilians in one area can leave civilians more vulnerable in other areas and runs the risk of creating zones of impunity.[82]

It is hard to see how the problem of capacity is likely to be resolved in the short term. Although contemporary peacekeeping requires large numbers of highly trained and well-equipped troops in order to be effective, those countries which are most able to provide such troops are increasingly disinclined to do so. At the end of the 1990s, around a quarter of all UN peacekeepers were contributed by 'the West', broadly defined to include states such as Australia and Japan. At the beginning of 2008, that figure had fallen to less than 10 per cent.[83] There is a variety of reasons for this. Western governments are preoccupied by non-UN missions in Iraq, Afghanistan and the Balkans; their leaders are less prepared to send troops to regions thought strategically insignificant; westerners are reluctant to place their troops under the command of non-westerners. The upshot is that there is a difference between the states which mandate peace operations and advocate the R2P, robust doctrines and civilian protection, and the states which actually contribute most of the troops to UN operations.

As the number of peacekeepers required continues to grow, the burden will fall on developing states, irrespective of whether these forces are best suited to the task. In the medium term, hopes are pinned on the development of regional capacities like the AU's African Stand-by Force (ASF), through which the AU plans to build five regional brigades capable of deploying 20,000 troops by 2010. The US, Britain, France and the UN have all invested in the development of an African peacekeeping capacity. The US established the Global Peace Operations Initiative in 2004 with the aim of training 75,000 peacekeepers, mainly from Africa, over fifteen years. To date, troops from a dozen African countries have received peacekeeping training under this programme, and in 2005 Americans trained some 14,000 African troops for deployment in Darfur.[84] Likewise, Britain's conflict prevention strategy involves the training of 17,000 African troops as peacekeepers and the French RECAMP programme is focusing on training the ASF. The development of regional capacity, in Africa especially, is an attractive option. Many sub-Saharan African states have endorsed the R2P, and a regional capacity to conduct civilian protection operations would provide a protective capacity, while also reassuring those who remain concerned about the R2P being a kind of western interventionism in disguise. However, the ASF timetable has already slipped by over twelve months, and the AU's inability to sustain a moderately sized force of 7,000 in Darfur suggests that it will be many years before it is capable of taking the lead in large operations. Moreover, training programmes are not being reinforced with initiatives to provide African forces with key capabilities such as air mobility and logistics, nor is there much being done to increase the financial sustainability of AU missions. The fact that some AU troops in Darfur went for six months without pay despite purportedly heightened levels of global engagement does not bode well. Finally, the donors' political interests have sometimes influenced the scope and nature of their assistance. For example, the US refuses to train South African peacekeepers because of that country's refusal to guarantee US personnel immunity from the ICC.[85]

Although the development of regional capacity is both politically and operationally important, it is no panacea for immediate problems relating to the staffing and resourcing of peace operations. Other options that have been canvassed include the creation of a 15,000 strong UN Emergency Peace Service (UNEPS) or an International Marshals service. Both proposals are in their infancy and, although there is real merit to both, they have high hurdles to clear before they can become credible proposals.[86] Not least, advocates would have to persuade reluctant states about the merits of granting the UN an independent military capacity, or even modest increments of it. In addition, there are difficult constitutional questions to address and myriad operational problems. Not least, the UNEPS proposal envisages a unit of 15,000 personnel, deploying globally to prevent genocide. It seems overambitious to believe that a force of that size would be large and effective enough to prevent genocide in places like Darfur, Rwanda and Bosnia.

This brings us to the question of what sort of doctrine is needed to guide peacekeepers in their civilian protection duties. Traditionally, states have opposed the formulation of UN doctrine, on the grounds that it is for themselves to determine such matters for their own armed forces. Moreover, the DPKO has lacked the strategic capacity to develop a peacekeeping doctrine. Brahimi's call for the DPKO to be given a capacity for strategic planning and analysis was sidelined, principally due to concerns about the potential for such a capability to challenge the decision-making authority of member states. However, important recent progress has been made – for instance, in terms of thinking about the meaning of key concepts such as 'impartiality'. In this, the DPKO's Best Practices Section – created to collect and disseminate the world's best thinking on peace operations and to conduct investigations about lessons learned – has played a key role. In 2003 the section released a handbook of guidelines for peacekeepers. The *Handbook on United Nations Multidimensional Peacekeeping Operations* referred to the fact that some peacekeeping operations 'may include the need to protect vulnerable civilian populations', but would do this only if given the capacity to do so. Moreover, the handbook did not elaborate on how peacekeepers might go about fulfilling that role, except in a brief discussion of the role of peacekeepers in providing a secure environment.[87] Thus:

> Military forces, as part of a UN peacekeeping operation, are often tasked with providing a secure environment to allow other aspects of the mission's mandate or peace process to be implemented. A secure environment is generally a precondition for moving ahead on several elements of peace agreements . . . As part of the task of providing a secure environment, the military component may be asked to provide a visible deterrent presence, control movement and access through checkpoints, provide armed escort for safety and to facilitate access, conduct cordon and search operations, control crowds or confiscate weapons.[88]

In December 2005, Kofi Annan called for the development of an inventory of terms and items of peacekeeping doctrine designed to address questions including the protection of vulnerable populations.[89] Shortly afterwards, in March 2006, member states signalled their willingness to address the question of UN doctrine, with the General Assembly's Special Committee on Peacekeeping calling upon the secretariat to prepare a glossary of terminology for 'further development of a peacekeeping doctrine, guiding principles and concepts'.[90] The development of what has become labelled 'capstone doctrine' for UN peace operations has progressed apace, being led by the DPKO's Best Practices Section. In the second draft, discussed at a March 2007 workshop in Accra, Ghana, civilian protection was identified in passing as one of six 'principles of peacekeeping'.[91] In the third draft, opened for public consultations, however, civilian protection was demoted from a 'principle' to one out of four 'cross-cutting responsibilities' which peacekeepers are expected to fulfil even if they do not have a specific mandate for it.[92] DPKO insiders report that the change in emphasis was driven by member states who were concerned that, when coupled with the R2P, strong references to the protection of civilians might provide a way for Western states to legitimise interventionism under the rubric of peacekeeping.[93] The doctrine also stopped short of specifying precisely how peacekeepers were to protect civilians.

The very idea that the UN should develop a capstone doctrine for peacekeeping and that this doctrine should include civilian protection marks a significant breakthrough even if the end product was significantly watered-down. It is perhaps unsurprising, though, that the UN has yet to develop clear guidelines for the way military peacekeepers should go about protecting civilians. As Victoria Holt and Tobias Berkman have recently demonstrated, key states such as Canada, the UK and the US, as well as organisations like NATO, have been slow to include specific guidelines on civilian protection in their own military doctrines. Whilst their doctrine points to civilian protection as a possible task or goal, none singles it out or elaborates on how military force should be used to accomplish it. Within the wider UN community, however, there is obvious scepticism about the expansion of peacekeeping so as to include the use of force for human protection purposes. For instance, speaking on behalf of the NAM, Morocco insisted that the 'establishment by the United Nations of any peace operation under Chapter VII of the United Nations Charter, or extension of a mandate, should not only be based on the consent of the parties, but also on the non-use of force, except in self-defence'.[94]

To summarise: there has been significant progress in thinking about the use of military peacekeepers to protect endangered populations. Learning from the disasters of Rwanda and Bosnia, it is almost routine nowadays for the Security Council to write the protection of civilians into peacekeeping mandates. Significant obstacles remain, however. First of all, civilian protection mandates remain vaguely worded and provide little in the way of specific guidance. As part of the UN's doctrinal consultations, it would be well worth repeating the work of the Interlaken process on the wording of the resolutions concerning sanctions – in other words, considering the sorts of language that ought to be used in peacekeeping resolutions and the development of standard meanings. Second, there is a clear crisis of capacity, which is caused by the growing demand for peace operations, by the West's reluctance to provide troops, and by the inevitable slowness of regional capacity building. A clear case can be made that those states who have championed the R2P should play more of a role in realising this principle by contributing more both to regional capacity building and to contemporary peace operations. Finally, although support for UN capstone doctrine is a significant breakthrough, more work needs to be done to advance that doctrine as well as to ensure that civilian protection receives the status it deserves and that the final product provides concrete guidance as to how peacekeepers should go about fulfilling the twenty-five protection related tasks identified by the Stimson Centre.

Conclusion

As this chapter has demonstrated, the 'reaction' component of the R2P involves much more than the non-consensual use of force, though there are some things which only the application of military force can do – such as to rescue from genocide an endangered population. Even here, though, it is important to follow Weiss and Hubert in distinguishing between measures aimed at coercing compliance and measures that seek to provide protection. In most cases, an emerging crisis might not warrant full-scale non-consensual force, with all the attendant risks. Sometimes the risks might be simply too great, or there might be insufficient consensus. In such situations there remain a host of measures that the international community might use to prevent or halt genocide and mass atrocities. These involve non-forcible measures such as targeted sanctions and humanitarian support to IDPs and the deployment of military forces with the consent, albeit sometimes coerced, of the host state.

The past decade has seen substantial improvements in the effectiveness of the measures discussed in this chapter. The Security Council's engagement with the R2P, the shift from comprehensive to targeted sanctions and the place of civilian protection in peace operations have all improved the world's ability to protect threatened populations. Significant political and practical obstacles remain, however. Politically, many states remain hostile to measures which they interpret as challenging traditional sovereignty, or which might enhance the UN's capacity for independent action. It is for this reason that measures seen to be helping governments to maintain order and realise their sovereignty have found it easier to win support than those measures that could be turned against states themselves. Typically, this principle has manifested itself in a paradoxical situation where member states are prepared to endorse robust interventionism on an ad hoc basis but are reluctant to support even relatively small initiatives to institutionalise measures designed to improve the effectiveness of those interventions. In many cases, effective action is possible without anyone having to resort to non-consensual force; but we should not be lulled into thinking that there will not be cases in the future where non-consensual force is necessary. In such cases, the criteria set out by the ICISS might help to guide debate; but they will not make it easier to forge a consensus, nor will they remove the need for political leaders to make difficult judgements.

Myriad practical challenges also remain. As the Security Council's use of targeted sanctions becomes more sophisticated, so its need for precise and up-to-date guidance will increase. The use of expert panels has been highly effective in improving the council's activities in this area, and there are good reasons for thinking that it should revisit the proposal for the creation of a permanent 'embargoes unit' to conduct this work on a systematic basis. Once again, though, such a unit smacks of building independent capacity for the UN and is therefore likely to run into opposition. The same dynamic could be seen in relation to civilian protection, where once again the Security Council had been proactive, by incorporating the use of military and police forces to protect civilians on a case-by-case basis, but has proved much less willing to improve the UN's institutional capacity.

Finally, the whole question of non-consensual military force – the original impetus behind ICISS, though not behind the broader idea of sovereignty as responsibility (see Chapters 1 and 2) – remains particularly thorny. Among the dozens of international initiatives geared towards realising the R2P, there has been minimal movement on this one. We still have no way of judging when the 'last resort' is reached, or how the 'balance of consequences' should be calculated. At what point should non-state actors be prepared to argue that consensual or non-military means have failed? And who should arbitrate between different judgements? In practice, political leaders will continue to make these judgements on the basis of the same balance of interests, expectations and humanitarian concerns that guided them prior to the release of the ICISS report. It might be wise, therefore, for R2P advocates to put aside the questions of criteria and decision-making, recognising certain inescapable political facts, and to focus instead on practical questions associated with improving the effectiveness of those measures designed to reduce the number of times when political leaders are confronted with a choice between standing aside and sending in the Marines.

6

Rebuilding

Beyond the obvious concerns about neo-imperialism set out in Chapter 2, the basic principle that international society has a responsibility to help states and societies in rebuilding after genocide or mass atrocities is one of the most uncontroversial ideas associated with the R2P. There is a clear link between assistance for rebuilding institutions, the rule of law, shattered economies and basic infrastructure and the strengthening of state sovereignty. In short, post-conflict rebuilding is chiefly about enabling and empowering states and societies to establish sustainable and legitimate peace. It is about building the local institutions necessary to protect civilians in the long term. This point was made most clearly by Donald Steinberg, Vice-President of the International Crisis Group, in a 2006 address on Burundi to the UN's Peacebuilding Commission (PBC). Steinberg proposed the following view:

> Some may worry that these measures would undercut Burundi's sovereignty. Instead, the exact opposite is the case. The PBC can empower the Burundian people and government to harness the good will and hard resources of the international community to end the cycle of violence, political unrest, and economic upheaval that has shadowed Burundi for most of the past half-century.[1]

It is easier to make the argument that the R2P strengthens sovereignty in the wake of protracted civil wars and state failure than it is to make the same argument in relation to the types of circumstances described in the previous chapters. This is not to say that the 'responsibility to rebuild' has avoided criticism. Some figures close to the R2P project question whether there is a link at all between the R2P and peacebuilding.[2] That connection, however, is made plain by a second set of criticisms of the R2P's approach to peacebuilding. Cosmopolitan-minded writers like Daniel Warner and Mark Duffield criticise the principle by arguing that, although the R2P recognises the fact that state sovereignty can breed human insecurity, its solution is simply to replace one type of state with another, whilst leaving the principle of sovereignty intact.[3] This is exactly what the R2P advocates – the idea that the best way to protect civilians from genocide and mass atrocities is through an international society of responsible states – and it is only through commitment to peacebuilding (and nation-building and state-building) on the part of the 'responsibility to rebuild' that the R2P engages directly with the question of how one builds a world of responsible states. Of course, this principle will not satisfy the critical cosmopolitans, but recent history teaches that for the foreseeable future responsible governments *are* the actors best placed to protect their citizens. Without its 'rebuilding' component, the R2P would be a doctrine of responsible sovereignty shorn of guidance about how responsible sovereigns might be fostered.

There is even less agreement on what form the 'responsibility to rebuild' should take and on the types of policies needed to build sustainable peace. On the one hand there is a broad neo-liberal consensus among the key agencies involved in post-conflict reconstruction (especially the World Bank) which holds that the key to long-term peace lies in rapid processes of democratisation and market liberalisation designed to attract foreign investment and to stimulate growth. In recent years, though, it has become increasingly clear that this model is deeply problematic. Rapid democratisation can produce triggers for renewed violence and might inadvertently legitimise those very elites who caused conflict and state collapse in the first place. Market liberalisation can weaken already fragile states and exacerbate economic inequalities, one of the key causes of civil war.

In addition to these questions about the most appropriate path to take, there are questions about the way in which international assistance is delivered. Some espouse a large and highly directive international engagement, typified by the transitional administrations set up in Kosovo and East Timor, whereby the UN assumed both the role of peacebuilder and that of sovereign. Others argue that these are impractical and expensive endeavours, which deliver uncertain results and deny local ownership. They prefer the 'light footprint' approach, developed by Lakhdar Brahimi as a strategy for post-war Afghanistan. Finally, there are myriad practical questions about how external actors can best support the transformation of societies torn by war into havens of stable peace.

There are three things we do know about peacebuilding, however. First, it is critically important for the *prevention* of genocide and mass atrocities. The single most important contributing factor to the outbreak of civil war is a past history of civil war, especially in the previous five years. A recent history of war can increase the likelihood of further war by as much as forty per cent. Indeed, almost fifty per cent of peace agreements collapse within the first five years.[4] Effective peacebuilding is therefore a necessary component of prevention.

Second, we know that, for all its other faults, the UN is relatively good at peacebuilding when it is given adequate resources and political support, and it has a significantly better track record than the US when it comes to nation-building. According to RAND, out of sixteen prominent cases of post-conflict rebuilding, eleven enjoy stable peace today. Of the nine UN-led endeavours (Congo, Namibia, El Salvador, Cambodia, Somalia, Mozambique, Eastern Slavonia, Sierra Leone and East Timor), RAND found that seven enjoy relatively stable peace today (Congo being one obvious exception). The American record is much more mixed. Only four out of the eight US-led missions resulted in stable peace (West Germany, Japan, Bosnia, Kosovo) whilst another four did not (Somalia, Haiti, Afghanistan, Iraq).[5] Of course, a more stringent test might add Sierra Leone and East Timor to the list of failures, and would certainly raise concerns about progress in Cambodia and El Salvador. Indeed, if something more substantive than the absence of widespread violence is taken to be the benchmark, the UN's record looks much less impressive. Charles Call and Susan Cook argued that, out of eighteen countries the UN was involved in between 1998 and 2002, thirteen were still classified as 'authoritarian' in 2002.[6] Likewise, Roland Paris argues that only two of the aforementioned missions (Eastern Slavonia and Namibia) could be described as 'unqualified successes'.[7] In a separate study which considered all the countries that had played host to UN missions, including small peace-making missions, Call concluded that such countries were no less likely to revert to war than countries which had not hosted a UN mission.[8] However, when these figures are controlled for the size and scope of the UN's engagement with a particular crisis, it becomes clear that the better resourced, mandated and politically supported a peacebuilding endeavour is, the more likely a stable peace becomes.[9]

Finally, although the practice of rebuilding is highly controversial, it is much easier to generate international consensus around the need to engage in rebuilding after armed conflict than it is to forge consensus on prevention or reaction. However, rebuilding is a long and costly endeavour, and it has proven very difficult to persuade states to provide the necessary resources over a long enough period of time. This problem is perhaps best exemplified by the fact that, whilst the world was quick to embrace the proposed new Peacebuilding Commission in 2005, it has proven less eager to provide the commission with the resources and funds necessary to fulfil its role effectively (see below).

This chapter evaluates in two parts the sorts of activities that are required in order to discharge the 'responsibility to rebuild'. The first part sets out the evolution of thinking on the relative merits of 'heavy' and 'light' approaches to international engagement with post-conflict rebuilding, focusing on transitional administrations and on the 'light footprint' approach. This section also outlines some of the practical dilemmas associated with rebuilding. The second part considers the efforts to enhance the UN's capacity to manage and plan rebuilding effectively, through the creation of the Peacebuilding Commission.

From Transitional Administrations to 'Light Footprints'

Transitional administrations and neo-liberalism

In the second half of the 1990s, the UN assumed sovereign responsibility for four territories: Bosnia, Kosovo, Eastern Slavonia and East Timor. Prior to this, the exercise of international authority over formerly war-torn territories had been limited to the provision of assistance to an interim government, a formal partnership with retreating occupiers (UNTAG in Namibia), and the exercise of control over belligerent parties, including the host government which remained sovereign (UNTAC in Cambodia).[10] What was different about these four transitional administrations was not just a significant up-scaling of international engagement – outside agencies assuming control of every arm of government, from security to sanitation – but their assumption of sovereign authority. The regulations governing the UN Mission in Kosovo (UNMIK), for instance, granted its special representative 'all legislative and executive authority with respect to Kosovo, including the administration of the judiciary'.[11] Likewise, the high representative in Bosnia was empowered to promulgate laws, appoint and dismiss government officials and remove elected representatives irrespective of their seniority if he/she judged them to be violating the Dayton Peace Accord or jeopardising its implementation. Through these missions, international actors assumed responsibility for all the elements of government administration, sovereign authority and peacekeeping as well as peacebuilding duties.[12] Several other peace operations, for instance those in Haiti, Liberia and the DRC, share many of the characteristics of transitional operations but lack this element of sovereignty.

The principal rationale behind the rebuilding efforts in each of these missions was that sustainable peace (and hence the prevention of future atrocities) requires more than just the provision of military security by peacekeepers. In addition to military security, stable peace requires the establishment of legitimate and effective government, the creation of growing and sustainable economies, and the transformation of civil society through – among other things – the reconciliation of deep-seated grievances. To achieve these things, the UN assumed control of all the elements and authority of the state and sought to build new, peaceful polities and communities.[13] In those similar cases where the UN did not assume sovereign authority, it has attempted to accomplish this same end through a mixture of control over, and partnership with, the host state.

In the late 1990s, the promulgation of transitional authorities appeared to be the natural next step in the UN's deepening engagement with the rebuilding of war-torn societies. However, it is becoming increasingly clear that this model was anomalous. Three of the four administrations were part of the world's response to the dissolution of Yugoslavia and the fourth, in East Timor, was conducted in a context of near unanimity among world leaders about the province's future status. What is more, as Richard Caplan points out, these four cases shared some striking contextual similarities: all territories were geographically small, and in each case the former ruler's claim to authority either had entirely collapsed or was subject to serious challenge. In addition, all four administrations were in areas which the western states considered to be strategically important, and the missions were led, endorsed and financially supported by westerners. As Paul Williams has argued, these reasons give some indication of why these four locales were the focus of so much effort and attention, whereas other areas, which were equally (or more) in need of transitional administration – most notably Somalia – have been overlooked.[14]

To what extent did the assumption of sovereign authority by the UN succeed in laying the foundations for a stable peace? Unsurprisingly, many different answers have been offered and many different explanations put forth – some of them quite contradictory. What can be said of all four missions is that, by 2008, living conditions in these areas were significantly better than they were before the missions were deployed. But, on the downside, violence, ethnic tension, economic fragility and government incapacity remain. Some areas – East Timor and Kosovo especially – have endured sporadic outbursts of deadly violence. In Kosovo, nineteen people were killed in riots sparked by allegations that Serbs had chased an Albanian boy into a river, where he drowned. Dozens were killed when East Timor descended into anarchy in 2006. Ethnic tensions are evident across the territories of all four missions, and all these territories are characterised by high unemployment and low economic growth. Of course, some have fared better than others. Eastern Slavonia was successfully reintegrated into Croatia, refugee return has been slow but has progressed, the economy has grown, unemployment has fallen and ethnic violence is rare. On the other hand, the economy of East Timor has barely grown at all, discontent and economic woes in the region have provoked mutinies, riots and gang violence, and the East Timorese police and military forces proved utterly incapable of maintaining order in 2006. Indeed, it is highly likely that the state would have collapsed, had it not received rapid international security assistance. But, despite these problems, there has been no generalised violence, all four areas are now governed by democratic governments, basic human rights are safeguarded in them, and economies – still poor – are better than once they were.[15]

State-building

There are two broad – and almost diametrically opposed – schools of thought on the limitations of transitional administrations as a way of building stable peace. The first group consists of what might be labelled 'state-builders'. They share the ICISS' premise that host states are the actors most able to protect their own people from harm and to promote their best interests, and that rebuilding should focus on helping the state to build the necessary capacity to fulfil its responsibilities. Indeed, two ICISS commissioners followed up their work on the R2P with a study on the centrality of state-building to the fostering of stable peace.[16] For the state-builders, the chief problem with the types of activities discussed above is not that they are excessively intrusive, but that they are not based on a sober assessment of what works best in post-conflict settings. Their view springs from the belief that the fragility – all too evident in many of the peacebuilding operations described above – is caused by a prevailing consensus *against* the primacy of state-building. Several analysts argue that the aforementioned UN operations are based on problematic neo-liberal assumptions about democratisation and economic liberalisation which actually impede the efforts to develop government capacity and to foster political reconciliation.

The missions described above were premised on the thesis of liberal peace: that is, the idea that liberal polities and societies are more stable and peaceful than their non-liberal alternatives. They attempted to foster a liberal peace by moving on rapidly to establish democratic government and to marketise the economy. According to Roland Paris, this approach to peacebuilding has several 'destabilizing effects'.[17] Paris argues that the rush to hold early elections before political reconciliation, institution building and the development of civil society can have two destabilising effects. First, the 'winner takes all' mentality, fostered by elections, encourages political intimidation, extortion, cheating and conflict – none of which is conducive to peacebuilding. Second, elections can entrench social divisions, as political parties are typically organised along ethnic lines. Where parties are elected on the basis of their ethnicity, elections can also lend the veneer of democratic legitimacy to the nationalist or patrimonial politics which helped to cause the conflict in the first place.

Likewise, economic liberalisation places a premium on competition (the essence of capitalism), which can exacerbate rivalries. Neo-liberalism's insistence on 'small states' can involve the withdrawal of already weak states from the provision of basic services and infrastructure, reducing indigenously driven human development, increasing dependence on aid and undermining the state's domestic legitimacy. In addition, attempts to privatise industries without the requisite institutional capacity to regulate complex financial transactions leads to 'crony capitalism', whereby ownership is corruptly transferred, often in return for political favours. Rather than dampening conflict, Paris argues, these policies exacerbate it and fundamentally weaken the host state's capacity to deal with it. The most vivid example of this was the near collapse of East Timor in early 2006, where a weak state was unable to maintain order in the face of unrest caused by a combination of political intrigue and economic inequality.

In response, 'state-builders' argue that the task of rebuilding after war should begin with the building of institutions, infrastructure and human capacity. Roland Paris, for instance, calls for an approach based on 'institutionalisation before liberalisation' whereby the competitive forces of elections and market economies are released only when state and society have the capacity to manage peacefully, regulate competition and mitigate its worst effects. To accomplish this end, Paris sets out six priorities:

1   Delay elections prepared to 'shut down' those civil society associations which promote hatred and intolerance.

2   Control hate speech: although free speech is a bastion of democracy, an entirely free press in a post-conflict environment can lead to the proliferation of factional outlets and to the dissemination of hate speech. Peacebuilders should deal with this by fostering responsible news outlets and by acting so as to 'shut down' forcibly hate speech outlets when they incite violence and genocide.

3 Adopt conflict-reducing economic strategies: economic liberalisation should be slowed down in order for its negative effects to be dampened (for instance corruption, clientalism, state incapacity, etc.) and should contain measures to guard against conflict-causing economic iniquities. These measures may involve economic redistribution, safety nets for the most disadvantaged, and the provision of education and public health.

4 The common denominator is the need to rebuild effective state institutions: the aforementioned recommendations are all based on the key priority of building effective state bodies. Democratisation and economic liberalisation require the rule of law, which in turn requires a police service, armed forces, a judiciary, a prison system, a constitution, parliamentary oversight capacity and so forth. They require free and open political participation: open media, freedom of movement, education, freedom of association, non-governmental capacity. They require institutions to oversee and police them. They require infrastructure to permit them to operate. In short, they require all those things which people in established democratic states take for granted. Without these capacities, democratisation and economic liberalisation are unlikely to deliver stable peace and much more likely to exacerbate tensions until conditions are ripe: elections have a chance to be an effective way of distributing political authority only when they can be conducted in a free and fair manner, when they do not produce violence, and when there are good grounds for believing that the twin principles of majority rule and absolute respect for the rights of minorities and of individuals rights – principles which are fundamental to any democratic politics – are deeply embedded and adhered to.[18]

5 Design electoral systems which reward moderation: peacebuilders should create constitutional arrangements which require the candidates for high office to seek support from different factions, thus rewarding political figures who promise to work for more than just their own constituency.

6 Promote good civil society: peacebuilders should provide logistical and financial support to those associations that cross factional boundaries.[19]

If anything, this approach would involve an even deeper level of engagement with post-conflict societies than the one already embarked upon by transitional administrations. As Paris himself notes, peacebuilders have traditionally been reluctant to interfere in the media (except in Kosovo, where a uniform code of conduct was imposed), have tended to steer clear of meddling in the affairs of political parties, and have expressed concerns that delayed elections could create democratic deficits. Nonetheless, the state-building position has been endorsed in many quarters. Simon Chesterman argued that his primary concern 'is not that transitional administration is colonial in character' but 'that sometimes it is not colonial enough'.[20] Likewise, Richard Caplan concluded that some transitional administrations precipitately downsized their engagement, leaving significant gaps in state capacity. This analysis proved highly prescient. Writing in 2004/5, Caplan identified especially serious gaps in the East Timorese government's capacity to maintain law and order – gaps brought about by the UN's precipitate withdrawal. That Caplan was quite right was made abundantly clear in 2006, when the country descended into anarchy and was only rescued by foreign intervention.[21] But there is also an obvious problem with this perspective – a problem which is evoked by Chesterman's reference to 'colonialism'.

Neo-colonialism and the democratic deficit?

A second group of critics maintains that the evident problems associated with rebuilding efforts are principally caused by the peacebuilders themselves. These writers see the echoes of colonialism as the most fundamental impediment to attempts to build peace through transitional administrations, to their non-sovereign equivalents, and to schemas such as the one espoused by Paris. From this perspective, the UN has played a quasi-imperial role, imposing political and economic systems without consulting the people who will be affected most. This creates a democratic deficit, only worsened by Paris' suggestion that elections should be further delayed.

It was for these reasons that Jarat Chopra – a former senior UN official in East Timor – accused the UN of setting up its own unaccountable and non-democratic 'kingdom' in East Timor.[22] Chopra argued that UNTAET's top-down approach excluded the East Timorese themselves from the process of state-building, with the result that international administrators had only a superficial impact on the country's institutions and political culture. It was this superficiality – brought about in part by UNTAET's quasi-imperial outlook and in part by problems related to its own capacity – that sowed the seeds of subsequent state failure, argued Chopra.[23] Rather than fostering sustainable democracy and self-government, the UN and other agencies are said to be fostering undemocratic practices, aid dependence and unsustainable polities by imposing ideologies, processes and institutions without reference to the local inhabitants. David Chandler – a staunch critic of the R2P (see Chapter 2) – has taken this argument a step further and argued that the agreements which provide peacebuilders with the broad-ranging powers described earlier lack legality and legitimacy, and are one-sided in that they bind to them the local parties, but not the international agencies charged with implementing them.[24] According to Chandler, the underlying ideology of this sort of endeavour is closely akin to racism, because it implies that certain groups are mere 'helpless victims of governments and the forces of the world market' and therefore unable to determine their own political affairs.[25]

Arguments like this did get an airing on the international stage, though they have not been as pronounced as one might expect. Traditionally, the Chinese have expressed concern that, by taking on these sorts of endeavours, the UN might become more of a 'supra-national government' than the state-based forum for collective security and cooperation that it was intended to be.[26] Despite these suspicions, China supported transitional administrations and the widening and deepening of peace operations to cover security, democratisation and state-building activities in the DRC, Haiti, Liberia and elsewhere. Among China's stated reasons for adopting this position are the conjoined facts that the Security Council is invested with the authority to do whatever it takes to maintain international peace and security and that state-building may be occasionally necessary. Importantly – and in line with the R2P – the Chinese argue that, far from damaging state sovereignty, such missions contribute to it by helping to build effective state bureaucracies.[27] The key point here is that, although the charge of quasi-imperialism has been levelled, this is not a charge which has had much political traction in terms of inhibiting consensus on engagement in particular crises. Nonetheless, the question of interference in the domestic affairs of sovereigns became an issue in relation to the creation of the Peacebuilding Commission (below).

This still leaves the difficult question of effectiveness posed by Chopra. It is well known that reform processes are most effective when they are 'owned' by the subjects of reform themselves and embedded within the relevant organisational, political and national cultures. This point was recognised by the ICISS. The commission broadly supported Paris' view that rapid democratisation and economic liberalisation could destabilise post-conflict societies. Indeed, one leading commissioner – Michael Ignatieff – supported the view that some form of neo-colonial trusteeship might be

necessary in certain cases.[28] However, the ICISS also recognised the importance of local ownership, arguing that post-conflict operations should seek
'a balance between the responsibilities of international and local actors'.[29]
International administrators should aim to 'do themselves out of a job' by
creating political processes and institutional mechanisms which require
local actors to take responsibility for their well-being, and they should avoid
the tendency to monopolise responsibility and to create dependence.
In a follow-up project on state-building led by two ICISS commissioners
(Thakur and Ignatieff, with Simon Chesterman), this ambition was translated into two key principles: legitimacy and ownership.

The importance of legitimacy and ownership

If government is to be effective and sustainable, Chesterman, Ignatieff and
Thakur argued, it has to be legitimate. Legitimacy in this context refers to
the extent to which the political leadership, state institutions and rule of law
enjoy the consent and support of the wider population.[30] There are two key
components to this kind of legitimacy. First, legitimacy is fostered by the
creation and development of institutions that 'fit' the wider community's
preferences. Institutions, laws and other political processes have to be con-
genial to the community rather than imposed by outsiders. In relation to
the rule of law, this creates potential difficulties for peacebuilders when
local institutions and practices fall short of international human rights standards for example, or when traditional forms of justice exist alongside the
formal system – as in East Timor. In the East Timor case, international
agencies attempted to bridge the divide by creating a panel of experts
comprised of East Timorese and international legal experts charged with
developing a new legal code. The panel developed a code which combined
international human rights standards with elements of Indonesian law
which had prevailed in East Timor before 1999. The state authorities also
permitted the continuation of traditional forms of justice for certain
crimes, including the use of village-based forgiveness rituals instead of war
crimes trials for some militia members.[31]

In relation to the founding of political institutions, this approach – which
has been used in part in Afghanistan and Iraq – involves creating a mechanism by which the local elites themselves design the political system. In
Afghanistan this was done in a non-democratic fashion, through a council
of tribal elders – the *Loya Jirga*. In Iraq, the US-led coalition attempted to
democratise the process by holding early elections to determine who would
play a role in constitution-writing. Although commendable in principle, the

Iraq model left the process open to political factionalism and created an opening for radicals and spoilers to shape the structure of government and to delay progress chronically.

The second element is 'ownership'. The ownership principle holds that the local population must be directly connected to peacebuilding. The local population should be engaged in decision-making as far as possible and should be informed and consulted about the direction of the whole process. Where decisions are made by external actors, it is important that those decisions are understood to be in the best interests of the local population, and clearly connected to the achievement of the final outcome. Ownership is best achieved by decentralisation – something akin to the EU principle of subsidiarity, whereby decisions should be taken as close as possible to those who will be affected by them to the utmost degree. Of course, as Chesterman, Ignatieff and Thakur point out, the urge to decentralise has to be balanced against the the need to build strong, stable and sustainable institutions in the centre and the need to foster national unity. After all, decentralisation can open the door to fragmentation.[32]

The 'light footprint'

A combination of concerns about the costs, effectiveness and legitimacy of transitional administrations and other forms of 'heavy' international assistance has prompted an important shift in emphasis in the way the UN approaches the question of post-conflict reconstruction. This is the so-called 'light footprint' approach, put forth by Lakhdar Brahimi. In 1999 Annan invited Brahimi to be his special representative in East Timor, heading the transitional administration there. Brahimi – who was serving as special envoy to Afghanistan at the time – declined the invitation, because he felt uncomfortable with being engaged in 'anything that looks like neocolonialism'.[33] After 9/11, Annan invited Brahimi to continue his work on Afghanistan and to lead the UN's contribution to the rebuilding of that country. This would be a very different operation from the one embarked on in East Timor. On the one hand, it was widely recognised that the Afghans would be much less receptive to heavy external interference than the East Timorese. On the other hand, world governments had little stomach for a major commitment to Afghanistan, and the US-led coalition was concerned that a large international presence in Afghanistan might hinder its ongoing military operations against the Taliban and al Qaeda. A new approach to post-conflict reconstruction was needed.

In October 2001, Brahimi insisted that 'the UN is not seeking a transitional administration or peacekeeping or anything like that' in Afghanistan. Instead, the principal aim of this new model was to bring Afghan parties together and to assist them in rebuilding their country.[34] The guiding principle of this 'light footprint' approach was that the UN mission should focus on supporting local capacity with as small an international staff as possible.[35] Its advocates argued that the 'light footprint' approach avoided the appearance of neo-colonialism – which made it easier for the mission to fulfil the legitimacy and ownership requirements set out above – and was much less expensive than the full-blown transitional administrations. According to one estimate, the 'light footprint' approach cost $52 per capita in the first two years, whereas the transitional administration in Kosovo cost $814 per capita over the same period.[36] From the member states' point of view, the 'light footprint' acknowledged the wider needs of peace-building without advocating the wholesale assumption of government and its attendant costs. Moreover, assuming that the local authorities are considered legitimate by the host population – in many cases, a problematic assumption at best – the 'light footprint' approach leaves behind more legitimate political structures than its alternative does, because such structures have been built and shaped by indigenous political leaders.[37]

The 'light footprint' involves using international agencies to accomplish certain tasks – for instance the provision of security in some major cities, capacity building for the state bureaucracy and training and equipping a national army and a police service – whilst permitting indigenous leaders to develop their own preferred type of polity and to remain in control of the overall process. In sharp contrast to the situation in the Balkans and in East Timor, international agencies in Afghanistan did not insist upon the institution of a particular form of democracy and government, but left these decisions to tribal elders in the *Loya Jirga*. So long as certain basic conditions were satisfied (some form of democracy, an open economy, respect for basic human rights), international agencies were prepared to allow the Afghan government to control and direct the rebuilding effort.[38]

This model has been replicated in subsequent missions, which suggests that the basic principles of the 'light footprint' (external support for indigenous efforts) have become the basis for a new consensus on peacebuilding. In one of its largest operations, in the DRC, the UN's approach has focused on providing support to the government rather than assuming the reigns of government itself. In the security field, for instance, this has involved supporting the government's efforts to disarm and demobilise militia groups, to reform the security sector – a process which incorporated the formation of police services from scratch in some parts of the country such as the town of Bunia and was designed to improve the government's capacity to maintain order legitimately and effectively – and to root out spoilers, in joint operations with government forces. The DRC government remains entitled to pass and enforce laws and to use its security forces.

There are clear advantages to the 'light footprint' approach – not least its underlying principle that the purpose of international engagement is to facilitate the development of sustainable local capacity. There are also, however, a number of key problems. First, by placing authority in the hands of local elites, it runs the risk of legitimating spoilers. There is a danger that the 'light footprint' could help the perpetuation of a culture of impunity. One of the key partners in peace in Afghanistan was General Dostrum's 'Northern Alliance'. Dostrum was a notorious war criminal with a career characterised by mass atrocities. Likewise, DRC 'government forces' have themselves been implicated in massacres, some of which – for instance the killing of more than twenty civilians in Kilwa in 2003 – occurred during its period of cooperation with the UN. Second, as the comparative figures for Kosovo and Afghanistan noted above demonstrate, the 'light footprint' can serve as a cover for chronic under-investment and for a much reduced level of engagement. In Afghanistan, the 'light footprint' approach to security failed to prevent the resurgence of the Taliban and produced only 'modest gains' in relation to economic growth, education and infrastructure. Given this, it is not surprising that the opium trade has grown in the past few years. As RAND concluded, 'low input of military and civilian resources yields low output in terms of security, democratic transformation, and economic development'.[39]

Summary

There is clearly no easy answer to how best to go about rebuilding societies shattered by genocide and mass atrocities. While there is broad agreement that the focus should be on the building of indigenous capacities and that legitimacy and ownership are key components, there is much less agreement on how international agencies should go about building that capacity. In some respects there is a payoff between short-term effectiveness and ownership – the more one grants local ownership, the more reflective of local politics the peace process is likely to be. This can be both a strength and a curse. A strength because local ownership helps to ensure that the new institutions and processes reflect the values and concerns of the host population. A curse because it exposes peacebuilding to manipulation by some of the very actors who caused, and profited from, conflict in the first place. Clearly, what is needed in order to fulfil the responsibility to rebuild is a capacity to learn lessons from past missions, to plan for future missions, and to coordinate the activities of international agencies and local actors. Although rebuilding was not specifically referred to in relation to the World Summit's commitment to the R2P, it was aspirations such as these that lay behind the establishment of the Peacebuilding Commission in 2005. What is more, the World Summit's reference to the importance of international support for the building of state capacity in relation to the R2P was a clear nod in the direction of the responsibility to rebuild.

The Peacebuilding Commission (PBC)

Genesis

By early 2005, the establishment of a PBC was widely perceived by UN members as an 'idea whose time has come'.[40] The idea enjoyed broad polit-ical support, especially in Africa. Although the PBC was first mooted by the HLP, the idea of creating a Peacebuilding Unit within the DPA to support the UN's field operations had been put forth many times in the past and had suffered a similar fate to that of the proposals for an early warning unit. Kofi Annan recognised the need to develop a capacity to manage better the tran-sition from war to peace in his 2001 report on the exit and closure of peace operations. Annan noted that 'more than once during the last 10 years the United Nations has withdrawn a peacekeeping operation, or dramatically altered its mandate, only to see the situation remain unstable, or sink into renewed violence'.[41] The 'ultimate purpose' of a peace operation, Annan argued, was 'the achievement of a sustainable peace'. In the aftermath of civil wars, peace 'becomes sustainable, not when all conflicts are removed from society, but when the natural conflicts of society can be resolved peacefully through the exercise of State sovereignty and, generally, partici-patory governance'. Annan advocated a mixture of heavy involvement and 'light footprint': 'to facilitate such a transition, a mission's mandate should include peace-building and incorporate such elements as institution-building and the promotion of good governance and the rule of law, by assisting the parties to develop legitimate and broad-based institutions'.[42] To achieve sustainable peace, the Secretary-General argued, it was neces-sary to fulfil three objectives: consolidate internal and external security; strengthen political institutions and good governance; and promote eco-nomic and social rehabilitation and transformation.[43]

Although Annan stopped short of advocating institutional reforms in order to make the secretariat better able to provide guidance to the Security Council about the best way to achieve these objectives, there were moves to improve the UN's capacity in this area on an ad hoc basis. In October 2001, the UN established its first full-time Integrated Mission Task Force (IMTF) in New York, to facilitate joint planning among UN bodies and agencies for the new mission in Afghanistan. Unfortunately, the task force lasted only six months and was disbanded in February 2002, before the mission was fully deployed and Brahimi's plan for Afghanistan fully developed.[44] At the same time, the DPKO attempted to improve the coordination between peacekeepers and peacebuilders by developing an Integrated Mission Planning Process involving other UN agencies.[45] In the absence of a body designated to take the lead in developing peacebuilding strategies, progress was painfully slow, which prompted calls from some quarters for institutional reform. As Jehangir Khan, a former senior official in the DPA, put it: 'We desperately needed a high-level political body to support political processes and help countries implement peace accords. Historically, the Department of Political Affairs had been the lead UN body for peacebuilding, but it is not set up to be operational.'[46] These calls were echoed outside the UN. In October 2004, a meeting of NGOs and officials hosted by the International Peace Academy called for the UN to create an institutional 'home' for peacebuilding, where decisions could be taken and implemented.[47]

Recognising this need, the HLP called for the establishment of a Peacebuilding Commission supported by a Peacebuilding Support Office (PBSO), which was to be provided by the secretariat. The HLP couched its recommendations squarely in R2P terms, recognising the pivotal relationship between peacebuilding and the prevention of future atrocities identified at the beginning of this chapter. It recognised that there was 'no place in the United Nations system explicitly designed to avoid State collapse and the slide to war or to assist countries in their transition from war to peace', maintaining that this was no surprise, given the Charter's focus on relations between states. Nevertheless, the panel noted a clear international obligation to assist states in developing the capacity to perform sovereign functions effectively and legitimately.[48] This, the HLP argued, should be the task of the Peacebuilding Commission (PBC).

The HLP conceived that the PBC would have broad-ranging tasks. The commission should be charged with enabling the UN to act in a 'coherent and effective way', on a broad continuum of measures ranging from early warning and preventive action to post-conflict reconstruction. The PBC would identify countries at risk, organise and coordinate assistance, and oversee the transition from war to peace and from peacekeeping to peacebuilding.[49] It would fulfil the twin roles of conflict prevention and post-conflict reconstruction. In so doing, the PBC would facilitate joint planning across the UN system and beyond, would provide high-level political leadership (thus utilising peacemaking), and would increase the funds available for prevention and rebuilding.[50]

The proposal was broadly welcomed. Within the US State Department there was some initial resistance to the creation of 'yet another UN bureaucracy', but the proposal's backers prevailed, being helped in no small part by the US' abject failure to build peace in Iraq. From around autumn 2004, therefore, the Administration supported the proposal – though not without some important reservations.[51] Kofi Annan endorsed both the PBC and the Support Office, agreeing that the absence of such a body constituted 'a gaping hole in the United Nations' institutional machinery'.[52] Unsurprisingly, however, given the opposition to granting the UN an early warning capacity outlined in Chapter 4, there was little support for giving the PBC a mandate covering everything from early warning to post-conflict reconstruction. At the 2005 World Summit, only Angola defended the idea that the PBC would be incomplete without a conflict prevention component.[53] Some – especially the P5 – worried that these provisions impinged on the Security Council's prerogatives. In line with his preferred stance on prevention, Annan moved to distance himself from this part of the proposal. Indeed, the first iteration of Annan's reform agenda issued on 21 March 2005 omitted reference to the whole question of prevention. After informal consultations with member states, Annan addressed the question of prevention in an explanatory note issued in May as an addendum to 'In larger freedom'. Rather than a standing capacity to monitor members and identify those in need of support, Annan preferred a voluntary system whereby the UN would provide assistance on request. He argued that:

> Neither the Peacebuilding Commission nor the Support Office should have an early-warning function. There are other mechanisms in the United Nations for what has become known as 'operational prevention', i.e. the use of such tools as mediation and preventive peacekeeping when conflict has become imminent or has broken out in a small scale way.[54]

It is important to recognise that, in addition to the obvious political problems associated with the proposed prevention role for the PBC, there were some serious practical and institutional difficulties. Annan maintained that the UN already had functions designed to address early warning and conflict prevention, not least the organisation's capabilities in the areas of peacemaking (see Chapter 5) and preventive deployment (see Chapter 4). It would be better to strengthen these capacities, Annan argued, than to overlay them with new offices. Moreover, the development of additional offices dealing with conflict prevention might lead to inadvertent duplication and unhelpful interference in politically sensitive peacemaking activities. It would be difficult, analysts reasoned, for the DPA to conduct quiet diplomacy on behalf of the Secretary-General when an issue was before an inter-governmental body like the PBC.[55] Then there was the risk of duplication with the special representative for the prevention of genocide and mass atrocities (see Chapter 4). Finally, Annan argued that his proposed PBC model contained within it the capacity to act in support of prevention, through its advisory function.[56] Annan's preference was that the PBC would play an advisory role, providing ideas and inputs to the Security Council and ECOSOC; its core members should meet only infrequently; the majority of its work should be conducted through country-specific meetings; and it should be 'creative' in facilitating the participation of national actors and humanitarian representatives.[57]

Even this modest proposal proved too much for the General Assembly. In its final form, the PBC's mandate was limited to bringing together 'all relevant actors to marshal resources and to advise on and propose integrated strategies for post-conflict peacebuilding and recovery'.[58] The 2005 World Summit supported the creation of a Peacebuilding Support Unit, but insisted that it should be funded and staffed out of existing resources. The key driver of this restriction was the US, which argued against increased assessed contributions to fund the PBC/PBSO and insisted that the PBC's membership must reflect the financial contributions it received from member states.[59] In place of assessed contributions, the General Assembly created a new voluntary fund to support peacebuilding.

The most significant political dispute over the PBC concerned the question of where the commission would be situated institutionally. The HLP clearly envisaged the PBC as a subsidiary of the Security Council, calling for its establishment by the council under Article 29 of the Charter. The Security Council would 'consult' with ECOSOC on the formation of the PBC, but it would have ultimate responsibility for the new body. Tellingly, the HLP omitted the General Assembly from its proposed schema.[60] This proposal was not well received by the membership. India argued that the PBC should be entirely autonomous from the Security Council, so as to make it easier for states to seek the commission's assistance.[61] Others – most notably Iran – took this argument a step further and expressed concern at the expansion of the UN's capacity for interfering in the domestic affairs of states. Iran argued that the commission should only conduct country-specific meetings at the request of the member state concerned. The proposed link with the Security Council would give the PBC potentially far-ranging powers of interference in sovereign affairs on a non-consensual basis. Even Switzerland expressed doubts about the connection between the PBC and the Security Council, lamenting that the prominence given to the Security Council would further undermine the relevance of ECOSOC.[62]

Partly in response to these concerns, Annan rejected the idea that the PBC should be a subsidiary of the Security Council. Instead he proposed that the commission should be an 'inter-governmental' organ, comprising an equal number of members from the Security Council and ECOSOC and being subsidiary both to the General Assembly and to the Security Council.[63] This compromise failed to stem the debate, which dragged on into 2005. The Bush administration tempered the State Department's earlier enthusiasm for the PBC by insisting for the commission to be controlled by the Security Council: the Council should be responsible, namely, for determining when and where the PBC would become involved in post-conflict reconstruction. In particular, the US argued that the PBC should be subsidiary to the Security Council on matters on which the council was seized.[64] This position was strongly opposed by African governments. Africa's common position on UN reform (the 'Ezulwini consensus') insisted that the PBC be closely related to the ECOSOC and to the General Assembly, as well as to the Security Council. This position was endorsed by other key members of the G77, including Indonesia and Iran.[65] The views of other states generally sat somewhere between these two poles. Sweden supported the US position on the grounds that the PBC would need to coordinate its efforts with the UN's peace operations. On the other hand, Brazil used instrumental arguments to reject Security Council primacy, insisting that peacebuilding 'is best implemented by means of a core social and economic approach, rather than one based almost exclusively on political and security considerations'.[66]

The end-product was a framework almost identical to the one proposed by Annan, comprising the General Assembly, the ECOSOC and the Security Council. The PBC would be subsidiary to the General Assembly and Security Council and would act as an 'advisory body' for the Assembly and two Councils. It would report, however, only to the General Assembly. This model paved the way for complex negotiations about membership. In addition to equal representation from the Security Council and the ECOSOC, NAM members insisted upon strong representation for the General Assembly. Many Western states argued that representation should be based on the level of financial contributions. After much wrangling, a compromise was reached granting the General Assembly equal representation with the Security Council and the ECOSOC, and also membership rights for the top five financial contributors and for the top five troop contributors to UN peace operations.

The tripartite system: Commission, support office, fund

The PBC was formally established by concurrent Security Council and General Assembly resolutions (Resolution 1645, 20 December 2005 and Resolution 60/180, 30 December 2005, respectively). Created as an intergovernmental body, it was described by Vice-President of the International Peace Academy Necla Tschirgi as 'a very unusual and unique experiment'.[67] As set out in the two resolutions, the PBC was given three primary purposes:

1 to bring together all the relevant actors to marshal resources, to provide advice, and to propose integrated strategies for post-conflict peacebuilding;
2 to focus attention on the reconstruction and institution-building efforts necessary to ensure post-conflict recovery and sustainable development;
3 to provide recommendations and information for improving coordination among all the relevant actors.

The PBC's formal status is that of an 'advisory body' which operates on the basis of consensus among its thirty-one member states. The commission organises 'country specific meetings' to assess those needs of individual states which come onto its agenda. Countries may come onto the PBC's agenda at the request of the Security Council, of the ECOSOC or of the General Assembly; with the consent of the state concerned; and, in exceptional circumstances, at the request of the state concerned or at the request of the Secretary-General.[68] Even where consensus between PBC members and UN agencies is possible, the PBC lacks the formal authority to ensure the envisaged level of coordination between UN bodies and agencies. As one commentator put it, 'its influence within the UN stems entirely from the quality of its recommendations, the relevance of the information it shares, and its ability to generate extra resources'.[69] Of course, the PBC is not operating in a 'policy vacuum' but in an area already crowded with UN agencies and bodies, regional organisations, individual government donors and NGOs. Finding a place within this context, and within the limitations set by the General Assembly is the single greatest challenge facing the new body (see below).

As was conceived by Annan, the Peacebuilding Support Office (PBSO) would be given the role of preparing substantive inputs for commission meetings, of providing inputs for the planning process and of conducting best practice analysis and policy guidance where appropriate.[70] It would be staffed by twenty-one new appointments funded through the regular budget. Once again, however, the UN membership had a more circumscribed view, limiting the PBSO's role to 'gathering and analysing information relating to the availability of financial resources, relevant United Nations in-country planning activities, progress towards meeting short and medium-term recovery goals and best practices'.[71] Most notably absent was the policy guidance role envisaged by the Secretary-General. Nor, as noted earlier, were the members convinced by Annan's case for new appointments to staff the PBSO; this was due in part to financial concerns from the US and in part to concerns among the G77 that a strong and effective PBSO might interfere in domestic affairs. Under pressure, the UN's budget committees insisted that the PBSO's needs should be met from existing resources.

PBSO was placed under the leadership of Carolyn McAskie (Canada), assigned seven staff members, three seconded personnel and five UN employees redeployed from other areas. By early 2008, these redeployments had not yet taken place. The reduction from twenty-one to fifteen staff members was achieved by cutting professional and general services posts, which left a relatively 'top-heavy' office. The question of redeployment – one of the key problems associated with the failed ORCI experiment (see Chapter 4) – has also provoked concerns. Speaking on behalf of the G77, South Africa expressed apprehension about the impact of redeployment on the releasing department.[72] Others have raised the possibility that redeployment might encourage turf struggles between departments; they have also observed that the releasing departments might refuse to release high-quality professionals. In addition to salaries and associated personnel costs, the PBSO receives an annual operating budget of $1.2 million from the DPA.[73]

The third element of the UN's new peacebuilding capacity is the Peacebuilding Fund (PBF). The fund was created as an alternative to increased assessed contributions; it is managed by the head of the PBSO and administered by the UNDP. The actual decision-making process associated with the fund's distribution is quite cumbersome and involves country-level reports, steering committees comprising UN agencies, bilateral donors, NGOs and the host government, and requests by the PBC and/or Secretary-General. Initially it was envisaged that the fund would be used to support projects in countries under consideration by the PBC and other post-conflict states.[74] This remit was subsequently narrowed as a result of the relatively small number of donations actually received. According to a 2007 PBSO briefing, the PBF is now intended to fill an important funding gap between the conclusion of a peace treaty and the commencement of fully fledged peacebuilding measures. Rather than providing substantive funding, the PBF envisages its role as a 'catalytic' one – of helping to stimulate further funding by other agencies and donors.[75] The Secretary-General set a target of $250 million per year, and by May 2007 governments had formally pledged $221 million and the fund had actually received $137 million – though many of these pledges were multi-year ones. To date, the largest single donor to the fund is Norway, which has contributed $30 million.[76] By mid-2007 the fund had begun dispersing a small amount of this income on projects in Sierra Leone and Burundi – the PBC's first two cases. A little over $5 million (of a projected total of $25 million) had been assigned to Sierra Leone for capacity building in the police service and youth enterprise development. Burundi fared somewhat better, receiving $15.5 million for projects on the resolution of land disputes, on anti-corruption measures, on national reconciliation, on support for the role of women in the peace process, on the creation of a national human rights commission, on the improvement of the judicial system, on the disarmament of small arms, and on barracking the national army.[77]

The commission at work

It is too early to make definitive judgements about the extent to which the PBC, PBSO and PBF have improved the UN's capacity for rebuilding. Tschirgi maintained that the PBC model 'will have little money and authority' and 'will therefore be a much less effective body than what many had wished for'.[78] Gareth Evans, meanwhile, maintained that, despite these constraints, the PBC could play an important role in improving the UN's peacebuilding capacity – though only if member states embraced the commission as a 'full partner' in peace and provided it with adequate resources.[79] The PBC's first six months were characterised by diplomatic wrangling, conducted in a 'climate of suspicion' over procedures and membership.[80] It was not until October 2006 that the PBC started substantive work, beginning country-specific meetings on Sierra Leone and Burundi at the request of the Security Council. The scope of its work was expanded in 2007 so as to include $700,000 in emergency funds to support political dialogue in Côte D'Ivoire and $800,000 to support mediation in the Central African Republic. In October 2007, Ban Ki-moon further expanded the council's work by declaring that Liberia was also eligible to receive PBC assistance. On a positive note, McAskie maintained that, once the commission came to address substantive matters, 'the whole tone of the discussions and atmosphere changed 180 degrees. All members of the Commission were engaged on the issues of peacebuilding.'[81]

The commission's first country-specific meetings received 'conference room papers' identifying the critical challenges which faced the two countries. In relation to Sierra Leone, those challenges were identified as social and youth empowerment and employment, the consolidation of democracy and of good governance, and justice and security sector reform.[82] In Burundi, the main priorities were identified as the promotion of good governance, the strengthening of the rule of law and of the security sector, and the securing of community engagement.[83] Following up on these meetings, the PBC/PBSO worked with the respective governments towards developing plans to address these challenges. Specific measures were identified and $25 million allocated from the PBF (discussed earlier). Significantly, the World Bank and the IMF agreed to cooperate with the PBC and to extend credit to both countries.[84]

In relation to Sierra Leone, the commission has encouraged foreign governments to increase their overall commitment and has called on donors to broaden the donor base, to provide secure assistance, to relieve government debt and to meet consolidated peacebuilding objectives.[85] In the first half of 2007 the commission focused on preparations for the country's presidential elections. In particular, the PBC served as a forum for the UNDP and for Sierra Leonian officials, along with members of the UN's Integrated Office in Sierra Leone (UNIOSIL), to identify potential risks to the election and risks which might be generated by the election. The PBC hosted discussions on the development of strategies to reduce those risks, including measures to ensure that the election itself was managed fairly, transparently and effectively; a process of dialogue and confidence-building involving the electoral commission and political parties; measures to ensure freedom of speech in the media while also guarding against hate speech through the instigation and supervision of a government-sponsored code of conduct for the media; and measures to uphold the recommendations of the Truth and Reconciliation Council in order to discourage opposition spoilers. In addition to these measures already adopted by the government of Sierra Leone, the PBC advocated a range of other initiatives, aimed at reducing the risks related to elections. The PBC argued that the government should establish a National Human Rights Council to address grievances raised by political parties and individuals; develop a strategy for decentralising public policy and the electoral commission in order to make them both better able to respond quickly and effectively to regional concerns; and initiate a process of dialogue with political parties that would continue after the election.[86] Taken together, these measures constitute a reasonably comprehensive plan for dealing with the inherent risks associated with the holding of elections which were identified in the first part of this chapter. Early indications from Sierra Leone's presidential elections suggest that these measures succeeded in ensuring a largely free, fair and non-violent electoral process.

In the case of Burundi, the PBC initiated a wide-reaching programme of activities which was described earlier. The commission has continued to monitor and comment on the development of a strategic plan for peacebuilding. In mid-2007, the government of Burundi, in partnership with key national figures and international donors, developed a draft Strategic Framework for Peacebuilding in Burundi, which aimed to identify objectives and specific tasks designed to achieve those objectives, as well as clear measures which could be used to ascertain progress.[87] The PBC acted as one partner in this process, making a series of recommendations drawn from the informal country-specific meetings. Some practical and political tensions were evident, however, in the dialogue between the government of Burundi, other sponsors of the framework, and the PBC. On the practical level, some PBC delegates argued that the framework should be 'action-oriented' and liable to revision as circumstances changed. This contrasted with the Burundian view – also adopted by several agencies working in Burundi – that the framework should *not* be an action plan, but should instead set out an overarching strategic vision. These actors argued that individual programmes already had specific plans of action and that the framework would simply add an extra layer of bureaucracy, without making much of a concrete contribution to the peacebuilding effort in Burundi. Two types of political tension were also in evidence. Some delegates expressed concern about the way in which the proposed framework referred to neighbouring states. For example, the draft text referred to refugees in Tanzania as a 'threat to peace' and drew calls for revision from the PBC. Others, keen to avoid the de facto expansion of the PBC's remit, voiced concerns that some aspects of the proposed framework were broader than the scope of the PBC's mandate.[88]

Early signs therefore suggest that the PBC's political character makes it well suited for acting as a catalyst for attracting government donations for UN operations and as a forum for developing strategic priorities – and better suited for this than for providing operational guidance. Indeed, some commentators have noted that PBC meetings have already taken the form of pledging conferences which help to focus attention on specific countries and measures in need of support – a perception strongly resisted by the PBSO especially.[89] The early indicators also suggest that the PBC is unlikely to play a clear or decisive role in coordinating UN agencies. The PBC lacks the constitutional clout (that is, it does not have a mandate to coordinate UN agencies) the bureaucratic capacity and the financial power (in that its programmes are dwarfed by those run by the UNDP, UNHCR, UNICEF, WFP and the like) to be an effective coordinator. Its coordinating role is therefore rather one of providing a forum for agencies, donors and the states concerned to identify peacebuilding priorities, to develop strategic plans and to initiate relatively small but high-profile programmes.[90] The danger, then, is that the PBC might simply 'duplicate, confuse and divert scarce resources' already dedicated to particular countries.[91] Indeed, this very concern was raised by the African Development Bank at a meeting of the council in May 2007.[92]

Some members have insisted on the PBC working with the states concerned to develop Integrated Peacebuilding Strategies. Indeed, there is broad agreement that it is in the development of such strategies that the PBC will make its contribution. Speaking on behalf of the EU, Thomas Matussek insisted that 'promoting the development of a viable peacebuilding strategy which has broad ownership is where the Commission can really add value'. The NAM broadly agreed, calling for the PBC to develop 'holistic, coherent and inclusive' approaches to post-conflict reconstruction.[93] There is clear merit here, and, even as I am writing, the PBC is busily developing integrated peacebuilding strategies for Burundi and Sierra Leone. However, without the constitutional, bureaucratic or financial wherewithal to coordinate even UN agencies in the realisation of those strategies, it is hard to see how duplication can be avoided. As Richard Ponzio notes, Sierra Leone already has a Poverty Reduction Strategy, a Medium-Term Expenditure Framework, a Peace Consolidation Strategy, and bilateral strategies with the UK and EU on security and justice sector reform. It would be hard to disagree with Ponzio's view that these context-specific and locally negotiated strategies developed by indigenous authorities and actors actively engaged on the ground are likely to prove more effective than the centralised strategies developed by political figures in New York on the advice of a tiny support office.[94]

Nevertheless, there are ways for the PBC to make an effective contribution to post-conflict rebuilding even with the narrow confines of its mandate and resources. First, it could embrace its political nature and become an engine for augmenting donations and resources in support of programmes already in place. From Afghanistan to Angola, post-conflict reconstruction efforts are woefully under-resourced, and the PBC could play a useful role as a focal point for persuading governments to provide the necessary resources. The PBC could also play an important role in ensuring that states deliver on their pledges of assistance. In Burundi, for example, by early 2006 only 66 per cent of the $1.1 billion pledged by donors in 2000 had actually been disbursed.[95] The PBC's high profile and political standing makes it ideally suited to fulfilling this role. Indeed, during the council's deliberations on Burundi, Guinea-Bissau advanced precisely this argument.[96] In addition, the PBC also builds an important bridge between the Security Council and the World Bank. All too often, the security and economic wings of the UN have acted at cross-purposes – the latter using economic coercion to instil neo-liberal marketisation and the retreat of the state, while the former sought to enhance state capacity. Sometimes, as in the cases of Sierra Leone and Rwanda, World Bank policies have contributed to political instability and violence.[97] In both these cases, the World Bank and IMF promoted market-driven growth and focused on the collection of debt repayments, largely ignoring the destabilising political and social effects of their policies. In both cases, marketisation stimulated economic growth at the expense of widening economic inequalities, which sharpened political and ethnic differences. The World Bank's and IMF's focus on debt repayment encouraged already fragile states to cut vital services, which weakened them further.[98] By bridging the gap between security and economics, the PBC not only could work to mitigate these effects; it could also provide a forum for the articulation of consolidated peacebuilding strategies where the security, the governance and the economic dimensions reinforced one another rather than operating at cross-purposes.

Second, working alongside the DPKO, which recently strengthened its civilian component by establishing a separate office on the Rule of Law, the PBC/PBSO could explore ways of improving the organisation's capacity to augment peace operations with civilian capabilities in areas such as the rule of law, electoral management, parliamentary oversight, economic management and government effectiveness.[99] Ideally, the PBC should also play a key role in coordinating multi-agency programmes of aiding post-conflict societies – but there seems to be little political or bureaucratic support for this.

Conclusion

In the long term, the protection of civilians from genocide and mass atrocities is best secured through the exercise of responsible sovereignty.[100] The responsibility to rebuild is the element of the R2P which focuses on building and fostering the institutions, cultures and behaviours necessary for achieving responsible sovereignty in regions where the latter has been sorely lacking. Of all the measures associated with the R2P, it has proven easiest to build a broad consensus on the importance of capacity building in post-conflict reconstruction. One of the main reasons for this is that a clear case can be made that international assistance after armed conflict enables fragile states to develop the capacities necessary to realise their sovereignty. There is also a clearly emerging consensus on the best way to go about transforming communities shattered after war. Whilst democratisation and market-led growth are important, there is an increasing recognition that both can also sow the seeds of future conflict; there is therefore a need to develop strategies which may reduce the risks associated with them. It is telling, in this respect, that one of the earliest issues to come before the PBC was that of the development of 'risk reduction strategies' for Sierra Leone's 2007 presidential elections. The emerging consensus combines elements of the trusteeship mentality which has underpinned the UN's transitional administrations in the Balkans and East Timor with basic ideas from the 'light footprint' approach. It is widely recognised that only local elites and civil societies can build sustainable peace but that external actors have an important role to play in helping to develop the necessary capacities to facilitate locally managed peacebuilding. At the very least, external actors have a responsibility to ensure that its engagement with post-conflict societies does not sow the seeds of future conflict and instability, as programmes of rapid democratisation and economic liberalisation have tended to do in the past.

After protracted civil war where the state itself may have collapsed, this approach might involve the provision of leadership, assistance and supervision across every area of government. Where this sort of 'heavy engagement' is necessary, it is important that peacebuilding activities are guided by the twin principles of legitimacy and local ownership described earlier. Otherwise peacebuilders risk creating institutions which are culturally and physically divorced from the host population. Such institutions are unlikely to foster a sustainable peace. The main problem is not the proclivity towards neo-colonialism, but the world's relatively short attention span. Peacebuilding is an expensive and long-term endeavour, involving myriad agencies. One of the primary reasons for establishing the PBC was the hope that an institutional 'home' for peacebuilding might help to capture and hold the world's attention.

Given the broad support the PBC enjoyed, we might have expected it to be relatively immune from some of the political disputes which have dogged the efforts to enhance the world's capacity for engaging in the prevention of, and effective reaction to, genocide and mass atrocities. This has proved not to be the case. Agreeing with the commission in principle, states disagreed about its role and its place in the wider UN organisation. These debates reflected differences of opinion over the nature of peacebuilding itself and about the appropriate locus of authority within the UN. At the risk of over-generalising, western governments typically see peacebuilding as a political and security-led endeavour closely associated with the work of the Security Council. They are also relatively comfortable with enlarging the Security Council's remit to cover peacebuilding. By contrast, some key G77/NAM states remained deeply concerned about the increasing dominance of the Security Council and sought to use the PBC to reassert the authority of the General Assembly and of the ECOSOC. Moreover, as Brazil argued, these states typically see peacebuilding as an economic and social-led activity. Both sides of the debate were united by two considerations, however: they both supported the PBC in principle, and neither of them wanted it to develop a strong institutional capacity. As a result, the PBC has a narrow advisory role and lacks the authority or capacity to coordinate UN agencies, to conduct planning, or develop consolidated strategies. This has led some to doubt that the PBC will be able to develop a useful role and one that avoids duplicating the work of other organisations. These concerns notwithstanding, in the immediate term the PBC can play an important role in holding the attention of world leaders and in providing a catalyst for funding, in encouraging broad dialogue on lessons learned, and in identifying ways of improving the UN's civilian capacity to promote peace.

Conclusion

In the course of this book I have developed three principal arguments which I will briefly rehearse in this conclusion. First, in the process of transforming the R2P from a concept and recommendation proposed by an international commission into a global principle unanimously endorsed by world governments, the principle has changed in important respects from the way it was originally conceived by the ICISS. World leaders, we noted in Chapter 3, endorsed three pillars of the R2P: (1) The responsibility of the state to protect its own population from genocide, war crimes, ethnic cleansing and crimes against humanity, and from their incitement; (2) The commitment of the international community to assist states in meeting these obligations; (3) The responsibility of United Nations Member States to respond in a timely and decisive manner, using Chapters VI (Pacific Settlement of Disputes), VII (Action with Respect to Threats to the Peace), and VIII (Regional Arrangements) of the UN Charter as appropriate, when a state is manifestly failing to provide such protection. It is important to recognise the scope of the international society's actual commitment to the R2P and to distinguish *actual* commitment from the commitment we would like to see.

In important respects, the World Summit document amounted to much less than had been hoped for, which led some to argue that international society has adopted only 'R2P lite' – the basic concept shorn of much of its substance. Certainly the international commitment to 'stand ready' to respond to genocide and mass atrocities was simply an affirmation of already existing Security Council practice. By 2005, there were very few states prepared to argue that the Security Council lacked the authority to intervene in such humanitarian emergencies. Indeed the council had already declared its commitment to protect civilians in Resolution 1265, passed in 1999. The idea that the Security Council might act to protect civilians was therefore hardly revolutionary. What is more, as adopted by the World Summit, the R2P had no criteria for the use of force, no guidelines about how to proceed when the Security Council was deadlocked, no code of conduct on the veto, and no comprehensive continuum of measures ranging from prevention to rebuilding. Given all this, it was hardly surprising that, in the immediate aftermath of the summit, Gareth Evans (among others) evinced deep disappointment.

However, we should resist the temptation simply to dismiss paragraphs 138 and 139 of the Outcome Document as 'R2P lite' for two main reasons. First, as Edward Luck has argued, international society endorsed the R2P as set out in the Outcome Document, and this creates a powerful mandate for reform. As such, for those interested in translating the R2P into practice, the starting point needs to be the summit's Outcome Document. At the risk of over-simplifying matters, when the overwhelming majority of the world's states speak of the R2P, they mean the R2P as set out in the World Summit Outcome Document, not the ICISS version of it, or any other iteration. There is certainly scope for encouraging governments to reconsider specific ICISS recommendations they have rejected. One of the principal objectives of the new Global Centre for the Responsibility to Protect, for example, is to clarify the applicability of the criteria designed to guide decisions about the use of force in particular crises. Whilst I am sceptical about the practical utility of criteria even if it were possible to persuade governments to endorse them (see Chapter 5) – and there are grounds for questioning whether this is the best use of time and resources it is certainly worthwhile to identify ICISS proposals which were not adopted by international society and to develop new advocacy campaigns to encourage their adoption. However, it is important to recognise the distinction between what the R2P *is* – in terms of what governments themselves have signed up to – and what various activists would *like it to be*. With its adoption by governments, the R2P has been altered in important ways, but adoption has also thrown open the potential for transforming rhetoric into reality.

This brings me to my second reason for thinking twice about the 'R2P lite' label. As Luck has argued, if we take the World Summit Outcome Document at face value and we go through it line by line, we will find not a 'lite' agenda but a 'heavy' one.[1] The admission of responsibility that governments made to their own citizens opens the door to the full range of R2P-related measures discussed in the previous three chapters, almost all of which are designed to encourage and assist governments in meeting their – now formally acknowledged – responsibilities to their citizens. As the previous chapters have demonstrated, there is much work to be done to improve the ability of the UN and regional organisations to give early warning of genocide and mass atrocities, use preventive diplomacy effectively, end impunity via international criminal proceedings and human rights monitoring and dialogue, use rapidly deployable peacekeepers to prevent atrocities and to protect civilians, use and develop a range of targeted sanctions to deter abuses and to deny the abusers the means to ply their trade, and transform shattered societies in the wake of mass killing. All of these measures were pointed to in the Outcome Document and involve tasks for individual member states, UN bodies including the General Assembly, the Security Council, the UN Human Rights Council and UN Peacebuilding Commission, UN agencies such as the UNHCR and UNICEF, as well as regional organisations and civil society groups.

We need to know more about what needs to be done to prevent genocide, to protect civilians, to deter spoilers and to foster dialogue; and we need to know what sorts of practical measures can achieve these goals. The previous three chapters touched briefly on some such issues, but properly translating words into deeds will require the development of detailed plans, and these will have to be followed by patient negotiations to sell them to relevant actors. Many of the specific proposals – such as the creation of an early warning unit in the DPA or a dedicated office to support sanctions committees – have been aired before but dropped for lack of support. The international commitment to the R2P can provide both a catalyst and a rationale for these proposals to be dusted off, revised and put forward again, with fresh impetus. However, to achieve all – or even some – of this will require significant intellectual, financial and diplomatic investment. This will be anything but 'lite'. But there is a real danger that phrases such as 'R2P lite' become self-fulfilling prophecies, and that focusing on those elements we would like to see incorporated into the R2P rather than operationalising those things which already are part of R2P will provide succour to those who seek to block moves designed to advance the R2P – be it in the Security Council, in the UN Human Rights Council, the UN Peacebuilding Commission, in the International Criminal Court or elsewhere. In order to avoid that, it is important that advocates quickly translate the R2P into realistic proposals for institutional and behavioural reform, covering the full range of prevention, reaction and rebuilding set out in the previous three chapters.

This brings us to what all this means for the future direction of R2P, and in particular to its relationship with the non-consensual use force. It is imperative that the R2P should not be conceived of as a substitute for humanitarian intervention. The R2P is a commitment which states make to protect their own citizens from genocide, war crimes, ethnic cleansing and crimes against humanity, and a commitment that, as members of international society, they will assist other states to fulfil their responsibilities, to use a range of diplomatic, humanitarian and other peaceful measures to prevent and protect, and to support the Security Council in its responsibility to take coercive measures when appropriate. It goes without saying that there is a place for non-consensual force in this schema, but the R2P involves a much broader range of measures, calibrated according to their contribution to the prevention of genocide and mass atrocities and protection of endangered populations.

There are two reasons for distinguishing so sharply between the R2P and humanitarian intervention. As has been made clear in the previous three chapters, measures to develop a capacity geared towards the protection of civilians are often blocked at every turn by states which are reluctant to accept external coercive interference in their domestic affairs. Of course, there are occasions when interference is necessary, but, if consensus is to be forged both on the R2P principle and on measures designed to realise it, it is important that the R2P should avoid the appearance of being humanitarian intervention in disguise. The second reason, set out in the introduction, is that the overall aim of the R2P has to be to reduce the frequency with which the protection of civilians from genocide and mass atrocities is dependent on the use of non-consensual force by outsiders. Non-consensual force is a highly unreliable form of protection, and one likely to inflict a high cost in human life. There will be cases where only the use of force will do, but, by developing the capacity to employ effectively the other measures detailed in the previous three chapters, world leaders can reduce the frequency of these cases and afford better protection to a greater number of civilians.

As the R2P develops and progresses, it will distinguish itself more clearly from humanitarian intervention. We should recognise that there are few – if any – institutional reforms capable of resolving difficult debates about whether or not to intervene militarily in those cases where world leaders appear to face a choice between sending in the Marines and doing nothing. In reality, though, that is never the first choice that leaders are presented with. Crises only get to that point because of decisions that local actors, foreign governments and international organisations have already taken. For example, there was a direct link between the Security Council's choice to make UNAMIR in Rwanda small, cheap and badly mandated and the UN's failure to prevent or halt the Rwandan genocide. Likewise, there was a direct link between international society's decision to lock Kosovar Albanians out of the Dayton peace process, and Darfurians out of the Naivasha peace process, and the onset of armed rebellion in Kosovo (in 1998) and Darfur (in 2003).[2] The R2P calls attention to these facts and proposes a system of prevention which would make leaders more aware of the consequences of their decisions and would present opportunities for early action to prevent genocide and mass atrocities. Thankfully, this part of the R2P agenda emerged strengthened from the World Summit. If the policy agenda outlined above and detailed in the previous three chapters were actually implemented, world leaders would be faced far less often with the choice between sending in the Marines and doing nothing; and, in the rare instances where international engagement failed to prevent a crisis, the world's prior engagement would make it much easier to forge consensus on the right course of action, even if that involved the use of force.

Finally, it is important nevertheless to sound a strong note of caution. Almost every measure – no matter how small – outlined in the previous three chapters has been opposed by some, and sometimes by many, governments. If it has come at all, progress has been painfully slow. Governments remain deeply sceptical about external interference in their domestic affairs and reluctant to grant the UN a capacity for independent action, no matter how limited. Even those governments that support the R2P and lack this scepticism have been reluctant to commit more than the bare minimum in terms of human and financial resources. If the R2P principle is to be advanced and its ambition operationalised, it is important for its advocates to lead by example, by committing resources and people to endeavours that fall outside their strategic interests. In Chapter 5, we noted a disconnection between states which advocate robust peace operations and civilian protection and states which actually contribute the vast majority of troops to UN operations. In Chapters 4 and 6 we noted a general reluctance to fund new initiatives by increased assessed financial contributions to the UN. The result is a series of weak and under-resourced initiatives, which are unlikely to fulfil their promise any time soon. This tepid support for institutional capacity building has political consequences too, as it tells the world's sceptics that the advocates of the R2P are less than ready to put their money, their peacekeepers, and their expertise where their mouths are.

Ultimately, a principle can be used and abused by skilled diplomats to satisfy almost any political agenda. The real test for the R2P is whether it can be transformed into a programme of action which delivers real protection to civilians in peril. There are strong indications that it can, and there has been notable progress, but careful diplomacy and a significant political commitment will be needed to overcome the many obstacles which stand in its way.

Notes

Introduction

1 Human Security Centre, 'Human security report 2005' (Vancouver: Human Security Centre, 2006).

2 Lee Feinstein, 'Darfur and beyond: What is needed to prevent mass atrocities' (Council on Foreign Relations, CSR No. 22, January 2007), p. 5.

3 The idea of presenting the issue in terms of future Rwandas and Kosovos was suggested to the author by Nicholas J. Wheeler.

4 I addressed the question of how moral and legal frameworks shape debates about the legitimacy of war in Alex J. Bellamy, *Just Wars: From Cicero to Iraq* (Cambridge: Polity, 2006), especially in Part Two.

5 This is a question I have addressed in greater detail in Alex J. Bellamy, 'Realizing the Responsibility to Protect', *International Studies Perspectives*, forthcoming; but the focus on the R2P's military aspects is demonstrated in Chapters 2 and 3 of this volume.

6 I owe this insight to Edward Luck.

7 E. g. S/PV.5319 (Resumption 1), 9 December 2005, p. 3, S/PV.5319, 9 December 2005, p. 19, S/PV.5319, 9 December 2005, p. 30.

8 Edward C. Luck, 'Introduction: The responsible sovereign and the responsibility to protect', in *Annual Review of United Nations Affairs, 2006/7* (Oxford: Oxford University Press, 2008), p. xxxiv.

9 S/PV.5703, 22 June 2007, p. 17.

10 International Commission on Intervention and State Sovereignty, 'The responsibility to protect: (Ottawa: IDRC, 2001), Vol. 1, para. 2.24; UN High-Level Panel on Threats, Challenges and Change, 'A more secure world: Our shared responsibility', A/59/565, 2 December 2004, para. 203.

11 See, for example, Junta Brunnee and Stephen J. Toope, 'Norms, institutions and UN reform: The responsibility to protect', *Behind the Headlines*, 63 (3) 2006, esp. pp. 2–3.

12 Ban Ki-moon, 'Annual address to the UN General Assembly', SG/SM.11182, 25 September 2007.

13 Joseph Legro, 'Which norms matter? Revisiting the "failure" of internationalism', *International Organization*, 51(1) 1997, p. 33.

14 For instance, see Nicholas J. Wheeler, 'The humanitarian responsibilities of sovereignty: Explaining the development of a new norm of military intervention for humanitarian purposes in international society', in Jennifer M. Welsh (ed.), *Humanitarian Intervention and International Relations* (Oxford: Oxford University Press, 2004), pp. 29–51; Nicholas J. Wheeler, 'The emerging norm of collective responsibility to protect after R2P and HLP', paper presented at the BISA Conference, University of Warwick, 20–2 December 2004.

15 UN High-Level Panel, 'A more secore world' (above, n10), para. 203.

16 Gareth Evans, 'When is it right to fight?' *Survival* 46, no. 3 (2004), pp. 59–82.

17 E.g. Martha Finnemore and Kathryn Sikkink, 'International norm dynamics and political change', *International Organization*, 52 (4) 1998, p p. 887–918 and Friedreich V. Kratochwil, *Rules, Norms and Decisions: On the Conditions of Practice and Legal Reasoning in International Relations and Domestic Affairs* (Cambridge: Cambridge University Press, 1989).

Chapter 1 Sovereignty and Human Rights

1. This section draws its ideas and some of its text from Alex J. Bellamy, 'The responsibility to protect', in Paul D. Williams (ed.), *Security Studies: An Introduction* (London: Routledge, 2008).
2. Both cited by Nicholas J. Wheeler, *Saving Strangers: Humanitarian Intervention in International Society* (Oxford: Oxford University Press, 2000), pp. 90–1.
3. Both cited by Simon Chesterman, *Just War or Just Peace? Humanitarian Intervention and International Law* (Oxford: Oxford University Press, 2001), p. 80.
4. UNSC, S/PV.4988, 11 June 2004, p. 4.
5. UNSC, S/PV.5158, 31 March 2005, p. 3.
6. Chesterman, *Just War or Just Peace?* (above, n3), p. 231.
7. See Wheeler, *Saving Strangers* (above, n2), pp. 78–110.
8. See Mlada Bukovansky, *Legitimacy and Power Politics: The American and French Revolutions in International Political Culture* (Princeton: Princeton University Press, 2002).
9. This is a paraphrased and simplified version of Brad Roth's argument. See Brad R. Roth, *Governmental Illegitimacy in International Law* (Oxford: Oxford University Press, 2000).
10. Heinrich von Treitschke, *Politik* (Leipzig: Insel, 1899), vol. 2, p. 100.
11. Paul Fauchille, *Traité de droit international public* (Paris: Libraire Arthur Rousseau, 1921), p. 428.
12. Cited by James W. Garner, 'Some questions of international law in the European war', *American Journal of International Law*, 9 (1) 1915, p. 77.
13. Coleman Phillipson, *International Law and the Great War* (New York: E. P. Dutton and Co., 1916), pp. 46–7.
14. Lloyd George, 'Through terror to triumph: An appeal to the nation', speech delivered at the Queen's Hall London, 19 September 1914, pp. 4–6.
15. E.g. Victoria Brittain, 'Colonialism and the predatory state in the Congo', *New Left Review*, 236, July/August 1999, p. 133.
16. In Samuel H. Nelson, *Colonialism in the Congo Basin, 1880–1940* (Athens, OH: Ohio University Center for International Studies, 1994), p. 86.
17. See Tony Ward, 'State crime in the heart of darkness', *British Journal of Criminology*, 45 (4) 2005, p. 437.
18. Hedley Bull, 'Introduction', in H. Bull (ed.), *Intervention in World Politics* (Oxford: Clarendon Press, 1986), p. 3.
19. Barry Buzan, *From International to World Society? English School Theory and the Social Structure of Globalisation* (Cambridge: Cambridge University Press, 2004), p. 143.
20. Hidemi Suganami, 'Sovereignty, intervention and the English school', paper presented to the 4th Pan European Conference, University of Kent, 8–10 September 2001.
21. Kofi Annan, 'Two concepts of sovereignty', *Economist*, 18 September 1999.
22. Walzer, *Just and Unjust Wars: A Philosophical Argument with Historical Illustrations* (New York: Basic Books, 1977), p. 57.
23. Chesterman, *Just War or Just Peace?* (above, n3), p. 49.
24. Malcolm N. Shaw, *International Law*, fifth edition (Cambridge: Cambridge University Press, 2003), p. 227.
25. See Robert H. Jackson, *The Global Covenant: Human Conduct in a World of States* (Oxford: Oxford University Press, 2002), p. 291.

26 Cited by Ian Brownlie, 'Humanitarian intervention', in John N. Moore (ed.), *Law and Civil War in the Modern World* (Baltimore: Johns Hopkins University Press, 1974), pp. 217–21.

27 Chesterman, *Just War or Just Peace?* (above, n3), p. 231.

28 E.g. John Stuart Mill, 'A few words on non-intervention' [1859], in John Stuart Mill, *Essays on Politics and Culture* (edited by Gertrude Himmelfarb) (Gloucester: Peter Smith, 1973), pp. 368–84.

29 Gareth Evans, 'Foreword', in Ramesh Thakur, *The United Nations, Peace and Security: From Collective Security to the Responsibility to Protect* (Cambridge: Cambridge University Press, 2006), p. xiv.

30 Ramesh Thakur, 'A shared responsibility for a more secure world', *Global Governance*, 11 (3) 2005, p. 284.

31 Annan, 'Two concepts of sovereignty' (above, n21), p. 1.

32 Lynn Hunt, *Inventing Human Rights: A History* (London: W. W. Norton and Co., 2007), p. 20.

33 Thomas G. Weiss and David A. Korn, *Internal Displacement: Conceptualization and its Consequences* (New York: Routledge, 2006), pp. 71–3.

34 In Peter Balakian, *The Burning Tigris: The Armenian Genocide and America's Response* (New York: Perennial, 2004), pp. 307–8.

35 Atlantic Charter,12 August 1941. See Elizabeth Borgwardt, *A New Deal for the World: America's Vision for Human Rights* (Cambridge, MA: Harvard University Press, 2005).

36 Hunt, *Inventing Human Rights* (above, n32), p. 203.

37 Thomas G. Weiss, *Humanitarian Intervention: Ideas in Action* (Cambridge: Polity, 2007), p. 90.

38 See Sara E. Davies, *Legitimising Rejection? International Refugee Law in Southeast Asia* (The Hague: Martinus Nijhoff, 2007).

39 Francis M. Deng, 'The impact of state failure on migration', *Mediterranean Quarterly*, Fall 2004, p. 18.

40 Ibid., p. 20.

41 Roberta Cohen and Francis M. Deng, *Masses in Flight: The Global Crisis of Internal Displacement* (Washington, DC: The Brookings Institution, 1998), p. 275.

42 Deng, 'Impact of state failure on migration' (above, n39), p. 20.

43 Francis M. Deng, Sadikiel Kimaro, Terrence Lyons, Donald Rothchild and I. William Zartman, *Sovereignty as Responsibility: Conflict Management in Africa* (Washington, DC: The Brookings Institution, 1996), p. 1.

44 Ibid., p. 28.

45 Cited ibid., p. 9.

46 Ashton B. Carter, John M. Deutch and Philip D. Zelikow, 'Catastrophic terrorism: Elements of a national policy', Visions of Government for the Twenty-First Century Report, Harvard University, 1998.

47 Richard N. Haass, 'Defining US foreign policy in a post-post-Cold War world', The 2002 Arthur Ross Lecture, 22 April 2002.

48 Stewart Patrick, 'The role of the US government in humanitarian intervention', 5 April 2004, cited in Stuart Elden, 'Contingent sovereignty, territorial integrity and the sanctity of borders', *SAIS Review*, 26 (1) 2006, p. 15.

49 US Department of Defense, 'The national defense strategy of the United States of America', March 2005.

50 Tony Blair, 'Doctrine of the international community', speech to the Economic Club of Chicago, Hilton Hotel, Chicago, 22 April 1999.

51 John Kampfner, *Blair's Wars* (London: The Free Press, 2003), pp. 50–3.

52 Nicholas J. Wheeler, 'Legitimating humanitarian intervention: Principles and procedures', *Melbourne Journal of International Law*, 2 (2) 2001, p. 564 and n51.

53 UN Commission on Human Rights, 'Responses of governments and agencies to the report of the UN Special Representative for internally displaced persons', E/CN.4/1993/SR.40, 1993.

54 Ibid.

55 James Traub, *The Best Intentions: Kofi Annan and the UN in an Era of American Power* (London: Bloomsbury, 2006), p. 91.

56 See chapters by Brian Urquhart, Quang Trinh and Ian Johnstone in Simon Chesterman (ed.), *Secretary or General? The UN Secretary-General in World Politics* (Cambridge: Cambridge University Press, 2007).

57 Kofi Annan, 'Intervention', Ditchley Foundation Lecture, 26 June 1998.

58 Traub, *Best Intentions* (above, n55), p. 97.

59 Ibid., p. 98.

60 Cited in Stanley Meisler, *Kofi Annan: A Man of Peace in a World of War* (London: Wiley, 2007), pp. 177–8.

61 Ibid., p. 179.

62 Final document of the XIII Ministerial Conference of the Movement of Non-Aligned Countries, Cartagena, Colombia, 8–9 April 2000, pp. 41–2.

63 Cited by Meisler, *Kofi Annan* (above, n60), p. 178.

64 Traub, *Best Intentions* (above, n55), p. 99.

65 Ibid., p. 100.

66 Kofi Annan, 'Annual report of the Secretary-General to the General Assembly', 20 September 1999.

67 Traub, *Best Intentions* (above, n55), p. 101.

68 Annan, 'Annual report' (above, n66).

69 Cited in Traub, *Best Intentions* (above, n55), p. 101 and Meisler, *Kofi Annan* (above, n60), p. 186.

70 Traub, *Best Intentions* (above, n55), p. 101.

71 International Council on Human Rights Policy, 'Human rights crises: NGO responses to military interventions' (Versoix: International Council on Human Rights Policy, 2002).

72 The idea of seeing the two strands described in this chapter as having distinct origins was suggested by Edward Luck.

Chapter 2 The International Commission on Intervention and State Sovereignty

1 Lloyd Axworthy, *Navigating a New World: Canada's Global Future* (Toronto: Alfred A. Knopf, 2003), p. 191.

2 Kofi Annan, '"We, the peoples": The role of the United Nations in the 21st century', Report of the UN Secretary-General, 2000, pp. 47–8.

3 Address by Prime Minister Jean Chrétien to the Plenary Session of the Millennium Summit of the United Nations, 7 September 2000.

4 Lloyd Axworthy, 'Humanitarian intervention and humanitarian constraints', Hauser Lecture on International Humanitarian Law, New York University School of Law, 10 February 2000.

5 Canadian Ministry of Foreign Affairs, 'Axworthy launches international commission on intervention and state sovereignty', 14 September 2000.

6 Canadian Ministry of Foreign Affairs, 'Axworthy'. See Ramesh Thakur, Andrew F. Cooper and John English (eds), *International Commissions and the Power of Ideas* (Tokyo: United Nations University Press, 2004).

7 Jennifer Bond and Laurel Sherret, *A Sight for Sore Eyes: Bringing Gender Vision to the Responsibility to Protect Framework*, United Nations International Research and Training Institute for the Advancement of Women, March 2006.

8 Ramesh Thakur, 'Intervention, sovereignty, and the responsibility to protect', in Thakur, Cooper and English (eds), *International Commissions* (above, n6), p. 183.

9 Ottawa (November 2000), Maputo (March 2001), New Delhi (June 2001), Wakefield, Canada (August 2001), Brussels (September 2001).

10 Detailed in Gareth Evans and Mohamed Sahnoun, 'Foreword' to International Commission on Intervention and State Sovereignty (ICISS), 'The responsibility to protect' (Ottawa: IDRC, 2001), p. viii. This is the published version of an earlier 'Report from the Ottawa Roundtable for the International Commission on Intervention and State Sovereignty' (see below, n25).

11 Thanks to Nick Wheeler for information on the Wilton Park meeting.

12 Evans and Sahnoun, 'Foreword' (above, n10), p. viii.

13 Jeffrey Boutwell, 'Report on the Pugwash study group on intervention', Sovereignty and International Security meeting, Venice, Italy, 10–11 December 1999.

14 Hugh Beach, 'Secessions, interventions and just war theory: The case of Kosovo', *Pugwash Occasional Papers*, 1, 2000.

15 Boutwell, 'Report' (above, n13).

16 Jeffrey Boutwell, Report on the 2nd Pugwash Workshop on intervention, sovereignty and international security, Como, Italy, 28–30 September 2000.

17 Vladimir Baranovsky, 'Humanitarian intervention: Russian perspectives', *Pugwash Occasional Papers*, 2, 2000.

18 Chu Shulong, 'China, Asia and issues of sovereignty and humanitarian intervention', *Pugwash Occasional Papers*, 2, 2000.

19 Radha Kumar, 'Sovereignty and intervention: Opinions in South Asia', *Pugwash Occasional Papers*, 2, 2000.

20 Adekeye Adebajo and Chris Landsberg, 'The heirs of Nkrumah: Africa's new investments', *Pugwash Occasional Papers*, 2, 2000.

21 Boutwell, 'Report (no. 2)' (above, n13).

22 Ibid., p. 11.

23 Jorge Heine, 'The responsibility to protect: Humanitarian intervention and the principles of non-intervention in the Americas', in Thakur, Cooper and English (eds), *International Commissions* (above, n6), pp. 238–43.

24 Independent International Commission on Kosovo, *Kosovo Report: Conflict, International Response, Lessons Learned* (Oxford: Oxford University Press, 2000), opening summary. This line of reasoning is also developed later in the report.

25 Report from the Ottawa Roundtable for the International Commission on Intervention and State Sovereignty (ICISS), Canadian Centre for Foreign Policy Development, 1011.9E, 15 January 2001 (for which see also above, n10).

26 Thomas Weiss, email to the author, 30 October 2007.

27 The extent to which the commissioners sought to distance themselves from 'humanitarian intervention' was conveyed to the author by Ramesh Thakur in a personal email.

28 ICISS, 'The responsibility to protect' (above, n10), p. 357.

29 Ramesh Thakur, 'The responsibility to protect and the global south', unpublished paper in the possession in the author.

30 Report from the Ottawa Roundtable (above, n25), p. 9.

31 This account was given by Gareth Evans.

32 Roundtable consultation with nongovernmental and other interested organisations', Geneva, 31 January 2001, in Thomas G. Weiss and Don Hubert, 'The responsibility to protect: Research, bibliography, background' (Ottawa: IDRC, 2001), p. 355. (This is Volume 2 of the ICISS report in n10.)

33 Ibid., p. 394.

34 Ibid., p. 360.

35 Ibid., p. 363.

36 Ibid., p. 386.
37 Ibid., p. 380.
38 Ibid., p. 368.
39 Ibid., p. 360.
40 Jeffrey Boutrell, 'Report on the Joint Meeting of the Pugwash Study Group on Intervention, Sovereignty and International Security and the International Commission on Intervention and State Sovereignty', 20–1 July 2001, Pugwash, Nova Scotia.
41 Ramesh Thakur, 'A shared responsibility for a more secure world', *Global Governance*, 11 (3) 2005, p. 284.
42 Weiss and Hubert, 'The responsibility to protect: Research, bibliography, background' (above, n32), p. 367.
43 Ibid., p. 378.
44 Ibid., p. 361.
45 Ibid., p. 381.
46 Mohamed Sid-Ahmed, 'Sovereignty and intervention', *Al-Ahram Weekly*, 7–13 June 2001.
47 Weiss and Hubert, 'The responsibility to protect: Research, bibliography, background' (above, n32), pp. 364–5.
48 Ibid., p. 395.
49 Ibid., p. 379.
50 Ibid., pp. 367–8.
51 Ibid., p. 363.
52 Ibid.
53 Ibid., pp. 393–4.
54 Stanlake J. T. M. Samkange, 'African perspectives on intervention and state sovereignty', *African Security Review*, 11 (1) 2002, p. 5.
55 Ibid.
56 ICISS, 'The responsibility to protect' (above, n10), p. 5.
57 Thomas Weiss, email to the author, 30 October 2007.
58 'Canada launches report of the international commission on intervention and state sovereignty', press release of the Canadian Permanent Mission to the UN, 18 December 2002.
59 Kofi Annan, 'The responsibility to protect', address to the International Peace Academy, 15 February 2002, UN press release SG/SM/8125.
60 ICISS, 'The responsibility to protect' (above, n10), p. xi.
61 Thomas G. Weiss, *Humanitarian Intervention: Ideas in Action* (Cambridge: Polity), p. 104.
62 Thomas Weiss, email to the author, 31 October 2007.
63 ICISS, 'The responsibility to protect' (above, n10), p. 19.
64 Ibid., p. 21.
65 Ibid., pp. 21–2.
66 Ibid., p. 23.
67 Ibid., p. 25.
68 Ibid., p. 26.
69 Ibid., p. 25.
70 Ibid.
71 Ibid., p. 32.
72 Ibid., p. 49.
73 Ibid., pp. 53–5.
74 Ibid., pp. xii–xiii.
75 Ibid., p. xii.
76 See Nicholas J. Wheeler, 'The humanitarian responsibilities of sovereignty: Explaining the development of a new norm of military intervention for humanitarian purposes in international society', in Jennifer M. Welsh (ed.), *Humanitarian Intervention and International Relations* (Oxford: Oxford University Press, 2004), pp. 29–51.

77 ICISS, 'The responsibility to protect' (above, n10), p. 55.
78 Ibid., p. 39.
79 Ibid., p. 40.
80 Ibid., p. 42.
81 Anthony Lewis, 'The challenge of global justice now', *Dædalus*, 132 (1) 2003, p. 8.
82 David Chandler, '*The Responsibility to Protect*: Imposing the liberal peace', in Alex J. Bellamy and Paul D. Williams (eds), *Peace Operations and Global Order* (London: Routledge, 2005), pp. 59–82.
83 Ibid., pp. 64–5.
84 Ibid., pp. 65–6.
85 Ibid., p. 67.
86 I owe this insight to Luke Glanville, whose doctoral thesis sets out this history in full.
87 Thomas Weiss, 'The sunset of humanitarian intervention? The responsibility to protect in a unipolar era', *Security Dialogue*, 35 (2) 2004, pp. 135–53 and Michael Byers, 'High ground lost on UN's responsibility to protect', *Winnipeg Free Press*, 18 September 2005, p. B3.
88 Weiss, 'The sunset of humanitarian intervention?' (above, n87), p. 139.
89 Ibid.
90 Ibid., p. 140.
91 Bond and Sherret, *Sight for Sore Eyes* (above, n7), p. 24.
92 Some commentators, it should be noted, thought the commission's cautious attitude on this question 'surely right', because of international opposition to a legal 'right' of intervention. See Adam Roberts, 'Intervention: One step forward in the search for the impossible', *International Journal of Human Rights*, 7(3) 2003, p. 146.
93 Jennifer Welsh, Carolin J. Thielking and S. Neil MacFarlane, 'The responsibility to protect: Assessing the report of the International Commission on Intervention and State Sovereignty', in Thakur, Cooper and English (eds), *International Commissions* (above, n6), pp. 204–5.
94 See Amitai Etzioni, 'Sovereignty as responsibility', *Orbis*, 50 (1) 2006, p. 80.
95 Ibid.
96 Ibid., p. 51.
97 Roberts, 'Intervention' (above, n88), p. 149.
98 Welsh, Thielking and MacFarlane, 'Assessing the report of the ICISS' (above, n93), p. 212.
99 Roderic Alley, *Internal Conflict and the International Community: Wars Without End?* (Aldershot: Ashgate, 2004), p. 159.
100 ICISS, 'The responsibility to protect' (above, n10), pp. 74–5.
101 Ian Johnstone, 'The Secretary-General as norm entrepreneur', in Simon Chesterman (ed.), *Secretary or General? The UN Secretary-General in World Politics* (Cambridge: Cambridge University Press, 2007), pp. 131–7.
102 ICISS, 'The responsibility to protect' (above, n10), p. xi and Ramesh Thakur, *The United Nations, Peace and Security: From Collective Security to the Responsibility to Protect* (Cambridge: Cambridge University Press, 2006), p. 257.
103 See World Federalist Movement–International Policy Group, 'Civil society perspectives on the responsibility to protect', Final report, 30 April 2003 and Noel M. Morada, 'R2P roadmap in Southeast Asia: Challenges and prospects', UNISCI Discussion Papers, No 11, May 2006.

Chapter 3 The 2005 World Summit

1 United Nations General Assembly, '2005 Summit Outcome', A/60/L.1, 20 September 2005, paras 138–9.
2 This phrase was suggested to me by Thomas Weiss in an email dated 30 October 2007.

3 I am grateful to Edward Luck for pointing this out to me.
4 Jennifer M. Welsh, 'Conclusion: Humanitarian intervention after 11 September', in Jennifer M. Welsh (ed.), *Humanitarian Intervention and International Relations* (Oxford: Oxford University Press, 2004), p. 180.
5 S. Neil Macfarlane, Carolin J. Thiekling and Thomas G. Weiss, '*The Responsibility to Protect*: Is anyone interested in humanitarian intervention?', *Third World Quarterly*, 25 (5) 2004, p. 983.
6 Yevgeny Primakov, 'UN process, not humanitarian intervention, is world's best hope', *New Perspectives Quarterly*, 2 September 2004.
7 Welsh, 'Conclusion' (above, n4), p. 204, n. 4.
8 Statement by Mr Nirupam Sen, Permanent Representative, at the informal thematic consultations of the General Assembly on the report of the Secretary-General entitled 'In larger freedom: Towards development, security and human rights for all' (A/59/2005) (On Cluster III Issues: Freedom to Live in Dignity) on 20 April 2005.
9 Statement by the chairman of the Coordinating Bureau [Malaysia] of the Non-Aligned Movement on behalf of the Non-Aligned Movement at the informal meeting of the plenary of the General Assembly concerning the Draft Outcome Document of the high-level plenary meeting of the General Assembly; delivered by H. E. Ambassador Radzi Rahma, *chargé d'affaires* of the Permanent Mission Malaysia to the United Nations, New York, 21 June 2005.
10 Statement by H. E. Ambassador Stafford Neil, Permanent Representative of Jamaica to the United Nations and Chairman of the Group of 77, on the report of the Secretary-General entitled 'In larger freedom', 6 April 2005.
11 Michael Ignatieff, 'Why are we in Iraq? (and Liberia? and Afghanistan?)', *New York Times Magazine*, 7 September 2003, pp. 2–7.
12 Gareth Evans, 'When is it right to fight?' *Survival* 46 (3) 2004, pp. 59–82.
13 Respectively Ian Williams, 'Intervene with caution', *In These Times*, 28 July 2003, p. 7; Richard Falk, 'Humanitarian intervention: A forum', *Nation*, 14 July 2003, p. 2; Bruce Jentelson, 'A responsibility to protect: The defining challenge for global community', *Ethnic Conflict*, 28 (4) 2007, p. 3; Karl Kaiser, 'A European perspective on the post Iraq new international order', paper presented at the Center for Strategic and International Studies, Jakarta, 29 July 2003; John Kampfner, interviewed by Tim Dunne; available at www.ex.ac.uk/ships/news/kampfner.htm; and The Fund for Peace, *Neighbours on Alert: Regional Views on Humanitarian Intervention*, Summary Report of the Regional Responses to Internal War Program, October 2003, p. 6.
14 David Clark, 'Iraq has wrecked our case for humanitarian wars', *Guardian*, 12 August 2003, p. 16.
15 Nicholas J. Wheeler, 'The emerging norm of collective responsibility to protect after R2P and HLP', paper presented at the BISA Conference, University of Warwick, 20–2 December 2004.
16 See 'British PM urges tougher stance against brutal regimes', *Agence-France Press*, 14 July 2003 and Kevin Ward, 'Process needed so countries know when to intervene to protect human rights', *CBS (Canada)*, 13 July 2003.
17 Speech by Chancellor Shroeder at the opening of the Federal College for Security Studies, 19 March 2004.
18 Cheryl O. Igiri and Princeton N. Lyman, 'Giving meaning to "never again": Seeking an effective response to the crisis in Darfur and beyond', CSR No. 5 (Council on Foreign Relations, New York, NY, September 2004), p. 21.
19 Maria Banda, 'The responsibility to protect: Moving the agenda forward', paper for the UN Association of Canada, March 2007, p. 10.
20 'Civil society meeting on the responsibility to protect', Final Report, Geneva, 28 March 2003, p. 9.

21 Ibid.
22 Memo to the author from Allan Rock, Permanent Representative of Canada to the UN (2004–6), 12 November 2007.
23 'Civil society meeting on the responsibility to protect', Final Report, Ottawa, 8 April 2003, p. 9.
24 Ibid.
25 WFM–IGC, 'Civil society perspectives on the responsibility to protect', Final report, 30 April 2003, p. 20.
26 Noel M. Morada, 'R2P roadmap in Southeast Asia: Challenges and prospects', UNISCI Discussion Papers, No. 11, May 2006.
27 William Pace (R2P–CS), letter to permanent missions to the UN, 11 July 2005.
28 WFM–IGC, 'Civil society perspectives' (above, n25), p. 21.
29 Ibid., p. 9.
30 Michael Byers, 'High ground lost on UN's responsibility to protect', *Winnipeg Free Press*, 18 September 2005, p. B3.
31 Paul Martin, Prime Minister of Canada, Address to the 59th General Assembly, 22 September 2004.
32 Ibid.
33 Government of Canada, 'Non-paper on *The Responsibility to Protect* and the evolution of the United Nations peace and security mandate: Submission to the UN High-Level Panel on Threats, Challenges and Change', undated, para. 4.1.
34 Ibid., para. 4.3.
35 Ibid., paras 5.1 and 5.2.
36 It is important to note that the debate about criteria for guiding decision-making in this way dates back to the 1970s; see especially Richard B. Lillich, 'Humanitarian Intervention: A Reply to Ian Brownlie and a Plea for Constructive Alternatives' in John N. Moore (ed.), *Law and Civil War in the Modern World* (Baltimore, Md: Johns Hopkins University Press, 1974), pp. 217–251 and more generally Richard B. Lillich (ed.), *Humanitarian Intervention and the United Nations* (Charlottesville, VG: University Press of Virginia, 1973).
37 Ramesh Thakur, 'A shared responsibility for a more secure world', *Global Governance*, 11(3) 2005, p. 284.
38 Ramesh Thakur, 'Iraq and the responsibility to protect', *Behind the Headlines*, 62 (1) 2004, pp. 1–16.
39 This phrase was suggested to me by Thomas Weiss, in an email dated 30 October 2007.
40 Nicholas J. Wheeler, 'A victory for common humanity? The responsibility to protect after the 2005 World Summit', paper presented to a conference on 'The UN at sixty: Celebration or wake?', University of Toronto, 6–7 October, 2005, p. 4.
41 UN High-Level Panel on Threats, Challenges and Change, 'A more secure world: Our shared responsibility', A/59/565, 2 December 2004, para. 203.
42 Ibid., para. 198.
43 Yevgeny M. Primakov, 'Rather the United Nations than US unilateralism', *New Perspectives Quarterly*, 21 (2) 2004, pp. 3–4.
44 HLP, 'A more secure world' (above, n41), para. 203.
45 Ibid., para. 207.
46 Ibid., para. 257.
47 Kofi Annan, 'In larger freedom' (above, n8).
48 William R. Pace and Nicole Deller, 'Preventing future genocides: An international responsibility to protect', *World Order*, 36 (4) 2005, p. 25.
49 Annan, 'In larger freedom' (above, n8), para. 135. and para. 126.
50 Mohamed Bennouna (Morocco) speaking on behalf of the NAM, General Assembly press release, GA/PK/183. 31 January 2005, p. 6.

51 Statement by H. E. Ambassador Stafford Neil, Permanent Representative of Jamaica to the United Nations and Chairman of the Group of 77, on the report of the Secretary-General entitled 'In larger freedom', 6 April 2005.

52 Greg Puley, 'The responsibility to protect: East, west and southern African perspectives on preventing and responding to humanitarian crises', report for Africa Peace Forum, African Women's Development and Communication Network and Project Ploughshares, September 2005, p. 19.

53 Paul D. Williams, 'From non-intervention to non-indifference: The origins and development of the African Union's security culture', *African Affairs*, 106 (423), 2007, pp. 253–79.

54 See Ben Kioko, 'The right of interference under the African Union's constitutive act: From non-interference to non-intervention', *International Review of the Red Cross* 85 (6) 2003, p. 852. For a general introduction to the transformation of the OAU into the AU, see Samuel Makinda and F. Wafula Okumu, *The African Union: Challenges of Globalization, Security and Governance* (London: Routledge, 2007).

55 Declaration of African Heads of State and Governments, 8 July 2002.

56 Kioko, 'The Right of Intervention' (above, n54), p. 817.

57 For an excellent account, see Katherina P. Coleman, *International Organizations and Peace Enforcement: The Politics of International Legitimacy* (Cambridge: Cambridge University Press, 2007), pp. 116–92.

58 See, for instance, Philip Nel, 'South Africa: The demand for legitimate multilateralism', in Albrecht Schnabel and Ramesh Thakur (eds), *Kosovo and the Challenge of Humanitarian Intervention: Selective Indignation, Collective Action and International Citizenship* (Tokyo: UN University Press, 2000), pp. 245–59.

59 UNSC 5015th meeting, S/PV.5015, 30 July 2004, especially pp. 10–12.

60 E/CN.4/2005.8 27 September 2004, paras 22, 26 and 36.

61 S.PV/5040, 18 September 2004, pp. 2–3.

62 Final communiqué: African mini-summit on Darfur', Tripoli, Libya, 17 October 2004, p. 2.

63 African Union Executive Council, 'The common African position on the proposed reform of the United Nations', ext/EX.CL/2(VII), Addis Ababa, 7–8 March 2005, section B (i).

64 Ibid.

65 Ibid.

66 See Greg Puley, 'The responsibility to protect: East, west and southern African perspectives (above, n52), p. 4.

67 Sir Adam Roberts, 'The United Nations and humanitarian intervention', in Jennifer Welsh (ed.), *Humanitarian Intervention and International Relations* (Oxford: Oxford University Press, 2004), p. 90.

68 James Traub, *The Best Intentions: Kofi Annan and the UN in an Era of American Power* (London: Bloomsbury, 2006), p. 362.

69 Ibid.

70 Report of the Task Force on the United Nations, *American Interests and UN Reform* (Washington DC: United States Institute of Peace, 2005), p. 28.

71 Ibid.

72 Ibid., p. 29. On the question of Darfur, see Chapter 5 below and Alex J. Bellamy, 'A responsibility to protect or a Trojan horse? The crisis in Darfur and humanitarian intervention after Iraq', *Ethics and International Affairs*, 19 (2) 2005.

73 Task Force on the United Nations, *American Interests and UN Reform* (aboved, n70), p. 32.

74 Traub, *Best Intentions* (above, n68), p. 363.

75 Statement of the Honorable John R. Bolton, US Permanent Representative of the United Nations, 'Lessons learned from the September 14–16 United Nations high-level

event', Hearing before the House International Relations Committee, 28 September 2005, p. 4.

76 Personal email from John Dauth.

77 Statement by Ambassador Stafford Neil, Permanent Representative of Jamaica to the United Nations, Chairman of the Group of 77, on Cluster 1 (Freedom from Want) of the Secretary-General's report 'In larger freedom: Towards development, security and human rights for all', New York, 25 April 2005.

78 Memo from Allan Rock to the author, 12 November 2007, and email to the author from John Dauth, July 2007.

79 Advanced Unedited Version (5 August 2005), A/59/HLPM/CRP.1 (Rev 2), paras 118–19 and Revised Draft Outcome Document (10 August 2005).

80 These provisions were in the Advanced Unedited Version (5 August 2005), paras 118–19.

81 Nicholas D. Kristof, 'A wimp on genocide', *New York Times*, 18 September 2005.

82 Pace and Deller, 'Preventing future genocides' (above, n48), p. 28.

83 Memo from Allan Rock to the author, 12 November 2007.

84 John Bolton, *Surrender is Not an Option: Defending America at the United Nations and Abroad* (New York: Threshold Editions, 2007), p. 204. John Dauth's view was communicated to the author in an email.

85 Ibid., p. 207.

86 Letter from John R. Bolton, the representative of the United States of America to the United Nations, to President Ping, president of the UN General Assembly, 30 August 2005.

87 Ibid.

88 For Bolton's account see Bolton, *Surrender is Not an Option* (above, n84), pp. 208–9; cf. Traub, *Best Intentions* (above, n68), p. 374. Bolton's reasoning is set out in a letter from John R. Bolton on the Millennium Development Goals, 26 August 2005.

89 Traub, *Best Intentions* (above, n68), p. 373 and Stephen John Stedman, 'UN transformation in an era of soft power balancing', *International Affairs*, 83 (5) 2007, p. 940.

90 Traub, *Best Intentions* (above, n68), p. 373.

91 See 'Position paper of the People's Republic of China on the United Nations reforms', 8 June 2005, p. 12.

92 Hu Jintao, president of the People's Republic of China, 'Building towards a harmonious world of lasting peace and common prosperity', Statement at the United Nations Summit, 15 September 2005.

93 Email from John Dauth, July 2007.

94 See Yevgeny Primakov, 'Best hope' (above, n6).

95 Memo from Allan Rock to the author, 12 November 2007.

96 Statement by the chairman of the Coordinating Bureau [Malaysia] of the Non-Aligned Movement (above, n9).

97 See Ifikhar Ali, 'Annan's reform plans criticized by other developing countries', *The Nation*, 8 April 2005.

98 Traub, *Best Intentions* (above, n68), p. 386.

99 Memo from Allan Rock to the author, 12 November 2007.

100 See comments by the *chargé d'affaires* of South Africa's permanent mission to the UN, Xoliso Mabhongo, at the informal meeting to consider the draft outcome document, 20 April 2005.

101 See Statement by Augustine Mahinga to the United Nations at the informal thematic consultations of the General Assembly on Cluster III: Freedom to Live in Dignity, 20 April 2005.

102 Memo from Allan Rock to the author, 12 November 2007.

103 Bolton, *Surrender is Not an Option* (above, n84), p. 209.

104 Howard LaFranchi, 'At UN, Bolton softens his tone', *Christian Science Monitor*, 12 September 2005.
105 Stedman, 'UN transformation' (above, n89), p. 940.
106 Bolton, *Surrender is Not an Option* (above, n84), p. 210.
107 Ibid., p. 941.
108 Ibid. and Traub, *Best Intentions* (above, n68), pp. 386–7.
109 Personal email from John Dauth to the author, July 2007.
110 Memo from Allan Rock to the author, 12 November 2007.
111 See Michael Byers, *War Law: International Law and Armed Conflict* (London: Atlantic Books, 2005), pp. 40–50.
112 Todd Lindberg, 'Protect the people', *Washington Post*, 27 September 2005.
113 Cited in Mark Turner, 'UN "must never again be found wanting on genocide"', *Financial Times*, 16 September 2005.
114 Michael Byers, 'High Ground Lost' (above, n30), 18 September 2005.
115 Newt Gingrich and George Mitchell, 'Report card from America: UN reform', *International Herald Tribune*, 28 November 2005.
116 Bolton, *Surrender is Not an Option* (above, n84), p. 214.
117 Emma-Kate Symons, 'UN reform a disaster: Evans', *Australian*, 19 October 2005.
118 A point made by James Traub.
119 Personal email from John Dauth.
120 International Service for Human Rights, '2005 World Summit: World leaders fail their human rights test', June / September 2005.
121 Kofi Annan, Address to Universidade Nova de Lisboa, M2 Presswire, 13 October 2005.
122 Pace and Deller, 'Preventing future genocides' (above, n48), p. 17.
123 R2P–CS, 'West Africa R2P workshops', post-workshop report, September 2006.
124 Senate of the Ninety-Fourth Assembly of the State of Illinois and the House of Representatives, joint resolution LRB094 21932 RLC 60401, 9 January 2007.
125 Gareth Evans, 'Taking the responsibility to the next level: A proposal', 2007. Thanks to Gareth Evans for forwarding this document.
126 Stedman, 'UN transformation' (above, n89), p. 942.
127 This is an issue I explore in greater detail in Alex J. Bellamy, 'Realizing the responsibility to protect', *International Studies Perspectives*, 10 (1) 2009.
128 Morada, 'R2P roadmap in Southeast Asia' (above, n26).

Chapter 4 Prevention

1 This phrase is drawn from Lee Feinstein, 'Darfur and beyond: What is needed to prevent mass atrocities', Council on Foreign Relations, CSR No. 22, January 2007, p. 5.
2 Edward Luck, 'Prevention: Theory and practice', in Fen Osler Hampson and David Malone (eds), *From Reaction to Conflict Prevention: Opportunities for the UN System* (Boulder, CO: Lynne Rienner, 2001), p. 256.
3 Hague Agenda, *The Hague Agenda for Peace and Justice in the 21st Century* (The Hague: Hague Agenda, 1999).
4 Carnegie Commission on Preventing Deadly Conflict, 'Preventing deadly conflict – Final report' (Washington DC: Carnegie Commission on Preventing Deadly Conflict, 1997).
5 See Carnegie Commission (above, n4); Peter Wallensteen (ed.), *Preventing Future Conflicts: Past Record and Future Challenges* (Uppsala: Uppsala University,1998); and I. William Zartman, *Preventive Negotiation* (Lanham, MD: Rowman and Littlefield, 2001).
6 See, for instance, Paul Collier et al, *Breaking the Conflict Trap: Civil War and Development Policy* (Oxford: Oxford University Press/World Bank, 2003).

7 Hugh Miall, 'Global governance and conflict prevention', in Fergal Cochrane, Rosaleen Duffy and Jan Selby (eds), *Global Governance, Conflict and Resistance* (Houndmills: Palgrave, 2003), pp. 59–77.

8 Michael Lund, *Preventing Violent Conflict: A Strategy for Preventative Diplomacy* (Washington DC: US Institute of Peace, 1996), p. 35.

9 Gareth Evans, 'The unfinished responsibility to protect: Europe's role', paper presented to EPC/IPPR/Oxfam Policy Dialogue on Europe's Responsibility to Protect, Brussels, 5 July 2007.

10 'Report of the Secretary-General on the work of the organization', General Assembly, A/2911, 15 September 1955.

11 Carnegie Commission (above, n4).

12 Fen Osler Hampson and David M. Malone, 'Introduction: Making conflict prevention a priority', in F. O. Hampson and D. M. Malone (eds), *From Reaction to Conflict Prevention: Opportunities for the UN System* (Boulder: Lynne Rienner, 2002), p. 4.

13 D. Chigas, 'The OSCE', in A. Chayes and A. Chayes (eds), *Preventing Conflict in the Post-Communist World* (Washington DC: The Brookings Institution, 1996) and Alice Ackerman, 'The idea and practice of conflict prevention', *Journal of Peace Research*, 40 (3) 2003, pp. 339–47.

14 Tapio Kanninen and Chetan Kumar, 'The evolution of the doctrine and practice of early warning and conflict prevention in the United Nations system', in Bertrand Ramcharan (ed.), *Conflict Prevention in Practice: Essays in Honour of James Sutterlin* (Leiden: Martinus Nijhoff, 2007), pp. 50–4.

15 Kofi Annan, 'Prevention of armed conflict: Report of the Secretary-General', A/55/985-S/2001/574, 7 June 2001, paras 161–2.

16 Lund, *Preventing Violent Conflict* (above, n8), pp. 151–5.

17 S/2001/574, para. 169.

18 Kofi Annan, 'Interim report of the Secretary-General on the prevention of armed conflict, A/58/365-S/2003/888, 12 September 2003, para. 33.

19 Kofi Annan, 'Progress report on the prevention of armed conflict', A/60/891, 18 July 2006, summary.

20 UN High-Level Panel on Threats, Challenges and Change, 'A more secure world: Our shared responsibility', A/59/565, 2 December 2004, para. 25.

21 Kofi Annan, 'Action plan to prevent genocide', SG/SM/9197 AFR/893, 7 April 2004.

22 Task Force on the United Nations, *American Interests and UN Reform* (Washington DC: United States Institute of Peace, 2005), p. 33.

23 African Union, 'Common African position on the proposed reform of the United Nations', AU Executive Council, Ext/EX.CL/2(VII), 7–8 March 2005 and Non-Aligned Movement, 'Statement by chairman of the Non-Aligned Movement concerning the Draft Outcome Document of the high-level plenary meeting of the General Assembly', 21 June 2005.

24 Non-Aligned Movement, 'Statement' (above, n23), p. 2.

25 Reform the UN, 'State-by-state positions on the responsibility to protect', 15 August 2005, http://www.reformtheun.org/index.php/issues/100?theme=alt42005, p. 8.

26 S/PV.4334, 21 June 2001.

27 James S. Sutterlin, 'Early warning and conflict prevention: The role of the United Nations', in Klaas van Walraven (ed.), *Early Warning and Conflict Prevention* (The Hague: Kluwer, 1998), p. 125.

28 On the rapid escalation of violent conflict in general, see Peter Wallensteen and Margareta Sollenberg, 'Armed conflict, 1989–1999', *Journal of Peace Research*, 37 (5) 2000, p. 640.

29 Stephen Stedman, 'Alchemy for a new world order: Overselling "preventive diplomacy"', *Foreign Affairs*, 74, May/June 1995, p. 16.

30 Ken Menkhaus, 'Conflict prevention and human security: Issues and challenges', *Conflict, Security and Development*, 4 (3) 2004, p. 430.

31 57th General Assembly, 2003, Resolution 337. See Kanninen and Kumar, 'Evolution of the doctrine and practice' (above, n14), p. 60.

32 Peter Wallensteen, *Understanding Conflict Resolution: War, Peace and the Global System* (London: Sage, 2002).

33 Natalie Mychajlyszyn, 'The OSCE and conflict prevention in the post-Soviet region', in David Carment and Albrecht Schnabel (eds), *Conflict Prevention: Path to Peace or Grand Illusion?* (Tokyo: UN University Press, 2003), p. 145.

34 John L. Davies and Ted Robert Gurr (eds), *Preventive Measures: Building Risk Assessment and Crisis Early Warning Systems* (Lanham: Rowman and Littlefield, 1998), pp. 267–80.

35 A. Walter Dorn, 'Early and late warning by the UN Secretary-General of threats to the peace: Article 99 revisited', in Albrecht Schnabel and David Carment (eds), *Conflict Prevention: From Rhetoric to Reality, Volume 1: Organization and Institutions* (Lanham: Lexington Books, 2004), p. 328 and Derek Boothby and George D'Angelo, 'Building capacity within the United Nations: Cooperation on the prevention of violent conflicts', in Albrecht Schnabel and David Carment (eds), *Conflict Prevention: From Rhetoric to Reality, Volume 2: Opportunities and Innovations* (Lanham: Lexington Books, 2004), p. 253.

36 HLP, 'A more secure world' (above, n20), p. 37 (para. 98).

37 Simon Chesterman, 'Does the UN have intelligence?', *Survival*, 48 (3) 2006, pp. 149–64.

38 Howard Adelman, 'Humanitarian and conflict-oriented early warning: A historical background sketch', in Klaas van Walraven, *Early Warning and Conflict Prevention*, p. 45.

39 B. G. Ramcharan, *The International Law and Practice of Early Warning and Preventive Diplomacy* (The Hague: Kluwer, 1991), p. 67.

40 Boothby and D'Angelo, 'Building capacity' (above, n35), p. 252.

41 Kanninen and Kumar, 'Evolution of the doctrine and practice' (above, n14), p. 50.

42 Andrew Mack and Kathryn Furlong, 'When aspiration exceeds capability: The UN and conflict prevention', unpublished paper, p. 6.

43 Sutterlin, 'Early warning and conflict prevention' (above, n27), p. 124.

44 Boothby and D'Angelo, 'Building capacity' (above, n35), p. 252.

45 Independent Working Group on the Future of the United Nations, *The United Nations in its Second Half Century* (New York: Ford Foundation, 1995).

46 Annex A, A/50/853, 22 December 1995, paras 113, 120–1. Cited in John G. Cockell, 'Early warning analysis and policy planning in UN preventive action', in David Carment and Albrecht Schnabel (eds), *Conflict Prevention: Path to Peace or Grand Illusion?* (Tokyo: UN University Press, 2003), p. 186.

47 Report of the Secretary-General on the work of the organisation joint inspection unit: 'Strengthening the United Nations capacity for conflict prevention', 1997, paras 19 and 26. Analysis from Mack and Furlong, 'When aspiration exceeds capability', pp. 6–7 (above, n42).

48 Howard Adelman and Astri Suhrke, *The International Response to Conflict and Genocide: Lessons From the Rwanda Experience. Volume 2: Early Warning and Conflict Management*, Joint Evaluation of Emergency Assistance to Rwanda, Michelson Institute, Copenhagen, 1996, p. 80.

49 Cockell, 'Early warning' (above, n.46), p. 187.

50 Report of the Panel on United Nations Peace Operations, A/55/305 – S/2000/809, 21 August 2000, Section G.

51 Mark Malloch Brown, 'Administrator's statement on UNDP's role in crisis and post-conflict situations before the UNDP/UNFPA', New York, 2000, p. 17.

52 Mack and Furlong, 'When aspiration exceeds capability' (above, n42), p. 7.

53 This discussion is based on Boothby and D'Angelo, 'Building capacity', (above, n35), p. 260.

54 A/60/891, 18 July 2006, para. 110.
55 Simon Chesterman, *Shared Secrets: Intelligence and Collective Security*, Lowy Institute Paper, No. 10, 2006.
56 Bertrand G. Ramcharan, 'Preventive strategies, preventive diplomacy and the prevention of genocide: Some thoughts for the future', UNITAR, New York, 2 February 2007.
57 Boutros Boutros-Ghali, 'An agenda for peace: Preventive diplomacy, peacemaking and peace-keeping' (New York: UN, 1993), para. 23.
58 Human Security Centre, 'Human security report' (Vancouver: Human Security Centre, 2005), p. 153.
59 International Commission on Intervention and State Sovereignty, 'The responsibility to protect (Ottawa: IDRC, 2001), pp. 23–7.
60 Chester A. Crocker, *Peacemaking and Mediation: Dynamics of a Changing Field*, International Peace Academy Working Paper, March 2007, p. 9.
61 Ibrahim Gambari, 'Making good offices work better: Enhancing UN peacemaking capabilities', speech to the Statesmen's Forum, Washingon DC, 27 February 2006.
62 Ibid.
63 Ibid.
64 Ibid.
65 A/60/891, para. 110.
66 Juan Méndez , press conference, New York, 9 April 2006.
67 'Guidance note: Genocide prevention', results of the 26 July 2005 meeting between the UNA–USA and the special advisor on the prevention of genocide.
68 Juan Méndez, interview with Jerry Fowler, Holocaust Memorial Museum, 16 February 2006.
69 'Groups protest weakening of UN position against genocide', UN DPA, 14 February 2007.
70 Reported by Inner City Press, 15 February 2007.
71 'Ban appoints special adviser for the prevention of genocide and mass atrocities', UN News, 30 May 2007.
72 For details on Luck's perspective on the R2P and for the requirements of operationalisation see Edward C. Luck, 'Introduction: The responsible sovereign and the responsibility to protect', *Annual Review of United Nations Affairs 2006/2007* (New York: Oxford University Press, 2008), vol. 1, pp. xxxiii–xliv.
73 'United Nations human resources structures must be adapted to meet growing demands of peacekeeping, other field operations, budget committee told', press release on Fifth Committee Meeting of the 62nd General Assembly, GA/AB/3837, 4 March 2008.
74 Gareth Evans, 'The responsibility to protect: An idea whose time has come . . . and gone?', lecture to the David Davies Memorial Institute, Aberystwyth, 23 April 2008, p. 3.
75 I am grateful to Edward Luck and Thomas Weiss for these insights.
76 Gary J. Bass, *Stay the Hand of Vengeance: The Politics of War Crimes Tribunals* (Princeton: Princeton University Press, 2000), p. 221.
77 Richard J. Goldstone, *For Humanity: Reflections of a War Crimes Investigator* (New Haven: Yale University Press, 2000).
78 H. Ball, *Prosecuting War Crimes and Genocide: The Twentieth Century Experience* (Kansas: University Press of Kansas, 1999), pp. 195–6.
79 Ibid., p. 192.
80 See Jason Ralph, *Defending the Society of States: Why America Opposes the International Criminal Court and its Vision of World Society* (Oxford: Oxford University Press, 2007).
81 S/PV.4772, 12 June 2003, pp. 24–5.
82 Report of the International Commission of Inquiry on Darfur to the United Nations Secretary-General, Geneva, 25 January 2005, p. 4; available at www.reliefweb.int/library/documents/2005/ici-sud-25feb.pdf.

83 Peter Heinlein, 'UN Security Council deadlocked over Darfur', Voice of America News, 18 March 2005; available at www.voanews.com/english/2005-03-18-voa10.cfm.

84 Ibid.

85 S/PV.5158, 31 March 2005, p. 3.

86 Nick Grono, 'Briefing – Darfur: The international community's failure to protect', *African Affairs*, 105, 2006, p. 627.

87 Bertrand G. Ramcharan, 'Norms and Machinery', in Thomas G. Weiss and Sam Daws (eds), *The Oxford Handbook on the United Nations* (Oxford: Oxford University Press, 2007), pp. 450–1.

88 Report of the UN High Commissioner for Human Rights, 'Situation of human rights in the Darfur region of the Sudan', Commission on Human Rights, 61 sess., 7 May 2004, E/CN.4/2005/3, p. 3; available at www.unhchr.ch/huridocda/huridoca.nsf/e06a5300f90fa0238025668700518ca4/863d14602aa82caec1256ea80038e268/$FILE/G0414221.pdf.

89 E/CN.4/2005/3, p. 3.

90 Human Rights Watch, 'Darfur destroyed: Ethnic cleansing by government and militia forces in western Sudan' (New York: Human Rights Watch, May 2005), p. 55.

91 E/CN.4/2004.L11/Add7, 23 April 2004.

92 Report of the High-Level Mission on the situation of human rights in Darfur pursuant to Human Rights Council decision S-4/101, A/HRC/4/80, 7 March 2007, para. 2.

93 Report of the HLM, paras 19–20.

94 Report of the HLM, para. 76. Emphasis in original.

95 A/HRC/5/6, 8 June 2007.

96 The Independent Commission on Disarmament and Security Issues, 'Common security: A blueprint for survival' (New York: Simon and Schuster, 1982).

97 See Jean Krasnow, 'The quiet revolutionary: A biographical sketch of James S. Sutterlin', in Bertrand Ramcharan (ed.), *Conflict Prevention in Practice: Essays in Honour of James Sutterlin* (Leiden: Martinus Nijhoff, 2005), pp. 50–1.

98 Discussion based on Alex J. Bellamy, Paul D. Williams and Stuart Griffin, *Understanding Peacekeeping* (Cambridge: Polity, 2004).

99 R. Stefanova, 'Conflict prevention in Europe: The case of Macedonia', *International Spectator*, 32 (3/4), 1997, p. 101.

100 Based on Alex J. Bellamy and Paul D. Williams, 'The West and contemporary peace operations', *Journal of Peace Research*, 2009 (forthcoming).

101 Francois Grignon, 'The Artemis Operation in the Democratic Republic of Congo: Lessons for the future of EU peacekeeping in Africa', paper presented at 'The challenges of Europe-Africa relations: An agenda of priorities', conference held in Lisbon, 23–4 October, 2003, p. 3.

102 Marc Lacey, 'UN forces using tougher tactics to secure peace', *New York Times*, 23 May 2005.

103 H. Boshoff, 'The Democratic Republic of Congo on the eve of the second round of elections', situation report, *Institute for Security Studies – Africa*, 26 October 2006, and H-G. Ehrhart, 'Eufor RD Congo: A preliminary assessment', *ISIS Europe, European Security Review*, No. 32, March 2007.

Chapter 5 Reaction

1 Stephen John Stedman, 'UN transformation in an era of soft balancing', *International Affairs*, 83 (5) 2007, pp. 933–44.

2 Lee Feinstein, 'Darfur and beyond: What is needed to prevent mass atrocities', Council on Foreign Relations, CSR No. 22, January 2007, p. 5.

3 S/1998/318, 13 April 1998.

4 S/PV.4046, 16 September 1999.
5 Ibid., Resumption 1, 17 September 1999, p. 20.
6 Ibid., pp. 24–7.
7 Andrew Bonwick, 'Who really protects civilians?', *Development in Practice*, 16 (3) 2006, p. 272.
8 S/2005/740, 28 November 2005.
9 Draft Security Council Resolution on the Protection of Civilians, third iteration, 1 December 2005. I thank Joanna Weschler for providing this publication to me.
10 Security Council Report Update, 'Protection of civilians in armed conflict', No. 4, 13 January 2006.
11 S/PV.5319 (Resumption 1), 9 December 2005, p. 3.
12 Ibid., p. 10.
13 Ibid. (Resumption 1), p. 6.
14 Ibid., p. 11.
15 Ibid., p. 19.
16 Ibid., p. 30.
17 Security Council Report Update, 'Protection of civilians in armed conflict', No. 4, 13 January 2006.
18 S/PV.5476, 28 June 2006, p. 15.
19 Security Council Report Update, 'Protection of civilians in armed conflict', No. 1, 8 March 2006.
20 13 April 2006, Draft Resolution on the Protection of Civilians in Armed Conflict. I thank Joanna Weschler for putting this report at my disposal.
21 See Asia-Pacific Centre for the Responsibility to Protect, 'The responsibility to protect and the protection of civilians: Asia–Pacific in the UN Security Council', Briefing report, 22 June 2008, pp. 10–11.
22 Security Council Report Update, 'Protection of civilians in armed conflict', No. 5, 21 June 2006 and No. 1, 18 June 2007.
23 S/PV.5703, 22 June 2007, p. 17.
24 Ban, Ki-moon, 'Report of the Secretary-General on the protection of civilians in armed conflict', S/2007/643, 28 October 2007.
25 Thomas G. Weiss and Don Hubert, 'The responsibility to protect: research, bibliography, background' (Ottawa: IDRC, 2001), ch. 8.
26 International Commission on Intervention and State Sovereignty (ICISS), 'The responsibility to protect (Ottawa: IDRC, 2001), para. 4.3 (p. 29).
27 Gary Clyde Hufbaeur, Jeffrey J. Schott and Kimberley Ann Elliott, *Economic Sanctions Reconsidered* (Washington DC: Institute for International Economics, 1991).
28 E.g. Robert A. Pape, 'Why economic sanctions do not work', *International Security*, 22 (2) 1997, pp. 90–136. For an excellent overview see Thomas G. Weiss, 'Sanctions as a foreign policy tool: Weighing humanitarian impulses', *Journal of Peace Research*, 36 (5) 1999, p. 501.
29 David Cortright and George A. Lopez, *Sanctions and the Search for Security: Challenges to UN Action* (Boulder: Lynne Rienner, 2002), p. 24.
30 Ibid., p. 75.
31 Ibid., p. 47.
32 S/1997/935, 28 November 1997, para. 72.
33 Margaret P. Doxy, 'United Nations sanctions: current policy issues', Report for the Center for Foreign Policy Studies, Canada, 1997, p. 12.
34 Kofi Annan, '"We, the peoples": The role of the United Nations in the twenty-first century', UN, 2000, p. 50.
35 Kim Richard Nossal, 'Liberal democratic regimes, international sanctions and global governance', in Raimo Väyrynen (ed.), *Global Governance and Enforcement: Issues and Strategies* (Lanham: Rowman and Littlefield, 2000); and J. Dashti-Gibson, P. Davis and B.

Radcliff, 'On the determinants of success of economic sanctions: An empirical analysis', *American Journal of Political Science* 41 (2) 1997, pp. 608–18.

36 Second report, 'The future of sanctions', International Development Committee, UK House of Commons, 27 January 2000.

37 Marc Bossuyt, 'The adverse consequences of economic sanctions on the enjoyment of human rights', UN Human Rights Commission working paper, E/CN.4/Sub.2/2000/33, 21 June 2000, paras 41–7.

38 Arne Tostensen and Beate Bull, 'Are smart sanctions feasible?', *World Politics*, 54 (2) 2002, p. 380.

39 Background paper on targeted sanctions prepared by the Targeted Financial Sanctions Project, Watson Institute at Brown University, for the Workshop on UN Sanctions, 16–17 July 2004, p. 3.

40 Lorretta Bondi, 'Arms embargoes', paper prepared for the first expert seminar of the Bonn International Centre for Conversion on Smart Sanctions: The Next Step, 21–3 November 1999, p. 12.

41 Ibid., pp. 13–15.

42 SC/7672, 25 February 2003, pp. 8–9.

43 Summary of Ban Ki-moon's plenary address to symposium on 'Enhancing the implementation of United Nations Security Council sanctions', UN, New York, 30 April 2007, p. 3. The Informal Working Group was established on 17 April 2000. See 'Note by the President of the Security Council', S/2000/319, 17 April 2000.

44 David J. R. Angell, 'The Angola sanctions committee', in David M. Malone (ed.), *The UN Security Council: From the Cold War to the 21st Century* (Boulder: Lynne Rienner, 2004), p. 195.

45 Ibid., pp. 196–201.

46 Report of the panel of experts on violations of Security Council sanctions against UNITA, S/2000/203, 10 March 2000.

47 Ken Epps, 'International arms embargoes', Project Ploughshares Working Paper, 2002, p. 7.

48 Statement by the chairman of the Informal Working Group on general issues of sanctions, S/2003/1197, 10 December 2003, p. 3.

49 Report of the Informal Working Group on sanctions, S/2006/997, 22 December 2006.

50 For detailed analysis, see Alex J. Bellamy, 'Responsibility to protect or Trojan horse? The crisis in Darfur and humanitarian intervention after Iraq', *Ethics and International Affairs*, 19 (2), 2005, pp. 31–54.

51 See Thomas J. Biersteker and Sue E. Eckert, 'Strengthening targeted sanctions through fair and clear procedures', white paper prepared by the Watson Institute Targeted Sanctions Project, Brown University, 30 March 2006.

52 DPKO, 'Capstone doctrine for United Nations peacekeeping operations', Draft 2 (New York: UN, 2006), p. 29.

53 See Tim Dunne, Marianne Hanson and Cameron Hill, 'The new humanitarian interventionism', in Marianne Hanson and William Tow (eds), *International Relations in the New Century: An Australian Perspective* (Melbourne: Oxford University Press, 2001), pp. 105–9.

54 See Moya Collett, 'Foreign intervention in Cote D'Ivoire: The question of legitimacy, in Coady and O'Keefe (eds), *Righteous Violence*, pp. 160–82.

55 Collett, 'Foreign Intervention'.

56 Feinstein, 'Dafur and beyond' (above, n2), p. 38.

57 Nick Grono, 'Briefing – Darfur: The international community's failure to protect', *African Affairs*, 105 2006, p. 630.

58 S/PV.5015, 30 July 2004, pp. 10–11.

59 S/PV.5027, 2 September 2004, p. 3.
60 Alex de Waal, 'Darfur's deep grievances defy all hopes for an easy solution', *The Observer*, 25 July 2004.
61 Alex de Waal, 'The book was closed too soon on peace in Darfur', *The Guardian*, 29 September 2006.
62 Alex de Waal, 'No such thing as humanitarian intervention: Why we need to rethink how to realize the "responsibility to protect" in wartime', *Harvard International Review*, 2007, p. 5.
63 Ibid., para. 36.
64 International Crisis Group, 'Getting the UN into Darfur', Africa Briefing No. 43, 12 October 2006, pp. 15–17.
65 There is a long tradition of thinking about last resort in these terms in the 'just war' tradition. See Alex J. Bellamy, *Just Wars: From Cicero to Iraq* (Cambridge: Polity, 2007), p. 123.
66 This argument was put forward by Justin Morris and Nicholas J. Wheeler, 'Justifying Iraq as a Humanitarian Intervention: The Cure Is Worse Than the Disease', in Ramesh Thakur and W. P. S. Sidhu (eds), *The Iraq Crisis and World Order: Structural and Normative Challenges* (Tokyo: United Nations University Press, 2007), pp. 163–75.
67 Speech by Russell Broadbent, MP in the House of Representatives, Australia. *Hansard*, 17 March 2008, p. 121.
68 Roberta Cohen, 'Developing an international system for internally displaced persons', *International Studies Perspectives*, 7 (2) 2006, p. 98.
69 Speech by Russell Broadbent, MP in the House of Representatives, Australia: *Hansard*, 17 March 2008, p. 122.
70 Report of the Secretary-General pursuant to General Assembly Resolution 53/55: The Fall of Srebrenica, A/54/549, 15 November 1999.
71 Ibid.
72 Ibid, para. 499.
73 UN Panel on Peace Operations, 'The report of the panel on United Nations peace operations', A/55/305–S/2000/809, 21 August 2000, p. viii.
74 This discussion draws on Paul D. Williams and Alex J. Bellamy, 'Contemporary peace operations: Four challenges for the Brahimi paradigm', *International Peacekeeping: The Yearbook of International Peace Operations*, Vol. 11, 2007, pp. 7–10.
75 'The report of the panel on United Nations peace operations' (above, n73), p. ix.
76 Victoria K. Holt and Tobias C. Berkman, *The Impossible Mandate? Military Preparedness, The Responsibility to Protect and Modern Peace Operations*, Washington DC: The Henry L. Stimson Centre, September 2006, p. 43.
77 Cited ibid., p. 47.
78 Boutros Boutros-Ghali, *An Agenda for Peace* (New York: United Nations, 1992), pp. 4 and 7.
79 'The report of the panel on United Nations peace operations' (above, n73), p. 111.
80 See Susan C. Breau, 'The impact of responsibility to protect on peacekeeping', *Journal of Conflict and Security Law*, 11 (3) 2007, pp. 450–2.
81 Williams and Bellamy, 'Contemporary peace operations' (above, n74), p. 10.
82 Ian Johnstone, 'Dilemmas of robust peace operations', in B. Jones and I. Johnstone (eds), *Annual Review of Global Peace Operations 2006* (Boulder: Lynne Rienner, 2006), p. 7.
83 Alex J. Bellamy and Paul D. Williams, 'The West and contemporary peace operations', *Journal of Peace Research*, 2009.
84 Feinstein, 'Darfur and beyond' (above, n2), p. 35.
85 Ibid., p. 36.
86 Robert C. Johansen (ed.), *A United Nations Emergency Peace Service: To Prevent Genocide and Crimes against Humanity* (New York: World Federalist Movement – Institute for Global Policy, 2006); and Richard H. Cooper and Juliette Voinov Kohler, 'The responsibility to

protect populations from atrocity crimes: The case for an international marshals service', Committee for Humanitarian Justice report, 2006.

87 UN Department of Peacekeeping Operations (DPKO), *Handbook on Multidimensional Peacekeeping Operations* (New York: UN, 2003), pp. 56–7.

88 Ibid., p. 60.

89 Kofi Annan, 'Implementation of the recommendations of the special committee on peacekeeping', A/60/640, 29 December 2005.

90 Report of the Special Committee on Peacekeeping Operations and its working group at the 2006 Substantive Session, A/60/19, 22 March 2006, para. 7.

91 Draft Capstone doctrine for United Nations peacekeeping operations – Draft 2 (2006).

92 DPKO, 'United Nations peacekeeping operations: Principles and guidelines' (Capstone Doctrine Draft 3), 29 June 2007.

93 Sebastian Kaempf, 'Report on UN fieldwork', report of interviews conducted at the DPKO between 7 and 12 April submitted to the author.

94 GA/PK/183, 31 January 2005, p. 6.

Chapter 6 Rebuilding

1 Donald Steinberg, 'Peacebuilding commission: Enhancing the sovereignty of Burundi', presentation to the UN Peacebuilding Commission, 11 December 2006.

2 This view was expressed to the author by Thomas Weiss in an email sent on 30 October 2007.

3 Daniel Warner, 'The responsibility to protect and irresponsible, cynical engagement', *Millennium: Journal of International Studies*, 32 (1) 2003 and Mark Duffield, *Development, Security and Unending War: Governing the World of Peoples* (Cambridge: Polity, 2007), p. 123.

4 Paul Collier, V. L. Elliott, Håvard Hegre, Anke Hoeffler, Marta Reynal-Querol and Nicholas Sambanis, *The Conflict Trap: Civil War and Development Policy* (New York: Oxford University Press for the World Bank, 2003), p. 7.

5 James Dobbins, Seth G. Jones, Keith Crane, Andrew Rathmell, Brett Steele, Richard Teltschik and Anga Timilsina, *The UN's Role in Nation-Building: From the Congo to Iraq* (Santa Monica: RAND, 2005), pp. xxv–xxvii.

6 C. T. Call and S. E. Cook, 'The democratisation of peacebuilding', *Global Governance*, 9 (2) 2003, p. 240.

7 Roland Paris, *At War's End: Building Peace After Civil Conflict* (Cambridge: Cambridge University Press, 2004), p. 151.

8 Charles T. Call, 'Institutionalizing peace: A review of post-conflict peacebuilding concepts and issues for DPA', unpublished paper, 31 January 2005, p. 8.

9 Michael W. Doyle and Nicholas Sambanis, *Making War and Building Peace: United Nations Peace Operations* (Princeton, NJ: Princeton University Press, 2006).

10 Jarat Chopra and Tanja Hohe, 'Participatory peacebuilding', in Tom Keating and W. Andy Knight (eds), *Building Sustainable Peace* (Tokyo: UNU Press, 2004), p. 242.

11 UNMIK/REG/1001/I, section 1, 25 July 1999.

12 See Richard Caplan, *International Governance of War-Torn Territories: Rule and Reconstruction* (Oxford: Oxford University Press, 2005).

13 See Simon Chesterman, *You, the People: The United Nations, Transitional Administration, and State-Building* (Oxford: Oxford University Press, 2004).

14 Paul D. Williams and Alex J. Bellamy, 'Contemporary peace operations: Four challenges for the Brahimi paradigm', *International Peacekeeping: The Yearbook of International Peace Operations*, Vol. 11, 2007, p. 11.

15 Yiber Bjaraktari, Arthur Boutellis, Fatema Gunja, Daniel Harris, James Kapsis, Eva Kaye and Jane Rhee, The PRIME system: Measuring the success of post-conflict police reform', Princeton University, January 2006.

16 Simon Chesterman, Michael Ignatieff and Ramesh Thakur (eds), *Making States Work: State Failure and the Crisis of Governance* (Tokyo: UNU Press, 2005).

17 Paris, *At War's End* (above, n7), p. 235.

18 Ibid., pp. 188–9.

19 Ibid., pp. 188–207.

20 Chesterman, *You, the People* (above, n13), p. 12.

21 Caplan, *International Governance* (above, n12).

22 Jarat Chopra, 'The UN's Kingdom of East Timor', *Survival*, 42 (3), 2000, pp. 27–39.

23 Jarat Chopra, 'Building state failure in East Timor', *Development and Change*, 2002, p. 995.

24 David Chandler, *Faking Democracy After Dayton* (London: Pluto Press, 2nd edn, 2001), p. 87.

25 Ibid. Also William Bain, *Between Anarchy and Society: Trusteeship and the Obligations of Power* (Oxford: Oxford University Press, 2003).

26 Bates Gill and James Reilly, 'Sovereignty, intervention and peacekeeping: The view from Beijing', *Survival*, 42 (3) 2000, p. 43.

27 See Stefan Staehle, 'China's participation in the United Nations peacekeeping regime', unpublished MA thesis, George Washington University, 21 May 2006.

28 Michael Ignatieff, *EmpireLite: Nation Building in Bosnia, Kosovo and Afghanistan* (London: Vintage, 2003).

29 International Commission on Intervention and State Sovereignty (ICISS), 'The responsibility to protect (Ottawa: IDRC, 2001), Vol. 1, para. 5.30.

30 Chesterman, Ignatieff and Thakur, 'Conclusion: The future of state-building', in Simon Chesterman, Michael Ignatieff and Ramesh Thakur (eds), *Making States Work: State Failure and the Crisis of Governance* (Tokyo: UNU Press, 2005), p. 364.

31 Hansjorg Strohmeyer, 'Collapse and reconstruction of a judicial system: The United Nations missions in Kosovo and East Timor', *American Journal of International Law*, 95 (1), pp. 46–63.

32 Chesterman, Ignatieff and Thakur, 'Conclusion' (above, n30), p. 364.

33 Cited in James Traub, *The Best Intentions: Kofi Annan and the UN in an Era of American Power* (London: Bloomsbury, 2006), p. 160.

34 Ibid.

35 A/56/875-S/2002/278, 18 March 2002.

36 Traub, *Best Intentions* (above, n33), p. 164.

37 Williams and Bellamy, 'Contemporary peace operations' (above, n14), p. 16.

38 Chesterman, *You, the People* (above, n13), pp. 89–92.

39 James Dobbins, John G. McGinn, Keith Crane, Seth G. Jones, Rollie Lal, Andrew Rathmell, Rachel M. Swanger and Anga Timilsina, *America's Role in Nation-Building: From Germany to Iraq* (Santa Monica: RAND, 2003), p. 6.

40 Jessica Almqvist, 'A peacebuilding commission for the United Nations', Fundación par alas Relaciones Internationales y el Diálogo Exterior (FRIDE) policy paper, Madrid, June 2005.

41 S/2001/394, 20 April 2001, para. 4.

42 Ibid., paras 8 and 10.

43 Ibid., para. 20.

44 Richard Ponzio, 'The United Nations Peacebuilding Commission: Origins and initial practice', Disarmament Forum working paper, 2007, p. 7.

45 DPKO/HMC/2004/12, 23 January 2004.

46 Interviewed by Ponzio, 'UN Peacebuilding Commission' (above, n44), p. 7.

47 Niamh Gibbons, 'An expert view on the peacebuilding commission: A unique and unusual experiment', Center for UN Reform Education, 21 December 2005.

48 UN High-Level Panel on Threats, Challenges and Change (HLP), A more secure world: Our shared responsibility', A/59/565, 2 December 2004, p. 83.

49 Ibid., p. 83.

50 Ponzio, 'UN Peacebuilding Commision' (above, n44), p. 8 and Susan C. Breau, 'The impact of responsibility to protect on peacekeeping', *Journal of Conflict and Security Law*, 11 (3) 2007, p. 455.

51 Stewart Patrick, 'The peacebuilding commission and the future of US–UN relations', comments to the Annual Meeting of the UN Association of the USA, 9 June 2006.

52 K. Annan, 'In larger freedom: Towards development, security and human rights for all', A/59/2005, 21 March 2005, para. 114.

53 Statement by the President of Angola at the 2005 World Summit.

54 Annan, 'In larger freedom' (above, n32), para. 17.

55 Almqvist, 'Peacebuilding commission' (above, n40), p. 7.

56 Ibid.

57 Annan, 'In larger freedom' (above, n32), Add.2, paras 31–4.

58 World Summit Outcome Document, para. 98.

59 S/PV.5187, 26 May 2005.

60 HLP, 'A more secure world' (above, n48), para. 263.

61 A/60/PV.66, 20 December 2005, pp. 9–10.

62 Ibid. Also see Simon Chesterman, 'From state failure to state-building: Problems and prospects for a United Nations peacebuilding commission', *Journal of International Law and International Relations*, 2, 2005, pp. 155–69.

63 Annan, 'In larger freedom' (above, n32), paras 114–7.

64 S/PV.5187, 26 May 2005.

65 Common African Position on the Proposed UN Reform, para. 4. Also see Almqvist, 'Peacebuilding commission' (above, n40), p. 5, note 15.

66 Quoted ibid.

67 Niamh Gibbons, 'An expert view' (above, n47).

68 General Assembly Resolution 60/180, 30 December 2005, para. 15

69 Ponzio, 'UN Peacebuilding Commission' (above, n44), p. 8.

70 A/59/2005/Add.2, para. 21.

71 General Assembly Resolution 60/180, 30 December 2005, para. 23.

72 See C. S. R. Murthy, 'New phase in UN reforms: Establishment of the peacebuilding commission and human rights council', *International Studies*, 44 (1) 2007, p. 52.

73 'UN Peacebuilding Commission', Henry L. Stimson Centre Peace Operations Fact Sheet Series, 2007, p. 3.

74 Ibid.

75 'The UN Peacebuilding Fund (PBF)', presentation by the Peacebuilding Support Office, 3 July 2007.

76 Murthy, 'New phase in UN reforms' (above, n72), p. 48.

77 'The UN Peacebuilding Fund' (above, n75).

78 Gibbons, 'An expert view' (above, n47).

79 Gareth Evans, 'What difference would the peacebuilding commission make: The case of Burundi', presentation to EPC/IRRI Workshop on the Peacebuilding Commission and Human Rights Council, Brussels, 20 January 2006.

80 Security Council Report, 'Special research report: Peacebuilding commission', 13 June 2006.

81 Interview with Assistant Secretary-General Carolyn McAskie, by Center for UN Reform Education, 4 June 2007.

82 Conference Room Paper for the Country Specific Meeting on Sierra Leone, PBC/2/SIL/CRP.1, 10 October 2006.

83 Conference room paper for the country-specific meeting on Burundi, PBC/2/BUR/CRP.2, 10 October 2006.

84 Murthy, 'New phase in UN reforms' (above, n72), p. 53.

85 Chairman's summary of the country-specific meeting of the peacebuilding commission, 13 December 2006, para. 14.
86 'PBC update: First lessons learned on Sierra Leone', Center for UN Reform Education, 20 February 2007.
87 PBC/1/BD1/2. 21 May 2007.
88 'PBC country-specific meeting discusses draft of Burundi's strategic framework', Center for UN Reform Education Briefing, 11 June 2007.
89 Ponzio, 'UN Peacebuilding Commission' (above, n44), p. 10.
90 'The UN Peacebuilding Commission: Benefits and challenges', Background paper prepared by the International Peace Academy for the Regional Seminars organised by the Friedrich-Ebert-Stiftung, 6 June 2006.
91 Ponzio, 'UN Peacebuilding Commission' (above, n44), p. 10.
92 PBC/1/BD1/SR.1, 18 May 2007, para. 44.
93 A/61/PV.86, 6 February 2007, pp. 6–8.
94 Ponzio, 'UN Peacebuilding Commission' (above, n44), p. 10.
95 Evans, 'What difference would the peacebuilding commission make?' (above, n79), p. 5.
96 PBC/1/BD1/SR.1, 18 May 2007, para. 68.
97 Paul D. Williams, 'Peace operations and the international financial institutions: Insights from Rwanda and Sierra Leone', in Alex J. Bellamy and Paul D. Williams (eds), *Peace Operations and Global Order* (London: Frank Cass, 2005), pp. 103–23.
98 Ibid., p. 118.
99 Suggested by Ponzio, 'UN Peacebuilding Commission' (above, n44), p. 10.
100 A view shared by Edward Luck. See Edward C. Luck, 'Introduction: The responsible sovereign and the responsibility to protect', *Annual Review of United Nations Affairs 2006/2007* (New York: Oxford University Press, 2008), vol. 1, pp. xxxiii–xliv.

Conclusion

1 See Edward C. Luck, 'The responsible sovereign and the responsibility to protect', *Annual Review of United Nations Affairs 2006/2007* (New York: Oxford University Press, 2008), vol. 1, pp. xxxiii–xliv.
2 For example, see Alex J. Bellamy, *Kosovo and International Society* (London: Palgrave, 2002); Paul D. Williams and Alex J. Bellamy, 'The responsibility to protect and the crisis in Darfur', *Security Dialogue*, 36 (1) 2005; and Alan J. Kuperman and Timothy Crawford (eds), *Gambling on Humanitarian Intervention: Moral Hazard, Rebellion and Civil War* (London: Routledge, 2006).

Bibliography

Ackerman, Alice (2003), 'The idea and practice of conflict prevention', *Journal of Peace Research*, 40 (3).

Adebajo, Adekeye and Chris Landsberg (2000), 'The heirs of Nkrumah: Africa's new investments', *Pugwash Occasional Papers*, Vol. 2.

Adelman, Howard and Astri Suhrke (1996), *The International Response to Conflict and Genocide: Lessons From the Rwanda Experience*, Vol. 2: *Early Warning and Conflict Management*, Joint Evaluation of Emergency Assistance to Rwanda, Michelson Institute, Copenhagen.

Alley, Roderic (2004), *Internal Conflict and the International Community: Wars Without End?* (Aldershot: Ashgate).

Almqvist, Jessica (2005), 'A peacebuilding commission for the United Nations', Fundación par alas Relaciones Internationales y el Diálogo Exterior (FRIDE) policy paper, Madrid, June.

Annan, Kofi (1998), 'Intervention', Ditchley Foundation Lecture, 26 June.

Annan, Kofi (1999), 'Annual report of the Secretary-General to the General Assembly', 20 September.

Annan, Kofi (1999), 'Report of the Secretary-General pursuant to General Assembly Resolution 53/55: The fall of Srebrenica', A/54/549, 15 November.

Annan, Kofi (1999), 'Two concepts of sovereignty', *Economist*, 18 September.

Annan, Kofi (2000), '"We, the peoples": The role of the United Nations in the twenty-first century', Report of the UN Secretary-General.

Annan, Kofi (2001), 'Prevention of armed conflict: Report of the Secretary-General', A/55/985-S/2001/574, 7 June.

Annan, Kofi (2003), 'Interim report of the Secretary-General on the prevention of armed conflict', A/58/365-S/2003/888, 12 September.

Annan, Kofi (2004), 'Action plan to prevent genocide', SG/SM/9197 AFR/893, 7 April.

Annan, Kofi (2005), 'Implementation of the recommendations of the Special Committee on Peacekeeping', A/60/640, 29 December.

Annan, Kofi (2005), 'In larger freedom: Towards development, security and human rights for all', A/59/2005, 21 March.

Annan, Kofi (2006), 'Progress report on the prevention of armed conflict', A/60/891, 18 July.

Axworthy, Lloyd (2000), 'Humanitarian intervention and humanitarian constraints', Hauser Lecture on International Humanitarian Law, New York
University School of Law, 10 February.

Axworthy, Lloyd (2003), *Navigating a New World: Canada's Global Future*
(Toronto: Alfred A. Knopf).

Bajraktari, Yiber Arthur Boutellis, Fatema Gunja, Daniel Harris, James Kapsis,
Eva Kaye and Jane Rhee (2006), *The PRIME System: Measuring the Success of
Post-Conflict Police Reform*, Princeton University, January.

Bain, William (2003), *Between Anarchy and Society: Trusteeship and the Obligations
of Power* (Oxford: Oxford University Press).

Balakian, Peter (2004), *The Burning Tigris: The Armenian Genocide and America's
Response* (New York: Perennial).

Ball, H. (1999), *Prosecuting War Crimes and Genocide: The Twentieth Century
Experience* (Kansas: University Press of Kansas).

Ban Ki-moon (2007), 'Annual address to the UN General Assembly',
SG/SM.11182, 25 September.

Ban, Ki-moon (2007), 'Report of the Secretary-General on the protection of
civilians in armed conflict', S/2007/643, 28 October.

Banda, Maria (2007), 'The responsibility to protect: Moving the agenda
forward', paper for the UN Association of Canada.

Baranovsky, Vladimir (2000), 'Humanitarian intervention: Russian perspectives', *Pugwash Occasional Papers*, Vol. 2.

Bass, Gary J. (2000), *Stay the Hand of Vengeance: The Politics of War Crimes
Tribunals* (Princeton: Princeton University Press).

Beach, Hugh (2000), 'Secessions, interventions and just war theory: The case
of Kosovo', *Pugwash Occasional Papers*, vol. 1.

Bellamy, Alex J. (2002), *Kosovo and International Society* (London: Palgrave).

Bellamy, Alex J. (2005), 'A responsibility to protect or a Trojan Horse? The crisis
in Darfur and humanitarian intervention after Iraq', *Ethics and International
Affairs*, 19 (2).

Bellamy, Alex J. (2006), *Just Wars: From Cicero to Iraq* (Cambridge: Polity).

Bellamy, Alex J. (2009), 'Realizing the responsibility to protect', *International
Studies Perspectives*, 10 (1).

Bellamy, Alex J. (2009), 'The responsibility to protect', in Paul D. Williams (ed.),
Security Studies: An Introduction (London: Routledge).

Bellamy, Alex J. and Paul D. Williams (2009), 'The West and contemporary
peace operations', *Journal of Peace Research*, 46.

Bellamy, Alex J., Paul D. Williams and Stuart Griffin (2004), *Understanding
Peacekeeping* (Cambridge: Polity).

Bellamy, Alex J. and Paul D. Williams (eds) (2005), *Peace Operations and Global
Order* (London: Routledge).

Biersteker, Thomas J. and Sue E. Eckert (2006), 'Strengthening targeted
sanctions through fair and clear procedures', white paper prepared by

the Watson Institute Targeted Sanctions Project, Brown University, 30 March.

Blair, Tony (1999), 'Doctrine of the international community', speech to the Economic Club of Chicago, Hilton Hotel, Chicago, 22 April.

Bond, Jennifer and Laurel Sherret (2006), *A Sight for Sore Eyes: Bringing Gender Vision to the Responsibility to Protect Framework*, United Nations International Research and Training Institute for the Advancement of Women, March.

Bondi, Lorretta (1999) 'Arms embargoes', paper prepared for the first expert seminar of the Bonn International Center for Conversion on Smart Sanctions: The Next Step, 21–3 November.

Bonwick, Andrew (2006), 'Who really protects civilians?', *Development in Practice*, 16 (3).

Borgwardt, Elizabeth (2005), *A New Deal for the World: America's Vision for Human Rights* (Cambridge, MA: Harvard University Press).

Boshoff, H. (2006), 'The Democratic Republic of Congo on the eve of the second round of elections', situation report, *Institute for Security Studies – Africa*, 26 October.

Bossuyt, Marc (2000), 'The adverse consequences of economic sanctions on the enjoyment of human rights', UN Human Rights Commission working paper, E/CN.4/Sub.2/2000/33, 21 June.

Boutwell, Jeffrey (1999), 'Report on the Pugwash Study Group on intervention', Sovereignty and International Security meeting, Venice, Italy, 10–11 December.

Boutrell, Jeffrey (2001), 'Report on the joint meeting of the Pugwash Study Group on intervention, sovereignty and international security and the international commission on intervention and state sovereignty', 20–1 July, Pugwash, Nova Scotia.

Boutros-Ghali, Boutros (1992), *An Agenda for Peace: Preventive Diplomacy, Peacemaking and Peace-Keeping* (New York: UN).

Brittain, Victoria (1999), 'Colonialism and the predatory state in the Congo', *New Left Review*, 236, July/August.

Brownlie, Ian (1974), 'Humanitarian intervention', in John N. Moore (ed.), *Law and Civil War in the Modern World* (Baltimore: Johns Hopkins University Press).

Breau, Susan C. (2007), 'The impact of responsibility to protect on peacekeeping', *Journal of Conflict and Security Law*, 11 (3).

Brunnee, Jutta and Stephen J. Toope (2006), 'Norms, institutions and UN reform: The responsibility to protect', *Behind the Headlines*, 63 (3).

Bukovansky, Mlada (2002), *Legitimacy and Power Politics: The American and French Revolutions in International Political Culture* (Princeton: Princeton University Press).

Bull, Hedley (ed.) (1986), *Intervention in World Politics* (Oxford: Clarendon Press).

Buzan, Barry (2004), *From International to World Society? English School Theory and the Social Structure of Globalisation* (Cambridge: Cambridge University Press).

Byers, Michael (2005), *War Law: International Law and Armed Conflict* (London: Atlantic Books).

Byers, Michael (2005), 'High ground lost on UN's responsibility to protect', *Winnipeg Free Press*, 18 September.

Call, Charles T. (2005), 'Institutionalizing peace: A review of post-conflict peacebuilding concepts and issues for DPA', unpublished paper, 31 January.

Call, Charles T. and S. E. Cook (2003), 'The democratisation of Peacebuilding', *Global Governance*, 9 (2).

Caplan, Richard (2005), *International Governance of War-Torn Territories: Rule and Reconstruction* (Oxford: Oxford University Press).

Carment, David and Albrecht Schnabel (eds) (2003), *Conflict Prevention: Path to Peace or Grand Illusion?* (Tokyo: UN University Press).

Carnegie Commission on Preventing Deadly Conflict (1997), 'Preventing deadly conflict – Final report' (Washington DC: Carnegie Commission on Preventing Deadly Conflict).

Carter, Ashton B., John M. Deutch and Philip D. Zelikow (1998), 'Catastrophic terrorism: Elements of a national policy', Visions of Government for the Twenty-First Century Report, Harvard University.

Chandler, David (2001), *Faking Democracy After Dayton* (London: Pluto Press, 2nd edn).

Chesterman, Simon (2001), *Just War or Just Peace? Humanitarian Intervention and International Law* (Oxford: Oxford University Press).

Chesterman, Simon (2004), *You, the People: The United Nations, Transitional Administration, and State-Building* (Oxford: Oxford University Press).

Chesterman, Simon (2005), 'From state failure to state-building: Problems and prospects for a United Nations Peacebuilding Commission', *Journal of International Law and International Relations*, 2.

Chesterman, Simon (2006), 'Does the UN have intelligence?', *Survival*, 48 (3).

Chesterman, Simon (2006), *Shared Secrets: Intelligence and Collective Security*, Lowy Institute Paper, No. 10.

Chesterman, Simon (ed.) (2007), *Secretary or General? The UN Secretary-General in World Politics* (Cambridge: Cambridge University Press).

Chesterman, Simon, Michael Ignatieff and Ramesh Thakur (eds) (2005), *Making States Work: State Failure and the Crisis of Governance* (Tokyo: UN University Press).

Chigas, D. (1996), 'The OSCE', in A. Chayes and A. Chayes (eds), *Preventing Conflict in the Post-Communist World* (Washington DC: The Brookings Institution).

Chopra, Jarat (2000), 'The UN's Kingdom of East Timor', *Survival*, 42 (3).

Chopra, Jarat (2002) 'Building state failure in East Timor', *Development and Change*, 33 (5).

Chu Shulong (2000), 'China, Asia and issues of sovereignty and humanitarian intervention', *Pugwash Occasional Papers*, Vol. 2.

Clark, David (2003), 'Iraq has wrecked our case for humanitarian wars', *Guardian*, 12 August.

Coady, Tony and Michael O'Keefe (2005), *Righteous Violence: The Ethics and Politics of Military Intervention* (Melbourne: Melbourne University Press).

Cochrane, Fergal, Rosaleen Duffy and Jan Selby (eds) (2003), *Global Governance, Conflict and Resistance* (Houndmills: Palgrave).

Cohen, Roberta and Francis M. Deng (1998), *Masses in Flight: The Global Crisis of Internal Displacement* (Washington DC: The Brookings Institution).

Coleman, Katherina P. (2007), *International Organizations and Peace Enforcement: The Politics of International Legitimacy* (Cambridge: Cambridge University Press).

Collier, Paul, V. L. Elliott, Håvard Hegre, Anke Hoeffler, Marta Reynal-Querol and Nicholas Sambanis (2003), *Breaking the Conflict Trap: Civil War and Development Policy* (Oxford: Oxford University Press/World Bank).

Cooper, Richard H. and Juliette Voinov Kohler (2006), 'The responsibility to protect populations from atrocity crimes: The case for an international marshals service', Committee for Humanitarian Justice Report.

Cortright, David and George A. Lopez (2002), *Sanctions and the Search for Security: Challenges to UN Action* (Boulder: Lynne Rienner).

Crocker, Chester A. (2007), *Peacemaking and Mediation: Dynamics of a Changing Field*, International Peace Academy Working Paper, March.

de Waal, Alex (2004), 'Darfur's deep grievances defy all hopes for an easy solution', The *Observer*, 25 July.

de Waal, Alex (2006), 'The book was closed too soon on peace in Darfur', *Guardian*, 29 September.

de Waal, Alex (2007), 'No such thing as humanitarian intervention: Why we need to rethink how to realize the "responsibility to protect" in wartime', *Harvard International Review*, 21 March.

Dashti-Gibson, J., P. Davis and B. Radcliff (1997), 'On the determinants of success of economic sanctions: An empirical analysis', *American Journal of Political Science* 41 (2).

Davies, John L. and Ted Robert Gurr (eds) (1998), *Preventive Measures: Building Risk Assessment and Crisis Early Warning Systems* (Lanham: Rowman and Littlefield).

Davies, Sara E. (2007), *Legitimising Rejection? International Refugee Law in Southeast Asia* (The Hague: Martinus Nijhoff).

Deng, Francis M. (2004), 'The impact of state failure on migration', *Mediterranean Quarterly*, Fall.

Deng, Francis M., Sadikiel Kimaro, Terrence Lyons, Donald Rothchild and I. William Zartman (1996), *Sovereignty as Responsibility: Conflict Management in Africa* (Washington DC: The Brookings Institution).

Dobbins, James, John G. McGinn, Keith Crane, Seth G. Jones, Rollie Lal, Andrew Rathmell, Rachel M. Swanger and Anga Timilsina (2003), *America's Role in Nation-Building: From Germany to Iraq* (Santa Monica: RAND).

Dobbins, James, Seth G. Jones, Keith Crane, Andrew Rathmell, Brett Steele, Richard Teltschik and Anga Timilsina (2005), *The UN's Role in Nation-Building: From the Congo to Iraq* (Santa Monica: RAND).

Doyle, Michael W. and Nicholas Sambanis (2006), *Making War and Building Peace: United Nations Peace Operations* (Princeton NJ: Princeton University Press).

Doxy, Margaret P. (1997), 'United Nations sanctions: Current policy issues', Report for the Center for Foreign Policy Studies, Canada.

Duffield, Mark (2007), *Development, Security and Unending War: Governing the World of Peoples* (Cambridge: Polity).

Ehrhart, H.-G. (2007), 'Eufor RD Congo: A preliminary assessment', *ISIS Europe, European Security Review*, No. 32, March.

Elden, Stuart (2006), 'Contingent sovereignty, territorial integrity and the sanctity of borders', *SAIS Review*, 26 (1).

Epps, Ken (2002), 'International arms embargoes', Project Ploughshares Working Paper.

Etzioni, Amitai (2006), 'Sovereignty as responsibility', *Orbis*, 50 (1).

Evans, Gareth (2004), 'When is it right to fight?', *Survival* 46, No. 3, pp. 59–82.

Evans, Gareth (2006), 'What difference would the peacebuilding commission make: The case of Burundi', presentation to EPC/IRRI Workshop on the Peacebuilding Commission and Human Rights Council, Brussels, 20 January.

Evans, Gareth (2007), 'The unfinished responsibility to protect: Europe's role', paper presented to EPC/IPPR/Oxfam Policy Dialogue on Europe's Responsibility to Protect, Brussels, 5 July.

Evans, Gareth (2008), 'The responsibility to protect: An idea whose time has come . . . and gone?', lecture to the David Davies Memorial Institute, Aberystwyth, 23 April.

Falk, Richard (2003), 'Humanitarian intervention: A forum', *Nation*, 14 July.

Fauchille, Paul (1921), *Traité de droit international public* (Paris: Libraire Arthur Rousseau).

Feinstein, Lee (2007), 'Darfur and beyond: What is needed to prevent mass atrocities', Council on Foreign Relations, CSR No. 22, January.

Finnemore, Martha and Kathryn Sikkink (1998), 'International norm dynamics and political change', *International Organization*, 52 (4).

Garner, James W. (1915), 'Some questions of international law in the European war', *American Journal of International Law*, 9 (1).

Gibbons, Niamh (2005), 'An expert view on the peacebuilding commission: A unique and unusual experiment', Center for UN Reform Education, 21 December.

Gill, Bates and James Reilly (2000), 'Sovereignty, intervention and peacekeeping: The view from Beijing', *Survival*, 42 (3).

Gingrich, Newt and George Mitchell (2005), 'Report card from America: UN reform', *International Herald Tribune*, 28 November.

Goldstone, Richard J. (2000), *For Humanity: Reflections of a War Crimes Investigator* (New Haven: Yale University Press).

Grignon, Francois (2003), 'The Artemis Operation in the Democratic Republic of Congo: Lessons for the future of EU peacekeeping in Africa', paper presented at 'The Challenges of Europe–Africa Relations: An Agenda of Priorities', conference held in Lisbon, 23–4 October.

Grono, Nick (2006), 'Briefing – Darfur: The international community's failure to protect', *African Affairs*, 105.

Hague Agenda (1999), *The Hague Agenda for Peace and Justice in the 21st Century* (The Hague: Hague Agenda).

Haass, Richard N. (2002), 'Defining US foreign policy in a post-post-cold war world', the 2002 Arthur Ross Lecture, 22 April.

Hampson, F. O. and D. M. Malone (eds) (2002), *From Reaction to Conflict Prevention: Opportunities for the UN System* (Boulder: Lynne Rienner).

Hanson, Marianne and William Tow (eds) (2001), *International Relations in the New Century: An Australian Perspective* (Melbourne: Oxford University Press).

Holt, Victoria K. and Tobias C. Berkman (2006), *The Impossible Mandate? Military Preparedness, The Responsibility to Protect and Modern Peace Operations* (Washington DC: The Henry L. Stimson Centre).

Hufbaeur, Gary Clyde, Jeffrey J. Schott and Kimberley Ann Elliott (1991), *Economic Sanctions Reconsidered* (Washington DC: Institute for International Economics).

Human Rights Watch (2005), 'Darfur destroyed: Ethnic cleansing by government and militia forces in western Sudan' (New York: Human Rights Watch).

Human Security Centre (2006), 'Human security report 2005' (Vancouver: Human Security Centre).

Hunt, Lynn (2007), *Inventing Human Rights: A History* (London: W. W. Norton and Co.).

Igiri, Cheryl O. and Princeton N. Lyman (2004), 'Giving meaning to "never again": Seeking an effective response to the crisis in Darfur and beyond', CSR No. 5 (New York: Council on Foreign Relations).

Ignatieff, Michael (2003), 'Why are we in Iraq? (and Liberia? and Afghanistan?)', *New York Times Magazine*, 7 September.

Ignatieff, Michael (2003), *Empire Lite: Nation Building in Bosnia, Kosovo and Afghanistan* (London: Vintage).

Independent Commission on Disarmament and Security Issues (1982), 'Common security: A blueprint for survival' (New York: Simon and Schuster).

Independent International Commission on Kosovo (2000), 'Kosovo report: Conflict, international response, lessons learned' (Oxford: Oxford University Press).

Independent Working Group on the Future of the United Nations (1995), *The United Nations in its Second Half Century* (New York: Ford Foundation).

International Commission on Intervention and State Sovereignty (2001), 'The responsibility to protect (Ottawa: IDRC).

International Council on Human Rights Policy (2002), 'Human rights crises: NGO responses to military interventions' (Versoix: International Council on Human Rights Policy).

International Crisis Group (2006), 'Getting the UN into Darfur', Africa Briefing No. 43, 12 October.

International Development Committee, UK House of Commons (2000), 'The future of sanctions', second report, 27 January.

Jackson, Robert H. (2002), *The Global Covenant: Human Conduct in a World of States* (Oxford: Oxford University Press).

Jentelson, Bruce (2007), 'A responsibility to protect: The defining challenge for global community', *Ethnic Conflict*, 28 (4).

Johansen, Robert C. (ed.) (2006), *A United Nations Emergency Peace Service: To Prevent Genocide and Crimes against Humanity* (New York: World Federalist Movement – Institute for Global Policy).

Jones, B. and I. Johnstone (eds) (2006), *Annual Review of Global Peace Operations 2006* (Boulder: Lynne Rienner).

Kaiser, Karl (2003), 'A European perspective on the post Iraq new international order', paper presented at the Center for Strategic and International Studies, Jakarta, 29 July.

Kampfner, John (2003), *Blair's Wars* (London: The Free Press, 2003).

Keating, Tom and W. Andy Knight (eds) (2004), *Building Sustainable Peace* (Tokyo: UN University Press).

Kioko, Ben (2003), 'The right of interference under the African Union's Constitutive Act: From non-interference to non-intervention', *International Review of the Red Cross*, 85 (6).

Kratochwil, Friedreich V. (1989), *Rules, Norms and Decisions: On the Conditions of Practice and Legal Reasoning in International Relations and Domestic Affairs* (Cambridge: Cambridge University Press).

Kristof, Nicholas D. (2005), 'A wimp on genocide', *New York Times*, 18 September.

Kumar, Radha (2000), 'Sovereignty and intervention: Opinions in South Asia', *Pugwash Occasional Papers*, Vol. 2.

Kuperman, Alan J. and Timothy Crawford (eds) (2006), *Gambling on Humanitarian Intervention: Moral Hazard, Rebellion and Civil War* (London: Routledge).

Lacey, Marc (2005), 'UN forces using tougher tactics to secure peace', *New York Times*, 23 May.

LaFranchi, Howard (2005), 'At UN, Bolton softens his tone', *Christian Science Monitor*, 12 September.

Legro, Jeffrey (1997), 'Which norms matter? Revisiting the "failure" of internationalism', *International Organization*, 51 (1).

Lewis, Anthony (2003), 'The challenge of global justice now', *Dædalus*, 132 (1).

Lillich, Richard B. (ed.) (1973), *Humanitarian Intervention and the United Nations* (Charlottesville VG: University Press of Virginia).

Lindberg, Todd (2005), 'Protect the people', *Washington Post*, 27 September.

Luck, Edward C. (2008), 'Introduction: The responsible sovereign and the responsibility to protect', in *Annual Review of United Nations Affairs, 2006/2007* (Oxford: Oxford University Press).

Luck, Edward C. (2008), 'The responsible sovereign and the responsibility to protect', *Annual Review of United Nations Affairs 2006/2007* (New York: Oxford University Press), vol. 1, pp. xxxiii–xliv.

Lund, Michael (1996) *Preventing Violent Conflict: A Strategy for Preventative Diplomacy* (Washington DC: US Institute of Peace).

Macfarlane, S. Neil, Carolin J. Thiekling and Thomas G. Weiss (2004), '*The Responsibility to Protect*: Is anyone interested in humanitarian intervention?', *Third World Quarterly*, 25 (5).

Makinda, Samuel and F. Wafula Okumu (2007), *The African Union: Challenges of Globalization, Security and Governance* (London: Routledge).

Malone, David M. (ed.) (2004), *The UN Security Council: From the Cold War to the Twenty-First Century* (Boulder: Lynne Rienner).

Menkhaus, Ken (2004), 'Conflict prevention and human security: Issues and challenges', *Conflict, Security and Development*, 4 (3).

Mill, John Stuart (1973), *Essays on Politics and Culture* (edited by Gertrude Himmelfarb) (Gloucester: Peter Smith).

Meisler, Stanley (2007), *Kofi Annan: A Man of Peace in a World of War* (London: Wiley).

Morada, Noel M. (2006), 'R2P roadmap in southeast Asia: Challenges and prospects', UNISCI Discussion Papers, No. 11, May.

Murthy, C. S. R. (2007), 'New phase in UN reforms: Establishment of the peacebuilding commission and human rights council', *International Studies*, 44 (1).

Nelson, Samuel H. (1994), *Colonialism in the Congo Basin, 1880–1940* (Athens, OH: Ohio University Center for International Studies).

Pace, William R. and Nicole Deller (2005), 'Preventing future genocides: An international responsibility to protect', *World Order*, 36 (4).

Pape, Robert A. (1997), 'Why economic sanctions do not work', *International Security*, 22 (2).

Paris, Roland (2004), *At War's End: Building Peace After Civil Conflict* (Cambridge: Cambridge University Press).

Phillipson, Coleman (1916), *International Law and the Great War* (New York: E. P. Dutton and Co.).

Ponzio, Richard (2007), 'The United Nations Peacebuilding Commission: Origins and initial practice', Disarmament Forum working paper.

Primakov, Yevgeny M. (2004), 'UN process, not humanitarian intervention, is world's best hope', *New Perspectives Quarterly*, 2 September.

Primakov, Yevgeny M. (2004), 'Rather the United Nations than US unilateralism', *New Perspectives Quarterly*, 21 (2).

Puley, Greg (2005), 'The responsibility to protect: East, west and southern African perspectives on preventing and responding to humanitarian crises', Project Ploughshares working paper, no. 5, September.

Ralph, Jason (2007), *Defending the Society of States: Why America Opposes the International Criminal Court and its Vision of World Society* (Oxford: Oxford University Press).

Ramcharan, Bertrand G. (1991), *The International Law and Practice of Early Warning and Preventive Diplomacy* (The Hague: Kluwer).

Ramcharan, Bertrand G. (ed.) (2007), *Conflict Prevention in Practice: Essays in Honour of James Sutterlin* (Leiden: Martinus Nijhoff).

Ramcharan, Bertrand G. (2007), 'Preventive strategies, preventive diplomacy and the prevention of genocide: Some thoughts for the future', UNITAR, New York, 2 February.

Roberts, Adam (2003), 'Intervention: One step forward in the search for the impossible', *International Journal of Human Rights*, 7(3).

Roth, Brad R. (2000), *Governmental Illegitimacy in International Law* (Oxford: Oxford University Press).

Samkange, Stanlake J. T. M. (2002), 'African perspectives on intervention and state sovereignty', *African Security Review*, 11 (1).

Schnabel, Albrecht and Ramesh Thakur (eds) (2000), *Kosovo and the Challenge of Humanitarian Intervention: Selective Indignation, Collective Action and International Citizenship* (Tokyo: UN University Press).

Schnabel, Albrecht and David Carment (eds) (2004), *Conflict Prevention: From Rhetoric to Reality*, Vol. 1: *Organization and Institutions* (Lanham: Lexington Books).

Schnabel, Albrecht and David Carment (eds) (2004), *Conflict Prevention: From Rhetoric to Reality*, Vol. 2: *Opportunities and Innovations* (Lanham: Lexington Books).

Shaw, Malcolm N. (2003), *International Law*, 5th edn (Cambridge: Cambridge University Press).

Sid-Ahmed, Mohamed (2001), 'Sovereignty and intervention', *Al-Ahram Weekly*, 7–13 June.

Staehle, Stefan (2006), 'China's participation in the United Nations peacekeeping regime', unpublished MA thesis, George Washington University, 21 May.

Stedman, Stephen John (1995), 'Alchemy for a new world order: Overselling "preventive diplomacy"', *Foreign Affairs*, 74, May / June.

Stedman, Stephen John (2007), 'UN transformation in an era of soft power balancing', *International Affairs*, 83 (5).

Stefanova, R. (1997), 'Conflict prevention in Europe: The case of Macedonia', *International Spectator*, 32 (3/4).

Steinberg, Donald (2006), 'Peacebuilding commission: Enhancing the sovereignty of Burundi', presentation to the UN Peacebuilding Commission, 11 December.

Strohmeyer, Hansjorg (2006), 'Collapse and Reconstruction of a Judicial System: The United Nations Missions in Kosovo and East Timor', *American Journal of International Law*, 95 (1).

Suganami, Hidemi (2001), 'Sovereignty, Intervention and the English School' paper presented to the 4th Pan-European Conference, University of Kent, 8–10 September.

Sutterlin, James S. (1998), 'Early warning and conflict prevention: The role of the United Nations', in Klaas van Walraven (ed.), *Early Warning and Conflict Prevention* (The Hague: Kluwer).

Symons, Emma-Kate (2005), 'UN reform a disaster: Evans', *The Australian*, 19 October.

Task Force on the United Nations (2005), *American Interests and UN Reform* (Washington DC: United States Institute of Peace).

Thakur, Ramesh (2004), 'Iraq and the responsibility to protect', *Behind the Headlines*, 62 (1).

Thakur, Ramesh (2005), 'A shared responsibility for a more secure world', *Global Governance*, 11 (3).

Thakur, Ramesh (2006), *The United Nations, Peace and Security: From Collective Security to the Responsibility to Protect* (Cambridge: Cambridge University Press).

Thakur, Ramesh, Andrew F. Cooper and John English (eds) (2004), *International Commissions and the Power of Ideas* (Tokyo: United Nations University Press).

Thakur, Ramesh and W.P.S. Sidhu (eds.) (2007), *The Iraq Crisis and World Order: Structural and Normative Challenges* (Tokyo: United Nations University Press).

Tostensen, Arne and Beate Bull (2002), 'Are smart sanctions feasible?', *World Politics*, 54 (2).

Traub, James (2006), *The Best Intentions: Kofi Annan and the UN in an Era of American Power* (London: Bloomsbury).

von Treitschke, Heinrich (1899), *Politik* (Leipzig: Insel).

Turner, Mark (2005), 'UN "must never again be found wanting on genocide"', *Financial Times*, 16 September.

UN Commission on Human Rights (1993), 'Responses of governments and agencies to the report of the UN Special Representative for internally displaced persons', E/CN.4/1993/SR.40.

UN Department of Peacekeeping Operations (2003), *Handbook on Multidimensional Peacekeeping Operations* (New York: UN).

UN Department of Peacekeeping Operations (2006), 'Capstone doctrine for United Nations peacekeeping operations', Draft 2 (New York: UN).

UN Department for Peacekeeping Operations (2007), 'United Nations peacekeeping operations: Principles and guidelines' (Capstone Doctrine Draft 3) (New York: UN).

UN High Commissioner for Human Rights (2004), 'Situation of human rights in the Darfur region of the Sudan', E/CN.4/2005/3, 7 May.

UN High-Level Panel on Threats, Challenges and Change (2004), 'A more secure world: Our shared responsibility', A/59/565, 2 December.

UN Human Rights Council High-Level Mission (2007), 'Report of the high-level mission on the situation of human rights in Darfur pursuant to Human Rights Council decision S-4/101', A/HRC/4/80, 7 March.

UN Panel on Peace Operations (2000), 'The report of the panel on United Nations peace operations', A/55/305-S/2000/809, 21 August.

US Department of Defense (2005), 'The national defense strategy of the United States of America' (Washington DC: US Department of Defense).

Väyrynen, Raimo (ed.) (2000), *Global Governance and Enforcement: Issues and Strategies* (Lanham: Rowman and Littlefield).

Wallensteen, Peter (2002), *Understanding Conflict Resolution: War, Peace and the Global System* (London: Sage).

Wallensteen, Peter and Margareta Sollenberg (2000), 'Armed conflict, 1989–1999', *Journal of Peace Research*, 37 (5).

Wallensteen, Peter (ed.) (1998), *Preventing Future Conflicts: Past Record and Future Challenges* (Uppsala: Uppsala University).

Walzer, Michael (1977), *Just and Unjust Wars: A Philosophical Argument with Historical Illustrations* (New York: Basic Books).

Ward, Tony (2005), 'State crime in the heart of darkness', *British Journal of Criminology*, 45 (4).

Warner, Daniel (2003), 'The responsibility to protect and irresponsible, cynical engagement', *Millennium: Journal of International Studies*, 32 (1).

Weiss, Thomas G. (1999), 'Sanctions as a foreign policy tool: Weighing humanitarian impulses', *Journal of Peace Research*, 36 (5).

Weiss, Thomas G. (2004), 'The sunset of humanitarian intervention? The responsibility to protect in a unipolar era', *Security Dialogue*, 35 (2).

Weiss, Thomas G. (2007), *Humanitarian Intervention: Ideas in Action* (Cambridge: Polity).

Weiss, Thomas G. and Don Hubert (2001), 'The responsibility to protect: research, bibliography, background' (Ottawa: IDRC).

Weiss, Thomas G. and David A. Korn (2006), *Internal Displacement: Conceptualization and its Consequences* (New York: Routledge).

Weiss, Thomas G. and Sam Daws (eds) (2007), *The Oxford Handbook on the United Nations* (Oxford: Oxford University Press).

Welsh, Jennifer M. (ed.) (2004), *Humanitarian Intervention and International Relations* (Oxford: Oxford University Press).

Wheeler, Nicholas J., (2000), *Saving Strangers: Humanitarian Intervention in International Society* (Oxford: Oxford University Press).

Wheeler, Nicholas J. (2001), 'Legitimating humanitarian intervention: Principles and procedures', *Melbourne Journal of International Law*, 2 (2).

Wheeler, Nicholas J. (2004), 'The emerging norm of collective responsibility to protect after R2P and HLP', paper presented at the BISA Conference, University of Warwick, 20–2 December.

Wheeler, Nicholas J. (2005), 'A victory for common humanity? The responsibility to protect after the 2005 World Summit', paper presented to a conference on 'The UN at Sixty: Celebration or Wake?', University of Toronto, 6–7 October.

Williams, Ian (2003), 'Intervene with caution', *In These Times*, 28 July.

Williams, Paul D. (2007), 'From non-intervention to non-indifference: The origins and development of the African Union's security culture', *African Affairs*, 106 (423).

Williams, Paul D. and Alex J. Bellamy (2005), 'The responsibility to protect and the crisis in Darfur', *Security Dialogue*, 36 (1).

Williams, Paul D. and Alex J. Bellamy (2007), 'Contemporary peace operations: Four challenges for the Brahimi paradigm', *International Peacekeeping: The Yearbook of International Peace Operations*, Vol. 11.

World Federalist Movement–International Policy Group (2003), 'Civil society perspectives on the responsibility to protect', Final report, 30 April.

Zartman, I. William (2001), *Preventive Negotiation* (Lanham, MD: Rowman and Littlefield).

Index